Journey Into
PEACE

A Language for
Peace, Progress, & Healing

Journey Into
PEACE

Michael M. Starr

Published by Executive Coaching Services

ISBN (paperback): 979-8-218-25289-2
ISBN (ebook): 979-8-218-32225-0

Book design and production by www.AuthorSuccess.com

Dedicated to
my daughters Natalie and Christina

Contents

Foreword

I am blessed to have been placed in positions of leadership throughout my Navy and civilian careers. After many decades serving in these assignments, it became clear to me that attributes that make a person better do the same in making an organization perform well.

Among the attributes I selected were self-projection, the ability to communicate, self-discipline, self-esteem, and self-awareness.

As I look back, I was on to something regarding behaviors, but I had only scratched the surface in defining a method to modify behaviors to enhance one's life and the ability to positively influence others.

Mike Starr has very ably analyzed his own life, experiences with others, and happenings that occur to each of us on a daily basis. His analysis has allowed him to provide a roadmap to a better life, greater fulfillment, and enhanced moral influence.

He has accomplished this by focusing significant attention on our communications. He truly realizes that words are powerful, and if used improperly can cause great harm. On the other hand, he shows that by modifying our use of language, we can enhance our ability to communicate and more efficiently reach consensus.

The author's self-analysis has led him to understand the absolute need for good, healthy routines in our lifetime. He provides a clear roadmap for creating a good habit.

Journey into Peace is certainly not a "how to" manual. It provides an in-depth, non-emotional accounting of one's life lessons learned during the journey, and provides doable actions to improve our communications and instill life-invigorating habits!

This *Journey into Peace* does just what it says; it provides a simple and clear path to leading a life of greater peace and happiness!

VICE ADMIRAL AL KONETZNI, JR. USN (ret)
Former Commander, Submarine Force, US Pacific Fleet

ON MY WAY TO KILIMANJARO,
I FOUND GOD WAS WAITING THERE FOR ME

On my way to Kilimanjaro, I found God was waiting there for me.
Not at Uhuru peak, but along the path for those seven days, those
seven days for me to see.

I asked how long God had been waiting on this trail, this path along
the way?
"I've been waiting sixty-nine years to have you here," God did calmly
speak and warmly say.

On my way to Kilimanjaro, I found God waiting there for me.
There was much to hear and much for me to see.
I asked God, "What is it I need to know? What is it I need to see?"
God responded, "All that's come before you was completely meant to be.
"All the suffering and happiness that you experienced these 25,000 days,
"That's what has brought you to me now, ready to hear what I have
to say."

"God, so grand here in this far-off land, what do you have for me to
know and face?"
"You can choose to serve or choose to run a lifelong lonely race.

"You may serve with love. You may serve with grace.
"For in the end, what is left behind will signify your trace."

I saw the time was near, the time was here,
To set aside my fears and wipe away my tears.
The time is now to make peace with all that's always been,
To let go of animosity and of regretted sin.

So, on a lighter note, I asked, "Is God a he or perhaps a she?"
God chuckled a response, "It matters not, and neither would it be."
I came to see that God was for me to find,
Not just within me or just inside my mind.

So once again, I pursued Divine wisdom and asked about love and
being kind.
God passed this message on to me: "Seek and search, and
you will answers find."

Like a warm spring breeze, God gave this Epiphany,
"It is the questions you ask that will lead you along.
"It is your pursuit that need be your song.
"Thus, will this clarify right from wrong."
Like the born-again morning sun rising over a distant ridge,
I clearly know it is for me to understand, for me to be the bridge.
All around me, people wish to know,
That they are important and can love on common ground.
This is what I must show.

As we parted ways, God did finally say,
"Go forward my son, go forward my friend. We will speak again someday."

—Mike Starr, July 2019

Introduction

Are we but Neanderthals with our current language?

The limits of my language mean the limits of my world.

—Ludwig Wittgenstein

Language has a remarkable impact on our thinking, actions, and relationships. My dog Rippy reminded me of this big time! We have two rescue dogs: Rippy and Lola. Rippy, a tan and white colored Chihuahua with darkened sad-looking eyes, is the latest addition to the family. I found that unlike Lola, he would shy away from my efforts to pet him. Now, five years later, Rippy still folds back his ears and retreats when anyone walks quickly toward him, or he may growl and then strike out and try to bite their ankles. I remember a few weeks after we adopted him, my wife Karen told me to "be *patient*" in response to my comment: "This is the most *unfriendly* dog we have ever had!"

I was right, yet I was wrong. I was about to poison my relationship with him.

HIGHER TRUTH

After some thought, I realized *patience* was a **useless word** and *unfriendly* was a **dangerous word.** The term "unfriendly" harms, as it prevents healing and progress because it lacks empathy. I corrected myself later and said to my wife that I now believed Rippy was fearful, insecure, and anxious. Perhaps he had been previously abused, or maybe it's baked into his DNA. The view that he's fearful, insecure, and anxious is more empowering and effective for both of us. It depersonalizes his behavior with me. It elicits compassion, which in turn improves my perspective of him. This shifted me from a binary, dead-end view of either all good or all bad to one that promotes a healthier interaction between the two of us. I am now mindful to move slowly toward him and be kind with my tone of voice. When I do so, he does not shy away or appear to be afraid. This is a **Higher Truth** about Rippy—fearful, insecure, and anxious versus unfriendly. Using better language about Rippy makes both of our lives more peaceful and our relationship healthier. This is an empowering alternate reality with our little ten-pound Rippy.

Language communication has evolved from the grunts of primitive cave people to a vocabulary of the more than one million choices currently in the English language. Our language has evolved wisely in some ways. In the sciences such as chemistry and physics, there has been continued logic and precision with language, in which new concepts stand on the shoulders of the older ones. Yet, in many other areas, our words have evolved haphazardly. The word *stupid*, which has its roots in the Latin *stupere*, originally meant amazed or stunned, rather than the inferior derogatory accusation it has come to mean today. Our language in relationships and interpersonal communications is especially fraught with ambiguity, misunderstanding, and disempowering interpretation.

OUR LANGUAGE IS FLAWED

I contend that the common language we use is seriously flawed and inadequate. Our words and language often create barriers that limit and stifle progress and improvement. Language can make things worse for us. Woven within many words are formulas for failure that interfere with successful communication and thinking. Saying someone is *unfriendly, mean,* or *stupid* limits possibilities for improvement and connection. This often is more about our feelings and less about another and who they are.

There is an incredible amount of opportunity for our growth and advancement with the use of language. Perhaps we are currently cave people, mere Neanderthals, with our current use of language? Like the Model T automobile and sailing ships, which were transportation marvels in their day, our current communication modes are now only at a rudimentary level of effectiveness. However, we do have exciting possibilities with how we can use words during our future evolutionary path.

On its most fundamental level, we use language to think and communicate. Our language allows us to learn "better" ways to connect with others and achieve mutually desirable outcomes. It is a magic flying carpet that has taken us far beyond our primal "fight or flight" instincts and reactions. It has helped us to advance from anarchy to civilization. We use it to express our feelings toward each other and within ourselves. We use language to understand what is happening around us and how to best respond. We use it to diagnose and create solutions to problems. In many ways, our use of language defines us by directing our behavior in response to perceived realities. Wise language can be the difference between harmony and animosity, progress and frustration, empowered hope and disempowered victimhood.

If we are not vigilant with language use and understanding, we can be deceived to believe exaggerated slanderous views of others. These views divide, disempower, and distract us from healthy relationships. They facilitate self-righteousness and become the antithesis of empathy and compassion. Worst of all they dehumanize our views of others which then paves the way for cruel and intolerant behavior. They are a path for conflict, frustration, and despair. Seeking "common ground" has become most "uncommon." It isn't that we have lost our way as much as that we have been using unhealthy language and it has caught up to us. We never really found a way to communicate effectively.

THREE KEY LANGUAGE CATEGORIES

The foundation for a peaceful, happier, and more productive life occurs when we become aware of how our terminology impacts our perceptions and thinking. It is especially important that we understand the following three categories of language:

1. *Useless words* that take us nowhere except in circles

2. *Dangerous/tyrannical* **words** that harm, divide, and confuse

3. *Wise, empowering words* that advance our personal progress and inner peace

During my lifetime I have seen much unnecessary pain experienced by people around me; by myself as well. I am now convinced that we can mitigate if not eliminate much of this suffering and conflict. We can do this through wise, empowering language which focuses on empathy, objective empowering acceptance, and boundaries with consequences.

In my seventy-plus years as a student of life, I have taken many journeys:

- Summiting Mount Kilimanjaro

- Canoeing from Pittsburgh to New Orleans

- Driving a nuclear submarine

- Witnessing of successful substance abuse recoveries

- Managing a $100 million-a-year manufacturing production line

None of these journeys have been as painful, challenging, and rewarding as my transition from anger and resentment to loving empathy and boundaries with consequences. I came to see that my language had created a prison. I embraced a curiosity to understand why others became as they did. As a result of my understanding, I achieved a new empathy for others by understanding why they became who they had become. This all led to an objective empowering acceptance. As a result, I was able to abandon self-righteous views of the people and the world around me and replace them with compassion, kindness, and respect. I now am free to soar.

WHAT IS POSSIBLE FOR YOU?

Are you looking for more peace of mind and achieving results that matter? Do you desire less drama and more joy in your life? Do you wish to find and promote harmony within yourself and with others you care about? I believe you will find in the pages ahead seeds that will grow to bear the fruit of increasing wisdom for you. You can live a life where each year is more bountiful than the last!

If you are intrigued by the possibilities available through using improved language and are interested in a future with growing peace of mind, purpose, accomplishment, and harmony, then this book is for you.

This book will show you how to make peace with the past, progress with the future, and enjoy today free of frustration, guilt, or resentment. By the time you finish reading this book you will:

- Learn how to use wise, empowering language to improve your relationships
- Have available to you over twenty "States of Being" that will serve as your sword, shield, and compass
- Know how to set effective boundaries
- Be able to better help others who are struggling with life challenges

- Achieve compassion and caring for yourself and others
- Achieve and sustain results that matter

Providing a means to reduce suffering and increase satisfaction is my mission.

Your friend,
Mike

War and Peace ... The Odyssey of Joanne and Metro 1939-1948

This was not a love story nor an adventure. It was a fight for survival during the ravages of tyranny by both the Nazi fascists and Communist socialists. A story of resilience, gratitude, and contribution that would continue for decades thereafter.

The tyranny of the 1930s and 1940s was responsible for unprecedented suffering and destruction in our human history. Stalin's Communist/Socialist and Hitler's Nazi Fascist ideologies were responsible for the deaths of over twenty million non-combatants and an additional twenty plus million combatants.[1] These deaths occurred with the Nazi Jewish Holocaust, the Communist Ukrainian Holodomor of 1933, the murder of perceived political threats, and the ravages of World War II combat.

World War II began on September 1, 1939, with the Nazi invasion of Poland. At this time, my future parents, Metro and Joanne, were strangers living thousands of miles apart in the USA and Europe. They both soon found themselves swept up in this ensuing chaos. They left their homes and families and found themselves fighting for survival. Those wartime experiences had a profound impact on their perspectives of life. Standing on their shoulders, I have developed an unshakable view of gratitude, empowerment, and human frailty. Two of history's most evil tyrants indirectly helped me define my foundational views of right and wrong.

I was born five years after the conclusion of World War II in 1950, the son of Ukrainian parents Joanne and Metro. Joanne was born into a Ukrainian community in Eastern Poland. Metro was a first-generation Ukrainian born in McKees Rocks, Pennsylvania, a small town just downriver of Pittsburgh.

In September 1939, Joanne was seventeen years old.

September 1, Germany invaded Poland.

September 3, Great Britain and France declared war on Germany.

September 17, The Soviet Communists invaded Poland and occupied Joanne's hometown of Zolochiv as part of Stalin's agreement with Hitler to invade and partition Poland.

After the Soviet occupation of her town, they imprisoned many Ukrainians as perceived political threats and deported many more to Siberian labor camps and Gulags. Her mother's two brothers were taken to a local prison, where they soon died (were murdered?), and her father's mother, two brothers, and their wives were sent to Siberian labor camps and never heard from again. Often townspeople were "missing" in the morning, having been taken away in the middle of the night . . . many were found later in mass graves outside the city. Joanne hid her bible in her home with an ever-present fear of being identified as an anti-communist "enemy of the state" by soldiers or being betrayed by neighbors. During the Communist occupation, she saw people hanging from trees near her town . . . one, her uncle with his eyes and tongue cut out; another, a young woman with her dead baby stuffed inside her blood-drenched, gutted corpse.

This was indeed a time of survival. During the Communist occupation, Joanne soon left her hometown to live in the larger city of Lvov. There she studied teaching and later became an elementary school teacher in a small village called Rykiv in the Carpathian Mountain region. She was expected to introduce the children to Communist ideology.

During this time of teaching, she was brought in by the local administrator and told she was not doing enough to indoctrinate the children to love Stalin and and Communist ideology. They stated they were planning to send her away for further training. Stalling for time, she then agreed to study the Communist Constitution and asked for a book to familiarize herself better. Not long afterward, she became aware of the advancing German troops that would invade the area. After the German occupation, she returned to her hometown of Zolochiv in the summer of 1941.

Joanne was now nineteen years old.

After this German invasion, hundreds of neighbors and townspeople were discovered in mass graves created by the Communists. They had executed hundreds prior to their retreat before this Nazi invasion in July of 1941.

Joanne got work with the Zolochiv City Council distributing food ration cards.

March 1942, Metro

Metro was drafted and joined the Army in March of 1942, three months after Pearl Harbor. He was thirty-one years old. He was trained at Fort Lewis in the state of Washington as a medic, a member of "Company

B," and later became part of the 103rd evacuation hospital. He left the US by ship on February 27, 1944, and arrived in Ireland ten days later. Three months later, the Allies invaded Normandy, code-named "Operation Overlord," on June 6, 1944. The medics stood alongside more than 130,000 fighting soldiers who arrived aboard 7,000 ships and landing crafts and landed on the Normandy shores.[2]

Whenever a soldier was wounded, the medics were at their side to aid them . . . distinguishable by their red cross armbands.

During the next year, from 1944 to 1945, Metro marched east with the U.S. Army through France, Belgium, and into Germany. His support medical unit advanced eastward past Normandy and through the Ardennes Campaign ("Battle of the Bulge"). His life then was about marching, tents, dirt, rain, and attending to the wounded and maimed. His life was about morphine, amputation, and sutures. Causalities and death were the daily visitors within the tents of his 103rd Evacuation Hospital unit.

By 1944, the Nazis were in retreat, and the Soviets were advancing from the east. Joanne decided to face the lesser of the two evils and left her hometown to go westward, away from the Communists. She soon traveled by rail aboard a cattle car and later unloaded at an intermediate train station along with hundreds of other Ukrainians. There they waited for three days with little to eat. They made soup from grass and foraged potatoes. They were subsequently loaded on cattle cars again to be taken to a Nazi factory labor camp near Strasshof (near the city of Vienna).

After arriving at their destination, Joanne and the others had to strip naked. There they stood outside for hours while the Germans made jokes, calling them animals. They were waiting to be "deloused" with oil. She was forced to work in a Nazi factory. Joanne had to make a daily walk of three miles from the dormitory building sleeping quarters to the factory. They all were required to wear oversized wooden shoes. They existed on the minimal nutrition given to the workers and slept on floors in "dormitory" buildings.

In 1945, Joanne was twenty-three years old, living in a refugee camp in Germany. Metro, at thirty-five years old, was fluent in speaking Ukrainian and had become a military translator for a Ukrainian refugee camp. It was here that he met my mother, Joanne, his future wife. As a result of his visits to this camp, he spoke to several local military and civilian leaders and wrote articles that were published back in the United States. He wrote of the plight of immigrants in post-World War II Germany, especially Ukrainians who were being returned to their homelands to live under a tyrannical Communist government. He was largely responsible for preventing Joanne from being sent back to Soviet Ukraine and assisting hundreds more Ukrainians with immigrating to the U.S., Canada, and Argentina.

1948

When Joanne arrived in the U.S., she was twenty-six and Metro was thirty-eight. They married the next year on May 21, 1949, in a small town called McKees Rocks outside of Pittsburgh, Pennsylvania.

Decades later, my father was reluctant to speak of the death and maiming of fellow soldiers he treated and attended to daily. I only heard him make perhaps a minute or two of commentary on that portion of his life experience. My mother and I spoke for hours on end about her experiences during that period, and her gratitude for being able to worship and speak as she chose in America.

Seventy-five years later ... 2023

Joanne and Metro have passed on, both dying at the age of ninety-three, twelve years apart. They always lived a life of self-reliance. They were forever grateful for the fundamental freedoms and opportunities available to them over their more than fifty years together following the second world war.

I am their son Myron, a.k.a. Mike. I am now seventy-three. I live in the United States, where significant threat has shifted from monumental foreign aggression to one where we are facing a significant degradation of our cultural and economic strengths.

Soon for you . . . shortly after reading and perhaps rereading this book:

You wake up full of hope and optimism, smiling, excited, and delighted. You know that your trajectory, i.e., your path forward, is full of success, peace of mind, and harmony. You embrace your relationship with yourself, others, and the world; these relationships are full of love and caring. You harbor little animosity, confusion, resentments, fear, anger, or disdain. Certainty, understanding, compassion, and enthusiasm fill you. Your new eyes see more clearly than ever before, having achieved a remarkable level of enlightenment that now serves as a light and beacon for others.

> *The real voyage of discovery consists not in seeing new landscapes, but having new eyes.*
>
> —Marcel Proust

My mission is to shine a light on a healthy road forward. It is not to detail my personal beliefs about why there is darkness in our world, but rather, I propose a path forward that moves us away from the *bad* and closer to the *good,* filling our lives with compassion, clarity, conviction, and empowerment. My hope is to provide the tools and encouragement to others to seek common ground for the common good.

May this book be a foundation and springboard for you to move forward with breakthroughs in your use of empowering, concise, and legitimate language. May you continue to build upon this foundation with your discernment of additional improvements to these suggestions. May you stand on the shoulders of these ideas and suggestions and be ever better.

CHAPTER 1

A Path for Heaven on Earth: "Betterism"

Am I more concerned with being right than doing right?

"Be the Stream"

Our language defines us and what we are capable of becoming. Our language can empower us and guide us to solutions and peace of mind. It can provide clarity as we move forward. The words we use or do not use also limit us, as they can be embedded with dangerous presumptions. Sadly, language is becoming increasingly tyrannical. This dangerous language leads us further into the darkness of despair, hatred, and division. Seeking common ground has become most uncommon.

—Michael Starr

Shortly after I turned sixty years of age, I had a shocking "dinosaur epiphany." Despite all that I had accomplished and experienced, I had missed something critically important as a leader, as a family member, and as a human being. I came to realize I was a modern-day brontosaurus. This lightning bolt of clarity was not about being outdated, but rather about looking ahead and not behind.

Throughout much of my life, I saw the path forward clearly illuminated by my objectivity, integrity, and selflessness. Yet, what was behind me was largely unnoticed. My quest for progress was not wise; it had a component of ignorance and neglect that greatly diminished the value of my successes. "Results with integrity" was my compass for deciding the direction and actions needed for progress. This beacon was one that steered me aground, unto the rocks of troubled accomplishments. When this startling realization occurred, I was stunned and full of remorse. My rock-solid certainty and confidence were shaken. It was as if a bright white flare had suddenly exploded in a black evening sky, revealing hidden secrets in my past and exposing something unnerving in my wake. The wind had shifted and was coming up from behind me now. There was a scent of decay in the air. This reveal was a tale of telling and not selling. This was a tale of a tail.

Many of us find dinosaurs an intriguing group of reptiles. They are generally known for their enormous size and the circumstances of their disappearance. I am especially fond of the calm brontosaurus, which lived in North America around 150 million years ago, during the Jurassic Period. They are estimated to have been seventy plus feet long, weighing over 30,000 pounds, and measuring up to twenty-eight feet in height. Its tail could be thirty feet long. The name *brontosaurus* means "thunder lizard."

GOOD INTENTIONS ARE NOT ENOUGH

I viewed this species as confident herbivores who had little fear. In some ways, I aligned with those gentle giants. I was not interested in competing with others, only with myself. I had little fear about being wrong or being disliked. Rather, I was focused on making progress for myself and the team. Perhaps it was due to my six-foot-two stature and the unconditional love from my mother that I was so self-assured and had little need for approval from others. I did my own thing in a rather happy-go-lucky manner. But, as was said by the French Abbot Bernard of Clairvaux, "the road to hell is paved with good intentions."

I have always had the desire to help others succeed. I am ethical, honorable, and an adept problem solver. I am someone you can count on to be true to my word. Despite these values and talents, I was inadvertently leaving a path of destruction and harm behind me as my trailing Brontosaurus tail whipped from side to side as I was moved ahead "fixing," "improving," and "helping."

> *What do you call a leader who gets too*
> *far ahead of his followers? A target.*
> —Unknown Soldier

I saw that despite my ability to achieve results with integrity, the loyalty of key subordinates and superiors was minimal at best. Taking time to reassure and acknowledge others along the path of change and progress was not one of my habits. My confidence in myself and in my strategies led to a focus of "telling and not selling" my ideas and initiatives for improvement. "They will understand this is for their own good in the long run," I would think. I'm sure many saw me as arrogant.

THE GOLDEN RULE WAS A MISTAKE

I was demanding of myself and of others. I expected the personal sacrifice of others to assist with the success of the team's objectives. There was no worse motto for me than the *Golden Rule*, "treat others as you wish to be treated yourself." I can assure you that most people did not want to be treated the way I did. I assumed that others would be happy with my leadership in achieving desirable outcomes by seeing that the "short-term pain" was worth the "long-term gain." The truth is, as I moved forward, I was knocking things over; damaging the feelings, egos, and confidence of those around me. Resentment was a common wake that trailed behind my progress forward. I was largely oblivious and insensitive to the insecurities and concerns of those I was leading.

> *The operation was a success, but the patient died.*
> —Old Medical Saying

It was only when calamitous family crises hit me like an inescapable burning asteroid impacting the Earth that I stopped and reassessed my values. With my family, I saw I was an unknowing accomplice in the demise of those I so dearly loved. Though their life challenges extended beyond me, I had not done nearly enough to limit the impact of their past and present suffering. I had been insensitive—not by design, but by ignorance and preoccupation with "important things." Facing a lifetime of unintentional sins can be traumatic and unbearable. It brought about great suffering for me. It was painful to accept what I had done.

Regret is a bitter pill to swallow, yet it can also become an opportunity and reason to change course and better move forward. Remorse can be a profoundly self-motivating experience to seek improvement; to seek to be better. Perhaps the penance for sins of the past is to become better people. As a result of my desire to move forward unencumbered by my past transgressions, I have discovered a wise philosophy of living I call *Betterism*.

BETTERISM... "BE THE STREAM"... SEEK WIN-WIN

Betterism is a philosophy of living which continually takes action for incremental progress. Like a stream, it is defined and exists only through ongoing forward movement. It is *the continual pursuit of more good and less bad in our lives.* It utilizes *wise selfishness*, which seeks win-win outcomes for all. *Betterism* is a lifestyle that both adds good and subtracts bad in our lives. It begins with a change in the way we think. To support this improved thinking and the subsequent perceptions arising from this, we must improve the language we use in our daily lives.

One important distinction within *Betterism* is a "state of being" I call **Be the Stream.** When we are acting as a stream, we are moving forward undeterred by obstacles ahead. We quickly pivot over, under, and around barriers, as the stream does with rocks, trees, and logs in its current path. When we are **Being the Stream,** we understand that detours are the shortest path forward and focus not on the obstacle but on what best detour to take next. We may later revisit the circumstances of a detour, as with a mistake made, so we can later learn from it, but in the moment of facing an obstacle we do not stagnate.

Perhaps you've had to live through your own personal calamities and serious setbacks. It can be devastating. Unfortunately, we often must go through hell to get to a better place, a heaven on Earth, on the other side of all that pain. There is a silver lining to these sufferings in our past.

During more than forty years of professional and family life, I have experienced an unacceptable level of suffering in myself, my family, my friends, and my coworkers. Severe injuries, substance abuse, conflict, and despair have taken place around me. I have seen this type of suffering in families, businesses, religious communities, and even the underwater life aboard a nuclear submarine. I have seen much tragic and unnecessary pain and hopelessness. With each struggle, I became more convinced that *there has got to be a better way.* I was increasingly convinced that much of this suffering was preventable.

After my "dinosaur epiphany" experience, I set out on a personal crusade to find out how we can proactively avoid the anguish of suffering from happening in the first place. As Benjamin Franklin said, "An ounce of prevention is worth a pound of cure."

These experiences are the genesis from which my *Journey into Peace* and the writing of this book began.

In my pursuit of a better way, I arrived at two conclusions and convictions:

1. This conclusion wasn't surprising: we are the root cause and source of many of our problems and dilemmas.

2. A more unexpected conclusion was: I came to see and believe that the everyday language we use was at the heart of our suffering. Our use of language is a powerful influence that drives us into or away from suffering, failure, despair, and conflict.

Our language defines us and what we can become. Our language can empower us and guide us to solutions and peace of mind. It can provide clarity as we move forward. The words we use or do not use also limit us, as they can be embedded with dangerous presumptions. Sadly, language is becoming increasingly tyrannical. This dangerous language leads us further into the darkness of despair, hatred, and division. Seeking common ground has become most uncommon.

OUR COMMUNITIES ARE SUFFERING

The current state of our culture with the amount of conflict, drug abuse, divorce, murder, suicide, hatred, and family illegitimacy rates is tragic. Empathy and compassion have faded as core cultural values, and are now increasingly being replaced with intolerant and self-righteous divisiveness. Civil debate is being replaced by shouting over one another and efforts to censor opposing views. The idea of *agreeing to disagree* is rapidly being lost in the public forum. Merit-based identity is being replaced with an oppositional identity, in which people define themselves by their opposition to ideas and individuals. In many cases, individuals develop a near-psychotic obsession with hurting, punishing, and canceling those they dislike or disagree with.

Today's state of affairs in our country (as of 2023) can seem bleak:

- 40 percent of births in the United States occur outside of marriage, up 28 percent from 1990 to 2016 (for whites 15 percent to 28 percent, for Hispanics 34 percent to 52 percent, for Blacks 63 percent to 69 percent).[3]

- Dramatic increase in suicide, with a 30 percent increase between 2000-2018 . . . it was the second leading cause of death for ages ten to fourteen and twenty-five to thirty-four.[4]

- Drug overdose deaths have continually increased over the last twenty years. In 2020, nearly 92,000 persons in the U.S. died from drug-involved overdoses.[5]

- More than half a million people experience homelessness in the US at any given time.[6]

- Twelve major cities hit all-time homicide records.[7]

- Hatred, intolerance, and pejorative commentary is rampant amongst media, educational institutions, and our political leaders.

- Twenty-three million Americans suffer from drug or alcohol addiction.[8]

- Over 40 million individuals (one in six) use pharmaceutical solutions, including psychiatric drugs, for emotional problems.[9]

This evidence supports the belief that many people around us, and perhaps we ourselves, suffer profoundly. This suffering manifests itself in anger, conflict, anxiety, hatred, and crime. However, this suffering can be markedly mitigated with wise language. I contend that there is a way to live life as a dance, with a slow crescendo of empowering music in our head that fills our thoughts and convictions with hope and excitement. The paths we take toward this heaven on Earth are forged by the routines and habits we develop.

I believe the philosophy of *Betterism*, with its use of wise empowering language, is the key to future harmony, health, happiness, healing, and progress. *Betterism* builds a type of periodic table for clearly seeing what is possible and empowering.

As the United States was recovering from the devastating Civil War, across the Atlantic, Russian chemist Dmitri Ivanovich Mendeleev was working toward finding one of chemistry's most important discoveries, the periodic table. His periodic table organized the then-currently-known elements, and even predicted the properties of three elements that had not yet been discovered. He was able to correct prevailing misconceptions of the times in the chemistry community. He showed a more accurate nature of matter.

Elements are the building blocks of all matter with their specific and unique properties. With his periodic table, Mendeleev explained how and why these building blocks act and interact with other elements and molecules. This revolutionary perspective became a springboard for many advances in chemistry in the decades ahead. In contrast, the "alchemists" of the post-Middle Ages wasted nearly 200 years looking for ways to create gold. Had those scientists of that era only known and understood the periodic table, they would have seen that their efforts were futile, that it was an impossible goal to achieve.

WORDS ARE THE BUILDING BLOCKS OF LANGUAGE

Specific elements are made of the same atoms which are the building blocks of all tangible things. Understanding their nature gives us clarity with what is possible. Similarly, words are the building blocks of language. Wisely used, words can be your key ingredients for success and progress. To best present the opportunities and possibilities for you, I will sort words into three categories. This will set the groundwork for assisting you with developing a healthy and wise lexicon as you progress toward inner peace and important accomplishments.

There are three categories of language:

1. **Useless language**

2. **Dangerous and tyrannical language**

3. **Wise empowering language**

Today's language is full of ambiguity, misconceptions, maliciousness, misdirection, and confusion. Dangerous and useless language distracts us and harms us. Can it be that simple? Is our language, and the use of words within it, the Pandora's box from which emanates much suffering, despair, and dispute? I believe this to be true. Does language precede perception? In many cases this is also true.

Does the language we speak determine how healthy and rich we will be? New research suggests so. A study by Keith Chen of Yale Business School shows how language can impact the behavior of people within a specific culture. The structure of languages affects our judgments and decisions about the future and this might have dramatic long-term consequences."[10]

LANGUAGE IS USED TO THINK AND COMMUNICATE

We use language to think our thoughts, communicate with others, and communicate with ourselves. Wiser language leads to better thinking, allowing us to see helpful ways forward. Effective communication leads to more clarity. Better language enhances our ability to observe and respond dispassionately to our circumstances. It improves our relationships with others. It guides us in defining the problem and prioritizing its importance. It is invaluable in achieving a correct diagnosis of issues, which leads to successful remediation. By wisely improving our language, we can achieve increased happiness and reduced suffering.

With Wise Empowering Language, we can truly achieve a heaven on Earth for ourselves. This heaven is not a destination, but rather a journey. The path for peace is *Betterism*. When language works for us and not against us, we are empowered to solve problems effectively and feel confident that our current decisions are the right ones. The fights with our loved ones end and understanding grows. When a fellow driver makes a dangerous maneuver, we can see them as possibly troubled and no longer label them as jerks. We move forward calmly, avoiding involvement with road rage and replacing it with empathy. This is true for me now, though I responded much differently when I was younger.

Though your decisions today are not perfect, they are the best for now. It has taken many years of experience to achieve the level of wisdom and skill you have currently. Bravo to you! You have much to be proud of and grateful for. I hope to provide you with a means to make even better decisions in the future, using Wise Empowering Language. The result will be more peace, progress, and healing. The example from the Introduction with our rescue dog Rippy showed how Wise Empowering Language can be a game changer.

LEARNING EXPERIENCES for GROWTH (LEGS)

Using empowered, legitimate, and concise language improves our thinking. This improves discernment of *what is*, leading to more successful responses. As a result, we can increase our peace of mind as well as facilitate progress in our relationships. Life becomes an empowered journey; a trek toward continuing progress. Mistakes and setbacks are opportunities to learn. They are *Learning Experiences for Growth* (LEGs). Habitual misbehaviors of others become navigation beacons where hazards are clearly seen. Our shortcomings can become our strengths. Often, our use of words can work against us. Useless verbs such as patience, procrastination, or forgiveness circle us round and round, going nowhere. Dangerous words such as loser, liar, quitter, or deplorable spiral us downward, deeper and deeper into the darkness. *Useless words* and *dangerous words* work against progress.

When I speak of heaven, it is not the heaven of the religious afterlife. I am addressing a secular heaven that we can live in before death.

This heaven is not a destination, but rather like the mountain stream, it only exists in movement; it exists only in continuous empowered progress. It is a way of achieving calm clarity as we observe the world and ourselves. When we see *what is* in an objective light without drama, we disentangle ourselves from a death grip of how we think things should be.

At the core of our stifled potential are self-imposed barriers. Perhaps we are like monkeys caught in the wild. A hunter will take a gourd and cut a small hole into it. The hole will be just big enough for a monkey to fit their hand through. Inside the gourd, they'll put nuts or sweets, something the monkey craves. Then they wait. Sooner or later, a monkey will come by and smell the bait. It will put its hand through the hole, grab a fistful of nuts, and then try to pull its hand back out. But it can't. The hole is small enough to put an empty hand through, but not big enough for a hand clutching a fistful of nuts. They're stuck. Even at the expense of capture, they continue their death grip on the bait. For us as a *Betterist*, being able to let go of dangerous and useless language is vital to our success.

Our response to events and circumstances around us is a direct result of our view of *what is*. We perceive reality in our own way and react based on that view. I contend that our interpretation of *what is* may likely be only one of several possibilities. Have you ever been confident in your judgment, to later realize that you did not have all the facts?

ALTERNATE REALITIES

Is it possible that there are *Legitimate Empowering Alternate Realities* (LEAR) that escape us, like an alternate dimension in a sci-fi movie? I say yes! Empowering alternate realities are accessible with the use of a wiser language. This wiser language provides a means for achieving more peace for you and those around you. Have you ever experienced a miscommunication with another because you were using words that had different meanings or implications for each of you? That is just the tip of the iceberg. I invite you to consider that your current experiences and communication skills can be even more enhanced and fortified with the next level of language use. Let's call this an advanced degree. Here you can attain a "master's level" ability with a new advanced skillset. I invite you to move toward a breakthrough with your communication skills.

Throughout this book, I ask that you have an open mind. Some concepts will appear counterintuitive. Some of the ideas may confront assumptions and preconceptions you have. This can be an uncomfortable experience; your values may be challenged. My intent, however, will always be to elevate your life by making a convincing case for this new way of using language.

A journey of peace, progress, and healing lies ahead for you. It has many possible paths. There are indeed *higher truths* as you change and improve your use of words and language. These higher truths are not only *Legitimate Empowering Alternate Realties*, but they are also wiser and more accurate realities. As we change our language, we change our perceptions of what is (as well as what was). When we change our perceptions of what is, we change our thinking, and our reactions and responses shift. We will then observe things around us differently, changing what we decide to do or not do. These decisions nurture real progress while achieving more good and less bad in our daily lives.

TODAY MAKES TOMMOROW and TOMMORROW MAKES TODAY

As a Betterist, you see that both the journey toward a destination and the destination itself together become the goal. Both give context to the other. Journey and destination become one. It becomes much more about WHAT and HOW and less about WHY. The definition of success shifts from "achieving a result" to a balanced way of life where today and tomorrow are one focus for us. Tomorrow makes today have meaning and today makes tomorrow have meaning.

Our successful journey in pursuing the reduction of suffering and the increase of joy and satisfaction requires empathy. It is critical that we have a compassionate view of the people and world around us. We accept things as they are, but not from a perspective of defeated resignation. We make peace with it and have an objective embracement of what is. Our higher truth becomes an empowering vantage point, where undesired realities actually become springboards for progress. We didn't choose those events or limits, but we honor them. We stop the futile resistance and instead surrender to what we cannot control. We move forward with enthusiasm and vitality and appreciation for our ability to see opportunities for forward movement. We recognize futile paths that are just not worth our effort . . . here we are indeed **Being the Stream** with an *Objective Empowering Acceptance* of what is.

As a Betterist, you will **Be the Stream**, moving continually and vibrantly forward. You will easily pivot around obstacles and take the necessary detours. You will see that detours are the shortest way forward and obstacles are great opportunities for improvement (LEGs). You focus on what is the best detour and not waste time or energy lamenting the reality of the detour. You will find a way to have a much better day-to-day life and achieve the peace and progress you desire and deserve.

CHAPTER 2

Surrender to Reality and Make Progress

Do I believe surrender is a weakness or strength?

"Be the win-win, Wisely Selfish Mediator"

The happiness of your life depends on the quality of your thoughts.

—Marcus Aurelius

Are you looking for less suffering and a more fulfilling meaning for your life? Do you wish to improve your relationship with another and perhaps with yourself, as well? Are you looking to help others who are struggling with life challenges? I suspect that if you are reading this book, you may be open and ready to accept a novel view of what has been limiting you with achieving peace, progress, and healing. Your language is the key to this future success.

We can be our own best allies and advocates, looking out for what is in our best interest. However, we are often our own worst enemy. Many of us have self-defeating perceptions, beliefs, and take actions that not only limit our impact on making things better, but actually sabotage us. Are we acting like Don Quixote, the fictional character in Miguel de Cervantes' book *Man of La Mancha* who had a distorted view of the world around him? He was incapable of calmly seeing "what is." In his desire for grandeur and significance, Don Quixote goes somewhat insane and assumes an identity of a chivalrous knight. In this dysfunctional journey, he jousts with windmills he believes are enemies. He is impassioned and committed, but it is a futile journey.

People frequently pursue a goal or dream with intensity and a single-minded laser focus. As a result of this drive toward achievement, they often neglect other important aspects of life such as their health, relationships, and peace of mind. The process of getting to a destination is just as important as the destination itself. This book is about how to achieve results that matter with a healthy balance between destination and journey.

WISE SELFISHNESS VERSUS FOOLISH SELFISHNESS

I experienced an eye-opening example of losing perspective when I was forty-one years old while living in Camarillo, California. I was having a follow up visit with my family doctor after an overnight stay at the hospital. Chest pains that were initially thought to be symptoms of a possible heart attack were actually work stress anxiety. During this visit, my doctor shared how he had once been a distinguished neurosurgeon who had worked at a prestigious medical institution near Los Angeles. One day he realized he had been divorced twice, his children hated him, and that he was constantly busy with little time to relax. Shortly thereafter, he gave up that high-paced, lucrative lifestyle and opened a private practice with a colleague in Thousand Oaks. His past life with its definition of success was "not worth it," he said. Perhaps his prior view of winning was a formula for losing. Early in his career, he had not yet distinguished the difference between *wise selfishness* and *foolish selfishness.*

The common use of the word "selfish" often falls in the category of *useless* language. We all have a self-interest in everything we do. Whether it be Mother Teresa tending to the poor or Genghis Khan marauding through Asia, both had a self-interest in what they did. One, however, was wisely selfish, while the other was not. With *wise selfishness,* we focus on win-win outcomes, looking to make life better for ourselves and others. *Foolish selfishness* largely discounts the well-being and nurturing of others around us and, in the long run, works against us. *Foolish selfishness* can also cause us to neglect our own well-being when we are single-mindedly focused on a specific achievement or when our efforts to help others cause us to neglect ourselves.

When we pursue win-win outcomes in dealing with others, we become a mediator who looks for common ground and common benefit between ourselves and others. Here we achieve a state of being I call **"Be the win-win, wisely selfish mediator."**

Achieving a win-win outcome requires a deep understanding and empathy for both ourself and others. On the other hand, when we marginalize another by defining them as a one-dimensional person, such as a "racist" or "loser," we sabotage our ability to achieve this *wise selfishness.*

With the tragic trend toward divisiveness and dismissiveness in our communities, we need empathy and healing now more than ever. The best place to start finding a better way to improve our progress, harmony with others, and inner peace is to improve our use of language. Let's begin with a distinction I call *The Natural Order of Things (NOOT).* Some may call it God's will, others the will of the universe, or others may proclaim what will be, will be. The natural order of things is the inevitable consequence of the history of reality. It is cause and effect. It includes the laws of physics, the laws of chemistry, and objective science. It is the result of many prior events. NOOT is the nature and nurture woven within us. It is our culture, experiences, environment, and genetic DNA.

IT WAS INEVITABLE (NOOT)

I contend that all of what has happened in our lives was inevitable. It was unavoidable and necessary to get to where we are today. This inevitability is what I call NOOT. By seeing the world from this vantage point, we can unshackle ourselves from emotions that short-circuit future progress. When we see that people cannot help being who they are, we will shift away from frustration and disapproval to understanding. We will better accept *what is* and establish *boundaries with empathy and consequences* (The EBC Symbiotic 3). We will become a much better person than we could have ever imagined.

Discerning the concept of NOOT is the foundation for your success through a surrender to what is and an empathy for all. Though the world has inevitably become as it is , just as we have inevitably become who we are, there is free will for us to improve our future trajectories. We can decide which is the wisest direction for progress at any given moment. With our surrender to the objective NOOT, the pursuit of *Betterism* (seeking more happiness and less suffering), and mindfulness of *wise selfishness* we can achieve healthy success.

By sharing the concepts and language of this book, I hope to:

- Encourage you to surrender to reality, not with a defeated sense of resignation, but rather by embracing an *objective empowering acceptance.*

- Develop an unprecedented level of understanding and empathy for both yourself and others.

- Provide strategies, or as I call them, Trails of Progress (TOPs), that empower, heal, and calm.

- Improve your probability for achieving both wise desires and healthy win-win intentional outcomes.

- Make decisions based on *wise selfishness,* not *foolish selfishness.*

IMPROVE THE INTERPRETATION, IMPROVE THE RESPONCE

One can model events we experience in three stages:

1. Occurrence —> 2. Interpretation —> 3. Response

If we can improve the interpretation of an occurrence, we will improve our response to it. This is the heart of the concept of *Legitimate Empowering Alternate Realities* (LEAR) with better paradigms of credible (legitimate), self-efficacy (empowering), and alternative views of what is (reality). With a newfound clarity, we can move forward confidently and calmly with the conviction that we are where we are supposed to be, doing what we are supposed to be doing, and going where we are supposed to go.

Language can advance us beyond binary limiting views of disdain and disapproval to mature understanding. It can protect us from negative self-fulfilling prophecies that put others on the defensive and poison relationships with toxic animosity or fear. It can be a shield that thwarts harm when we define and practice the use of tailored boundaries. It can be our sword helping us clear the wise path ahead. It can also be our compass that keeps us on a healthy course for success.

DEFINTION OF INSANITY

If you approach our rescue dog Rippy quickly, he will bolt from you or may bite you. Failure to remember and be mindful of Rippy's nature is a mistake. Similarly, in our relationships, we cannot let our guard down and think, "Well, it is going to be different this time."

The story of the frog and the scorpion illustrates this:

A scorpion asks a frog to give him a ride across the stream. The frog says, "No you will sting and kill me!"

The scorpion responds, "Why would I possibly do that? It would kill us both!"

They go back and forth for a while, then the scorpion finally succeeds in convincing the frog to give him a ride across the stream. Then, midstream, the scorpion starts to sting the frog. The frog yells out, "Why are you doing this? You are going to kill us both!"

The scorpion responds by saying, "A scorpion must be a scorpion."

As we redefine and reinforce "what is," we can minimize inevitable pain and disappointment. Rippy is best approached slowly with a gentle tone of voice . . . scorpions are best left alone to find their own way. There are times when we know that we would not choose the behaviors others have. We may not agree with their choices, but there is no need to demonize or denigrate, either. It is far better to accept and embrace the reality of what is to effectively interact with it. If you must go outside in the rain, take an umbrella and don't waste your time cussing at the clouds.

This is a book about problem solving and achieving rapid sustainable results. To do so, it is essential that we surrender to reality and concede to things being as they are, as they have been, and to stop fighting futile battles with what is. Don't be like Don Quixote. It is important we do so through love, compassion, boundaries, and especially empathy. Empathy is understanding others (and ourselves) with a compelling, dispassionate curiosity that asks, "why so?"

When we do this, we become unprecedentedly calm and clear with our observations. Here we extricate the drama and emotions that taint our observations and conclusions. It is about conceding that we are all selfish, then asking whether we are we being *wisely selfish* in seeking win-win, or if we are being *foolishly selfish*.

A NECESSARY DETOUR IS THE BEST WAY FORWARD

The term *object empowering acceptance* does not mean we agree or condone. It does mean we understand the NOOT that has caused events and people to be as they are. We are not resigned to defeat, but rather we are lifted up and enlivened. Here we are empowered to see that we can and will make progress only by going forward around the inevitability of things as they are. Wisely chosen detours are the best ways forward. Once again **"Being the Stream"** and pivoting around obstacles to continue forward as a Betterist, seeking less suffering and more satisfaction. *Objective empowered acceptance* allows us to see a treasure map that shows us where to avoid the quagmire quicksand of denial and jungle booby traps of failure so as to have a safe and successful way forward to the prize. Failure to surrender to reality only stalls us, if not prevents us, from getting to our desires and dreams. Refusing to surrender leads to failure, frustration, and conflict.

You will most likely see the concepts and views here as "unnatural" as well as uncomfortable and counterintuitive. The use of a new language will be awkward in the beginning. Yet, I ask you to be open to challenging the presumption of many commonly-used words. These concepts stand in your way and are obstacles to both your inner and intra-peace.

HOW CAN I MAKE THINGS EASIER FOR YOU?

In my more than thirty years of facilitating business problem-solving teams in manufacturing and maintenance, we nurtured teamwork and employee engagement/fulfillment to achieve record progress and results. Most importantly, we changed the language within the teams. The employees became strategic thinkers on a granular day-to-day scale. They were encouraged to focus on how their jobs could be made easier and bring these ideas to the weekly improvement team meetings. We focused on processes and communication and shifted focus away from personalities. This methodology served us well.

With one particular set of teams, we were looking for a way to improve through-put of re-manufacturing locomotives. Initially, team members focused on views like: "The other shift is screwed up," or "How can you expect us to _____when we have to work with _____?"

The teams' language and thinking were in woeful need of improvement to move away from blaming and seeing themselves as victims to being problem solvers.

The first step to make progress was to depersonalize the problems (which became known as obstacles). We used language that empowered and guided thinking toward root causes to do so. The focus moved to areas such as material availability, informational hand-offs between shifts and departments, proper tooling, and adequate manpower. Weekly and daily meetings were set with the key groups represented. A list of specific obstacles was updated weekly and posted with the status of resolving the obstacle and the owner responsible for following up and reporting on that improvement. The focus moved to making improvements to our processes and standards and away from blaming personalities. Our goal was to do things right the first time and avoid rework. The language on the production line and with management and vendors changed. We went from a through-put of two to three locomotives remanufactured each week to a consistent five per week with excellent quality and minimal rework.

These were real down-to-earth nuts and bolts (literally) work areas with budget money encompassing over $100 million per year and over 100 skilled craft employees working on three separate shifts. Employee engagement, safety, quality, and morale improved. Productivity soared, upper-level management's confidence improved, and future funding increased because there was faith in our ability to deliver. All that centered around a central theme question for the team members: *"How can we make your job easier?"*

Communicating with a new common language that was less accusatory, demeaning, and victim-related made a huge, positive difference.

Teamwork within the shift and between shifts skyrocketed. Employees felt heard and were actively engaged in ownership improvements in their work areas. The employees became excited with identifying obstacles and solutions. They came to understand the importance of working within boundaries. They recognized policy and resource limitations with money, manpower, facility infrastructure, and regulatory requirements. They also came to fully believe in the value and a need to comply with safety, quality, union, and environmental policies. By accepting the reality of what is, we were free to constructively move forward within those boundaries to mitigate and resolve hundreds of problems and obstacles by taking ownership for improvement and communicating needs. Partners for progress were created who worked together for the common good. A win-win mindset was there for employees, management, the company, the customers, and the community served by our products.

This same general process for progress works with personal relationships, as well. As with the manufacturing production teams, it is essential to get beyond the tendency to blame the other, to play the victim, or to be defensive or dismissive. Those behaviors are common components in unhealthy relationships. It is especially important to have boundaries focused primarily on process standards and requirements, rather than with another's behavior (more on this in future chapters). With a clear view of the real problems and a better language, people can focus individually and collectively on obstacles to their success. The path for progress begins with honesty and clarity about one's own fears, desires, and entitled expectations (covered in detail with the chapters ahead).

SHED NON-ESSESTIAL BAGGAGE

In July 2019, I traveled to Tanzania, Africa, where I took a guided photographic safari in the Serengeti and the Ngorongoro Crater. Following this four-day amazing experience, I next went on a ten-day, nine-night camping trek to the summit of Mount Kilimanjaro at 19,300 feet. While on safari, I traveled in a Range Rover and could carry a near unlimited amount of baggage and personal belongings. The trek up Mount Kilimanjaro required traveling as light as possible and shedding nonessential baggage (left behind in safe keeping at a local hotel).

This book's proposed adventure journey requires you to step out of the comfort of your figurative Range Rover and walk forward with your backpack of valuable essential equipment and tools for the trail ahead. To do so, it is important that you shed as much unnecessary baggage as possible and have the simplest, lightest, yet most effective gear with you.

One common type of baggage many have is the harboring of ill will towards another. This state of mind can severely limit our forward progress. It is the subject of a later chapter, "Forget Forgiving."

I believe that with the use of wise empowering language, you will use the best words possible to serve as your shield, sword, and compass to support your ongoing future progress with your *Journey into Peace.*

CHAPTER 3

Golden Keys, Silver Keys, and States of Being

How do I master a new language?

"Be the Student"

Some words spiral us up, some words spiral us down,
and some just have us go round and round.

—Michael Starr

Positively connecting with people is very important to me. When I traveled to Africa in 2019 to go on a four-day safari and a ten-day trek summiting Mount Kilimanjaro, I wanted to be able to interact with the Tanzanians. To do so, I began learning Swahili. During the picture-taking safari I rode in a large Range Rover, which was equipped with a snorkel and observation deck, with my remarkable guide Victor.

Victor had studied at university and was an expert on the flora, fauna, and geography of Tanzania. As we traveled in that behemoth khaki-colored Range Rover, Victor became my teacher and introduced me to many terms in the language of Swahili. While driving to and through Serengeti National Park, Ngorongoro Conservation Area, and Lake Manyara National Park, Victor reviewed what he had taught me the day before and quizzed me each day. I took notes in a small composition notebook. Repetition and practice are indeed the keys to retention.

Learning this new language began by correlating terms in my current language of English with equivalent ones in the new language. For example, "jambo" means hello and "asante sana" means thank you very much. My nickname during the subsequent Mount Kilimanjaro trek was "twiga," which means giraffe. Another example related to the theme for summiting Mount Kilimanjaro, which was to not hurry. We were reminded to go slowly and pace ourselves due to the lower oxygen levels at high altitude and physical exertion. "Slow" translated is "pole pole" (pronounced pole lee pole lee).

As I became more proficient in the Swahili language, I was able to express gratitude, joke, and greet the many Tanzanians I met and traveled with during that two-week period. Being able to communicate with these marvelous folks resulted in respect, trust, smiles, and laughter.

A BIT OF PRACTICE CAN LEAD TO QUANTUM LEAPS

To effectively use the ideas within this book, you, too, must learn a new language. A bit of diligence and practice can lead to quantum leaps with your relationships, responses, and ability to achieve important results. Though the views within this book are admittedly unconventional and somewhat awkward, I ask you to please give it some time to sink in. In the end, I believe you will be living your life at a level of unprecedented peace, progress, and healing.

One of the challenges with writing a book about the shortcomings of our current word use is the need to use the same commonly-accepted language to make the case. It is further complicated by the lexicon within this book that has no exact equivalency for us. This will be found with the terms such as *Betterism*, the *Natural Order of Things, and LEAR*. The contention that "forgiveness" and "patience" are *useless language* will at first be confusing or even heretical. This does make mastering this new language difficult; perhaps more challenging than learning Swahili. Please give these new perspectives time to germinate, and they will indeed sprout and blossom for you.

Often, revolutionary new ideas can be well expressed within the common language, as it was with Polish Astronomer Nicolas Copernicus and explorer Christopher Columbus. While Columbus was advancing his belief of a round Earth and exploration across the Atlantic, Copernicus was claiming that the sun, and not the Earth, was at the center of the solar system. Both had little need to use an improved language to make their cases. Yet this is not always so with newly-discovered concepts and perspectives.

To better describe new ideas in the sciences of chemistry, physics, psychology, and physiology, an improved language is often necessary. A language for breakthrough new concepts and perspectives often is needed to communicate a new view of cause and effect. Advances in the area of chemistry proposed the theory that all matter was made of elements. Researchers like Ernest Rutherford discovered elements were composed of identical atoms, each with a nucleus with neutrons and protons surrounded by orbiting electrons. Elements were defined by the number of protons in their atomic nucleus. Physicist Sir Isaac Newton proposed the ideas of laws of motion such as F=MA (force equals mass times acceleration). Psychology advanced concepts such as Freud's idea of ego and Maslow's hierarchy of needs. In 1847, a physician named Ignaz Semmelweis became a pioneer of antiseptic procedures. He realized the importance of disinfection and sterilization protocols and ordered chlorinated lime solution for hand washing in the hospital. Subsequently, mortality rates of childbed fever dropped significantly. The French chemist Louis Pasteur advanced the germ theory of disease with its cause-and-effect relationship. This led to pasteurization, a procedure for heating milk to eliminate pathogens. Terminology such as bacteria, electrons, ego, and self-actualization were created and defined to facilitate discernment that turned theory into functional reality.

HAVE AN OPEN MIND AND SEEK FIRST TO UNDERSTAND

Our ability to learn and use breakthrough views of the world around us hinges on letting down our defenses and limiting any initial resistance to new ideas that appear to be contrary to our current views and beliefs. After building a solid understanding of these new concepts, we can then challenge and test them for validity and credibility. Please have an open mind and seek to first understand the presented subject matter before challenging it and testing it out for yourself. If you do that, I believe this can be a life-changing experience for you.

In order to best promote the value of the wiser realities (*higher truths*) within this book, it is important to recognize three categories of words and concepts:

1. Useless words

2. Dangerous/Tyrannical words

3. Wise empowering words (some entirely new, some refined, and others redefined)

1. Useless words are ideas and concepts that lead nowhere. They are like alchemy with its futile efforts to produce gold from non-gold materials; they will not lead to the improvements you desire. Some examples of useless words are *willpower* and *forgiveness*. I suggest replacing *willpower* with *desire power* and *forgiveness* with *understanding,* as the original words convey an intention rather than an action that leads to a desired outcome.

2. Dangerous and tyrannical language leads to beliefs that are harmful and make matters worse, as with binary views of people being either all bad or all good. Using terms like "loser" or "hater" promotes this limiting either/or thinking. This language can cause us to dehumanize our view of others which can then lead to the justification of cruel and intolerant behavior towards them. History is replete with examples of commonly accepted practices and ideas later proven wrong and harmful. Lead piping used for indoor plumbing by the Romans, bloodletting with leeches, and surgical lobotomies were believed to be helpful in their era. We now know that they were not. When communities were faced with unexplainable events, often tyrannical language was created, as with the Salem witch trials, that promoted mob rule. More recently, in the 1960s, the American Heart Association promoted the belief that all fat in food was inherently bad. A low-fat, high-carb diet was espoused. This idea for dietary improvement actually produced an opposite and enormously negative impact on both heart and general health. This misguided belief resulted in the decline in heart health of the general population because all fats are not bad and certain carbs are unhealthy.[11]

3. Within the category of **wise empowering language**, some common language words are redefined, and others refined. It is also necessary that some completely new words are invented to best understand new paradigms. Wise empowering language has embedded within it a direction that encourages you to take meaningful action. It steers you away from victimhood and toward self-reliance. "Desire power" versus willpower is an example. Here, the intent is to focus on what it takes to acquire and sustain your *"desire"* versus the less meaningful term of "will power." The emphasis is on what you can do to increase your desire. Likewise, the term *dispassionate clarity* accents the importance of seeing the world around you in a way that transcends emotion, drama, blame, and judgment. NOOT (the Natural Order of Things) is a concept of *objective empowering acceptance* of the realities around you (as opposed to a resigned acceptance). Being able to see that events have played out as they had to is key. By having an objective view of what is, we are empowered and capable to best decide how to effectively interact with people and events.

A new, wiser view of the world around us can be a game changer, as was the concept of the Glycemic index. The Glycemic index was introduced in the late 1970s by Dr. David Jenkins of the University of Toronto. It defined the relationship between food and its rate of conversion in raising levels of blood sugar. This proved most helpful in countering the misdirection of the earlier recommendations of the American Heart Association. These new and refined words further our understanding and lead to advances in solving problems and improving the human condition. Language has a profound impact on how we think about our observations. It facilitates our ability to make progress and get better results. There is no better time than now to have our language mature and evolve to the next level of wise understanding to promote healthy relationships and personal progress.

REDUCE CONFLICT AND ACCELERATE ACCOMPLISHMENTS

My motivation for this book is to reduce avoidable suffering. My desire is to help you help yourself with new, wiser directions and decisions. Reducing suffering leads to having more joy, more inner peace, harmony with self and others, and the ability to achieve that which is important. The new language concept I am promoting can reduce conflict, increase love and compassion, and accelerate meaningful accomplishments. You are likely reading this book because you wish to find a better way. I believe that improving your language, as explained in this book, is a better way.

In order to succeed, the first step is understanding some key terminology. It was necessary in my Navy submarine life for me to understand new terms such as reactor scram, port and starboard, bow and stern, and *the head* (bathroom). The new language proposed in this book includes key terms. These key terms fall into the three categories: *golden keys*, *silver keys*, and *states of being*. *Golden keys* unlock the first set of doors to a better life for you; they are foundational. *Silver keys* are terms that further promote empowered wise views and are presented in the chapters ahead. Silver keys build on the foundation provided with the golden keys. *States of being* are easily remembered ways to see yourself in different situations. Emulating these states of being will empower you and sustain you as you face challenging circumstances .

I have three important desires I hope to achieve with this book:

1. To convince you that the language you use has a profound impact on your ability to respond and interact effectively with the world around you.

2. To provide you a foundational language (golden keys, silver keys, and states of being terminology) to serve as a springboard to better achieve the desires and dreams you deserve.

3. To inspire you to pass this new language to others in order to facilitate peace, progress, and healing in your communities.

The golden keys, silver keys, and states of being are the gateways to an exciting and satisfying new world. This is a world where success is accelerated, achieved, and sustained. Introducing these three categories of terminology early on in the book will facilitate your progress and increase the return on your investment of time spent reading the subsequent chapters. The ultimate goal is to assist you in achieving desirable outcomes for yourself, as well as strengthening your leadership influence.

Please have an open mind and do a bit of review and practice with this chapter. As that old saying went in the nuclear submarine program in the US Navy, "Repetition is the key to retention."

Golden Key Terms:

1. *Dispassionate Clarity*

2. *Objective Empowering Acceptance*

3. *Betterism*

4. *Desire Power*

5. *Natural Order of Things (NOOT)*

6. *Legitimate Empowering Alternate Reality (LEAR)*

7. *Intentional Simple Tiny Efforts for Progress (ISTEPs)*

8. *The EBC Symbiotic 3*

9. *The Relationship Trinity*

10. *Sacred Habits*

11. *Relationship Listening*

12. *Delightful Detours*

Summary of the Golden Keys terms:

1. Dispassionate Clarity

The objective observation and recognition of people and events around us devoid of blame, drama, or judgment. As we see others through the eyes of empathy and a view of the Natural Order of Things, we unshackle ourselves from emotions that hinder clarity and wise decision making.

2. Objective Empowering Acceptance

Believing that people and events are as they had to have become. This is not a resigned surrender to reality, but an empowered dance which makes the achievement of desired outcomes far more likely.

When we accept limits and boundaries, we realize that progress exists only by working around undesired and immovable obstacles. We stop futile battles and wasted resistance, and focus instead on taking paths for wise progress forward.

3. Betterism

A philosophy where journey and destination are an interwoven combination; inseparable. It seeks win-win outcomes in our interactions with others. With *Betterism*, we are empowered to seek out more joy, harmony, peace of mind, and meaning while at the same time reducing frustration, anger, conflict, despair, and listlessness. Ultimately, we feel empowered and excited about our growing clarity regarding ourselves and our world. We respond in ways that increase our fulfillment and contribute to others. We are brimming with hope and possibility. We have confidence that our path is wise and proper. We act in ways that are in the long-term best interest for ourselves. A *Betterist* is one who practices *Betterism*.

4. Desire Power

Willpower is a concept that assumes we can somehow use our state of mind to push through difficulties and achieve something. Willpower is not a sustainable activity, as it often lacks context with our lives. Desire power is often revealed with the use of the words "I want to" as opposed to the words "I need to." Desire power is the self-motivation that wakes us up at 4 a.m. to engage with exciting challenges and opportunities. This golden key focuses our efforts toward understanding ourselves. It addresses cognitive dissonance, which is the tension that occurs when we act in a manner diametrically opposed to our own values. Surrounding ourselves with people with healthy views and getting proper rest are two of many actions we take to facilitate our self-motivation and nurture our desire power. There is a subtle nuance between the terms "motivation" and "self-motivation." The emphasis is on the latter, self-motivation, to remind us and empower us that *if it is to be, it is up to me.*

5. Natural Order of Things (NOOT)

The presumption here is that all that has happened was inevitable. It was the result of DNA, the laws of nature, environmental evolution, and experiences. It is a natural and neutral reality. People cannot help but be who they are. The Natural Order of Things is the golden key to compassion, love, and understanding. It leads to a profound empathy toward others as well as ourselves. It limits conflict and protects us by facilitating wise boundaries with consequences. Though other people can't help being who they are, we ourselves have the ability to adjust and improve our current and future trajectories. We can discover better and more effective ways to respond to the events and behaviors around us.

A view of the world and the people within it through the eyes of Natural Order of Things evaporates away much of the confusion and exhaustion that accompany unrealistic expectations that later lead to conflict, anger, disappointment, frustration, despair, and self-righteousness. Here, we achieve a dispassionate clarity and make wise choices and decisions that optimize the time, energy, and resources available to us. It allows us to unshackle ourselves from drama, animosity toward others, and self-loathing. It limits the amount and degree of stifling disappointment in our lives, freeing up energy to be empowered and follow through with actions to make improvements for ourselves. It promotes focus on our time, energy, and effort toward being used for meaningful progress.

6. Legitimate Empowering Alternate Reality (LEAR)

This is an alternative view from our current reality. It is an empowered view that facilitates healing, peace of mind, and progress. This view is credibly legitimate. This perspective empowers us to act and respond wisely and calmly. It promotes a win–win situation for all parties involved.

7. Intentional Simple Tiny Efforts for Progress (ISTEPs)

These are incremental actions for making progress in areas we have determined to be important. They are often scheduled and committed to on a daily basis as part of a morning routine. They are small and simple enough to be sustainable. They are the actions that are a key component of *Betterism*. They are the flow of activity with **"Being the Stream,"** in which we are alive through forward movement. They are best scheduled as part of a daily habit, as with a morning routine.

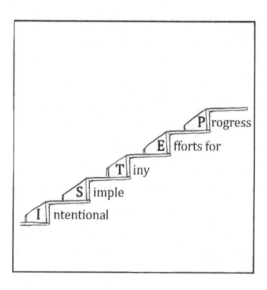

8. The EBC Symbiotic 3 = Empathy + Boundaries + Consequences

The EBC Symbiotic 3 concept provides a method for dealing with unpalatable or toxic behaviors in a calm and confident manner. We begin with building our understanding and empathy toward someone. We then establish clear boundaries for acceptable and unacceptable behavior. Lastly, we select consequences when our boundaries are crossed or encroached upon. These consequences must be implemented each and every time they are required. Consequences are a matter of what "I will do" as opposed to what "they need to do."

9. The Relationship Trinity

Relationships with another are comprised of three components:

- Our relationship with self

- Relationship of the other person with themselves

- Interactions between us

We best serve ourselves by putting our efforts into "being a better me." It is also wise to understand and accept the other person for who they are. The goal is to have our act together, so to speak, to minimize our tendency to project our personal unhappiness, discontent, and frustration upon another. Lastly, by accepting them for who they are, we are in a position to respond and interact wisely with them and develop boundaries with consequences when appropriate.

10. Sacred Habits

Habits are the things we do on auto pilot that simplify our journey forward by making progress automatic and effortless. Sacred habits are non-negotiable and essential for our ongoing progress. There are three recommended sacred habits promoted in this book. They are your morning routine, your week in review session, and use of the follow up setback system (FUSS).

11. Relationship Listening

This is a form of awareness and listening that is based on caring for others and their needs, desires, dreams, and concerns. It both acknowledges them and strives to understand not only the words, but the emotions and feelings behind these words. It recognizes the tendency to listen to respond, as opposed to listening to understand and respectfully acknowledge another. It communicates our caring for another.

12. Delightful Detours

Detours are inevitable and occur when the expected and planned path changes. Mistakes and setbacks are forms of detours. Examples of these unexpected events are road closures, a sudden work crisis, or a water leak in our home. We pivot quickly when they occur, focusing on the next best step forward instead of getting caught up in anger or frustration. Along with the pivot, we record the issue in our *Follow-Up Setback System* (FUSS) for later review. These can become *Learning Experiences for Growth* (LEGs). They are the shortest path forward and can be leveraged for future benefit of self and others.

Silver Keys

Silver keys are presented throughout the chapters ahead. These are common language words that are either redefined or refined. They will assist you with having empowering views and guide you toward progress. Below are a few examples of these silver key words that will be presented in future chapters:

What is: A calm, objective, and unemotional view of the state of things and occurrences, devoid of judgment or blame. Each event is seen with *dispassionate clarity,* and as such allows us to make the best decisions we can at that time.

Wise versus Foolish Selfishness: We all do things and take action from a position of self-interest and self-preservation. Wise selfishness efforts are those that seek win-win outcomes that help those around us as well as ourselves. They work toward the long-term interests of ourselves and others. Foolish selfishness occurs when we are consumed with self. This makes us short-sighted, with a need for immediate pleasure and satisfaction. Foolish selfishness does not consider the best interests of others and, in the long term, is not in our own best interests.

Durinfre: Duration— Intensity— Frequency: Our improvements are measured based on changes in duration, frequency, and intensity. The intent is to increase good occurrences and decrease bad occurrences. Three arguments a month is better than three per day. Exercising once a week for one hour is better than once a week for ten minutes.

Trails of Progress (TOPs): These are proposed processes and trajectories for forward advancement, as with improving a relationship or eliminating resentment.

Learning Experience for Growth (LEG): An alternative empowering term for mistakes and setbacks that facilitate improvement (learning from our mistakes). Here, we see an opportunity to become better by using the setback as a springboard for self-motivation to become better.

Higher Truth: A wiser view of "what is" that facilitates our being empowered to advance future peace and progress.

Velcro Learning: New ideas easily attach to established ideas and understanding. We understand that as we increase foundational understanding of a subject, we can more rapidly retain and understand future new learning associated with it.

Anchor Habit: An existing habit we use as an attachment point when starting a new habit.

Self-Exorcism: A process for moving past animosity and upset with another relating to experiences in the past. The anguish we often feel is a result of our points of view. We are often the source of our unhappiness, and by building understanding and empathy of another, these negative feelings evaporate.

Follow-Up Setback System (FUSS): A method for keeping mishaps and undesired outcomes on our personal radar for future assessment and possible action for improvement. Best reviewed periodically after the mistake or setback, possibly during the *Week in Review Session* meeting held with yourself.

Contra Identity: Defining ourselves by our opposition to others who have views with which we disagree. A strong predisposition toward being against as opposed to being for something or someone. We feel important and right by making others unimportant and wrong.

Opportunity Cost: The time, energy, and resources spent on "X" cannot be used for "Y."

States of Being

Most chapters within this book will have recommendations for a state of being. The states of being will assist you with visualizing an empowering and wise perspective of yourself as it relates to the focus of that chapter. You are encouraged to call up that image and be that concept when facing an applicable challenge or interest. This view will empower you to take wise next steps.

A few examples of states of being are:

Be the stream: Detours are the shortest way forward. We are alive and vibrant only when we are moving forward, as with a mountain stream.

Be the waiter: Make your case wisely and succinctly, then move on.

Be like Betty: Continually compete against yourself, looking to make things better.

Be the self-motivation maestro: Surround yourself with things, people, and activities that excite and energize you.

Be like a school of fish: Pivot quickly when an obstacle is encountered yet record it in your FUSS log for later analysis to see what can or should be done in the future.

Words and language can be nutritional and medicinal. Words can also be placebos or even toxic. They can advance us, stall us, or harm us. They can damage relationships and limit our ability to remediate harm. Woven into the very fabric of many words are embedded solutions or distractions. In some cases, words promote a disease that harms. This book will elaborate on the three categories of words: useless, dangerous, and wisely empowering. It will also reveal the fundamentals for achieving an optimistic path toward peace and progress while recognizing the often-obscured tyranny of words with the misdirection and toxins they contain. As we recognize useless and harmful words that hurt or drain us of energy, we then can focus on positive action. We then have a clearing, where prior obstacles and obstructions have been removed—a place for building positive lives for ourselves. We have the space to put our energy into meaningful actions for improvement that move us ever closer to the peace, progress, and the healing we desire.

CHAPTER 4

Betterism, the Pursuit of More Good and Less Bad

What am I pursuing?

"Be Like Betty"

Perfection Is the enemy of the good.

–Voltaire

Our personal language often creates self-fulfilling prophecies. There are subtle nuances with many of our commonly used words that steer us to either make progress, waste our energy, or be hurtful. Like Mendeleev's periodic table, which paved the way for advances in chemistry, a wise empowering language is the foundation for forward progress. It can provide clarity with both the past and the present. It can nurture our satisfaction with today and our aspirations for tomorrow. It guides us toward healthy decisions and responses. Words can help heal and encourage. Language can also be self-destructive and create unhealthy relationships with unrealistic expectations.

When we see someone as *inexperienced,* we are inclined to understand why they may be unsuccessful with a particular challenge. Within this word is embedded an understanding why the behavior is what it is, and we in turn have empathy. In this case, we tend to have a caring, calm, and slow approach when communicating with them. We are likely to act in a manner that guides and nurtures their path forward toward being "experienced." The view of another as *ignorant* tends to move us with compassion, as well. They just don't know and never had the opportunity to understand things that we assume and may take for granted. Once again, we understand why and have empathy for them. These perspectives support healthy relationships.

These views of another are more likely to be helpful for them and build up their confidence as opposed to a hurtful label such as *stupid,* which shuts down healthy and constructive communication.

Terms such as unfriendly, idiot, racist, or narcissist tend to put others in a binary category of all bad and zero good. A better alternative point of view is:

- "Are they concerned with being rejected, or perhaps they are preoccupied with a serious personal upset?" versus "unfriendly."

- "They are not learning from their past mistakes, I wonder why?" versus "idiot."

- "I am not sure why that comment regarding John's performance was made, I want to know more." versus "racist."

- "That person's behavior in today's meeting did not take into consideration its impact on me, why was that so?" versus "narcissist."

The questions with the alternative thoughts above can lead us to a deeper, more accurate understanding and empathy for others. They better serve us with finding a *higher truth.* These questions will restrain us from jumping to simplistic conclusions that alienate and poison later interactions. These questions can also provide a perspective that will optimize our future communications and relationships with them.

A TREND TOWARD DENEGRATION

There is a strong tendency these days to quickly denigrate and label someone in a negative manner, anxious to find them guilty until proven innocent. Once a public narrative erupts with an accusation, the well is often forever poisoned, and finding them innocent is off the table. It is difficult for many people to back away from a premature defamation they may have made. After several years of reviewing millions of records, millions of dollars spent, and a multitude of lawyers investigating the "Russian Collusion" accusation, these investigators found no substantial evidence to support the accusation. Despite all that investigative work, many clung to this story line that "no evidence was found, YET!" They had so enrolled themselves in this conclusion they could not see a way to back away and say, "I was wrong". Dangerous language can box us in and limit our ability to get out of a dark place.

Often, the motivation toward labeling someone with a quick negative label is rooted in our own insecurity and desire for importance. It is a tempting approach toward others, as it enhances our identity as being good because another is bad. I call this view a *contra identity;* a view of self in opposition to a negative view of others.

Each of us is an intricate mosaic of many roles and beliefs. We are complex tapestries interwoven with a multitude of experiences and genetic material, in many ways magnificent, yet flawed and imperfect. We are a collage of multiple abilities and shortcomings. Dangerous language tends to slam the brakes on meaningful communications and healthy relationships. It can isolate one flaw and magnify it way out of proportion. It limits our desire and curiosity to better understand and appreciate one another.

DARYL DAVIS AND THE KKK

Daryl Davis is a black R&B musician who engaged self-proclaimed racist KKK members in dialog. He chose to talk with them from a position of understanding. He pursued a communication with them to understand why they thought as they did. As a result of his use of language seeking to understand, he fostered respectful relationships with several Klan members. From that point, he then proceeded to better educate them. As a result, he convinced a number of these KKK members to leave and denounce the organization. Daryl is an activist focused on making things better; he seeks to find and guide others toward more good and less bad. He was looking to make things better rather than be satisfied to sit on a throne of self-righteousness.

In order to facilitate your understanding and progress, I have coined a term I call *Betterism*. It is a golden key word, a foundational word for understanding and applying the principles within this book. *Betterism* is simply defined as the pursuit of *being better*. Like a coin, it has two sides: destination and journey. Unlike a crusade that is consumed with a specific outcome, the continual pursuit matters with *Betterism*. Inherently, pursuit demands a destination; something to pursue. Without a destination, there is no meaningful pursuit, only aimless wandering. The destination together with the journey are symbiotic and together they become the goal. With *Betterism,* we always have at least one wisely chosen goal with its specific journey and destination at any time. Here we live our lives to *feel alive* by continually moving forward with joy and fulfillment. Here we are *being the stream,* where we are defined by forward movement and constant motion that proceeds effortlessly around, over, and under obstacles we encounter. Often, later in life, people second guess their direction and efforts after they have achieved a desired outcome. It is not that their destination was necessarily wrong, but more that their journey toward that destination was not wisely taken.

Language can take us on futile paths that do little but have us go in circles. It can have us thinking we are on a path of progress when we are on a carousel going nowhere but round and round. We can be like the alchemists of the 1700s that wasted their time and efforts with a dead-end goal. Their efforts to create gold was folly and impossible to achieve. *Try* and *should* are two examples of words that tend to promote futility and frustration. There is a world of difference between saying "I will try to exercise more" versus "I am committing to going to the gym Monday and Thursday immediately after work."

Likewise, the word *patience* tends to be a dead-end word as it is not a doable action. When we find ourselves in a circumstance where things are proceeding much slower than our initial expectation, it is prudent to have a curiosity to ask why it is so. We then can come to an understanding and view that things must now move at a different pace and direction than originally anticipated. This acceptance of the current circumstances eliminates frustration and anger and focuses us to leverage our energy on how to best facilitate this revised progress. We see that the detour is the shortest way forward and we now work on deciding which detour is the best one to take. The process of developing an understanding of *what is* does lead to an outcome that many would label as *patience*. In our commonly-used language, the outcome or destination is often confused with the path and means of getting to that result. Patience is not a path toward a desired outcome, just as *forgiveness* is not a verb of action, they better characterize the final resultant outcome.

Words can be subtly dangerous for us as well. They may have inadvertently evolved to be harmful. Additionally, some words are intentionally designed to divide and confuse. The term *hate speech* easily becomes a means for censorship. Who is the arbiter of this definition? This term can easily be used for denigrating and diminishing others who have different cultural or political views. This term short circuits civil dialog and debate much like a crushing blow from a fly swatter to the fly. Perhaps a better language would focus on what is true or not true supported by facts and not opinion. *Climate denier* or *anti vaxxer* likewise are yet other terms that divide and lead to a stillborn debate. This dangerous language is commonly accepted as legitimate yet is more akin to the common accepted belief by the Romans that the lead pipes used for bringing water to their homes were a good thing. For decades, use of asbestos was touted as a wonder substance and used in hundreds of products and applications. Commonly accepted ideas, words, or practices are not always legitimate or helpful. It is very common, yet alarming to many, that literally overnight multiple news organizations simultaneously introduce absolutely identically worded new catch phrases that are politically charged and motivated such as *manufactured crisis, existential threat, Russian collusion,* or *racist* to describe a current event or individual.

Our language impacts our perceptions, thinking, and responses. Empowering wise language can lift up others and ourselves by providing hope and possibility. Likewise, we can unknowingly and routinely put others down as well and damage self-worth, teamwork, healthy relationships, and our own self efficacy. Like the definition of insanity, it can also take us round and round on a carousal to nowhere. Let us choose wisely to be the winners who roll up our sleeves to improve things as opposed to the whiners who complain, blame, and shame.

Hopefully, we use language that empowers us and takes us to a positive place where we become *healers first* and *revealers last.* As healers, we are continually seeking and moving in a direction to improve things for ourselves and others. This role has us committed to the possibility of achieving win-win solutions and reducing suffering. Here we are committed to a pursuit of more good and less bad (*Betterism*). In contrast, as *revealers,* folks tend to be much like Henny Penny, the chicken who received attention and self-importance by declaring "the sky is falling." For the revealers, others' suffering, joy, and need for acknowledgment take a back seat to their quest for self-importance and uniqueness with their so-called enlightened views of the next apocalypse.

THE AFRICAN DISCOVERY

In the year prior to my retirement as a locomotive maintenance manager I decided to plan an after retirement adventure, I decided to climb to the summit of Mount Kilimanjaro. I found the allure of Africa and the uniqueness of this Ernest Hemingway subject irresistible. Shortly after my sixty-eighth birthday, in June of 2018, my preparations began. Mount Kilimanjaro, located in Tanzania, is the tallest mountain on the African continent. Its iconic snowcapped peak stands out majestically over hundreds of miles of the surrounding landscape. Unlike the much higher Mount Everest, which is embedded in the Himalayan Mountain Range, Mount Kilimanjaro is a standalone beacon singularity that can be clearly and completely viewed from its base to its peak. Often used as a backdrop for elephants, giraffes, and numerous African wildlife by photographers and artists, it symbolizes the grandeur of this remarkable continent. At its peak of 19,341 feet, oxygen levels are near 50 percent of those available at sea level. It can be a treacherous geology to climb with ice, below-freezing temperatures and near gale force winds at the summit of the Kibo volcanic crater called Uhuru Peak.

One year after my decision to summit Mount Kilimanjaro, in July 2019, at the age of sixty-nine, I arrived at the Kilimanjaro International Airport in Tanzania knowing I was as ready as I reasonably could be. Though I was uncertain as to my ability to make it to the top, I was confident that the real work was done and from here on it was to be what it would be. I knew that whether I made it to the top or not, that I would be at peace with the outcome. I did the right things with what was most in my control, selecting that destination and working the preparatory process wisely. The outcome was uncertain, yet the odds were wisely set up for success. Like a sports player, I was on the field on game day, ready to play and enjoy the adventure underfoot. Upon my landing in Tanzania in the dark of the midnight sky, I remember saying to myself, "Let the game begin."

I had little anxiety about the journey ahead.

There were those who doubted and felt my desire and plan at the age of sixty-eight to be foolhardy. They believed that I would not complete the trek to the summit. Those doubting and concerned included my general practitioner and a childhood best friend. My trusted general practitioner, who has helped keep me healthy for nearly twenty years said, "Are you sure you need to do this . . . that's some hefty altitude up there."

As the departure date to Africa drew close, my dear friend asked me, "How far do you think you will get?"

This question was a bit disempowering as it implied that reaching the summit was in question.

Yet, there were those who believed in my adventure as worthy of pursuit. My wife Karen and my heart doctor cheered me forward. My wife was excited to be part of the preparations with local hiking and eagerly flew to Flagstaff, Arizona, to do altitude training there with me as we climbed Humphreys Peak (nearly 10,000 feet higher than any peak in our home state of Arkansas at an elevation of 12,600+ feet). My heart doctor was enthusiastic as well, and told me of his preparation to climb Mount Everest years before (his permit for climbing unfortunately had been revoked by the Chinese government due to the then-current politics shortly before his arrival).

Before leaving the Little Rock Airport for my flights to Tanzania, my wife gave me two sealed envelopes with the request that I not open them until my arrival in Africa. They contained encouraging cards that expressed her belief in me and her admiration of my quest and confidence in my success. I took them up the mountain, and every evening took them out of my backpack and read them. Having healthy attitudes around me was reassuring.

From the outset, I was determined to give it my best and focus on what was in my control. I selected a time of year to climb when the weather would likely be a minimal problem. I researched and sought out advice on how best to be ready. After this, I just let it be what it would be, as there were many variables and uncertainties that were out of my control with weather, my body's response to high altitude, and my stamina in the reality of ten days of trekking, much of which was done at altitudes over 12,000 feet.

I spent nearly a year with my planning, preparations, and training for this mountain hike adventure. It was essential that my attitude, exercise, equipment, and medical readiness were done with a clear understanding of what was helpful, what was harmful, and what was frankly just a waste of time, effort, and money. It is the same with our language and words that fall in these three categories of helpful, harmful, or a waste of time.

During the year of preparation, I researched written material and YouTube videos, as well as sought out experts to discuss best practices for my pre-Africa arrival efforts. This all led to a very healthy diet and a "weekly exercise routine" with hiking over fifteen miles and three visits to the gym with a personal trainer who coached me with resistance and aerobic training. Decisions on equipment and clothing led to visits to the local outdoor store Ozark Outdoor Supply in Little Rock, as well as Amazon purchases aplenty (several every week for months). From backpack fitting and selection, to socks, to boots, to water containers, to down jacket, to sleeping bag choices were but a few of dozens and dozens of purchases. I also needed to assure myself I was healthy enough to accomplish this mission. Thinking I may have had a minor hernia, I visited with my trusted general practitioner (GP) and received a referral for further evaluation. I found I actually had a double hernia and needed surgery for both, which I received well in advance of the trip overseas. My GP also arranged for a treadmill test with a heart specialist (which I passed with flying colors). My GP gave me a prescription for "traveler's diarrhea," which proved to be invaluable during my photo safari in the Serengeti and the Ngorongoro Crater several days before starting the climb up the mountain. With a team of friends and experts, wise planning and preparation, fantastic support with the "Peak Planet" organization, and the remarkable leadership and talents of our Lead Guide Caspar, I did succeed with the ten-day ascent and descent of the mountain in July of 2019.

> *"When we commit to reaching a destination or outcome, we begin a three-phase experience:*
> *1. exciting anticipation,*
> *2. the thrill and challenge of the journey, and*
> *3. fond memories and lessons learned with the experience."*
>
> –Michael Starr

In retrospect, I came to see that far more important than reaching Mount Kilimanjaro's Uhuru Peak was the year-long process of planning and preparation with its feelings of excitement and purpose. The anticipation of the adventure ahead and actions taken were full of fun, friends, and fulfillment during the year leading up to the actual trek. The "real goal" was both the journey of preparation and the summiting. The destination gives meaning and context to the journey, while the journey is the aliveness we experience in our lives in each moment of *now*. I believe one of the important messages of this book lies with living a life of *Betterism,* with its ongoing pursuit of more good and less bad. As a Betterist, one actively seeks more laughter, harmony, peace of mind, optimism, and less frustration, anger, acrimony, and despair. We must take intentional paths and trajectories to accomplish that. *Betterism* is a lifestyle of continual movement forward by **Being the Stream**, existing within the context of the pursuit and motion. We are reminded with Betterism to **Be Like Betty** and chose an action for improvement each day. With this view, we need only stay grounded with the compass of integrity embedded in our wisely thought-out constitution of right and wrong with our *ten convictions,* undeterred by the obstacles before us and seeing the detour as necessary and the shortest route forward.

THE PATH AHEAD

Throughout this book, I endeavor to improve your clarity and effectiveness with words so as to develop a healthy, harmonious, and impactful language for you. There will be suggested Trails of Progress (TOPs) recommended for you. Those paths will give meaning to the goal of practicing *Betterism* as well as creating a nurturing and nutritious view of optimistic confidence for your present and future self. You will be encouraged to take *Intentional Simple Tiny Efforts for Progress* (ISTEPs) each day. You will create a wise *Language Periodic Table* with empowering words and concepts called Golden Keys, Silver Keys, and States of Being that will positively impact your thinking. You will identify ten convictions which will lie at the foundation of your communications, thinking, responses, and decisions. As a result, you will find more peace and progress for yourself and for the people around you, as well. You will better recognize the difference between words and concepts that empower versus harm versus waste your time and energy.

With our individual quests to make progress, we often proceed with unrealistic expectations for grand quantum leaps forward. We can be easily discouraged and dissuaded by setbacks and disappointing expectations. The quest with a trajectory of *Betterism* in our life process is one looking for incremental improvement. It not only anticipates but embraces delightful detours with our path forward. It improves in small steps with more happiness and less suffering each month.

Rather than expecting things to be always good and near perfect, it is far better to be more realistic and pursue "a bit" better with our experiences measured by their incremental improvements. A bit better can be measure objectively or subjectively with the duration, intensity, and frequency (*durinfre)* of reoccurrence. As with Betty in the following tongue twister, she sought to make today's batter better by seeking a better butter.

Betty Botter

Betty Botter had some butter,
"But," she said, "this butter's bitter.
If I bake this bitter butter,
it would make my batter bitter.
But a bit of better butter—
that would make my batter better."

So she bought a bit of butter,
better than her bitter butter,
and she baked it in her batter,
and the batter was not bitter.
So 'twas better Betty Botter
bought a bit of better butter.

I believe the moral to this tongue twister story is when things are not what you desire, "go for a bit of better."

As Betterists, we are empowered to seek out more good and less bad in our lives. We pursue a lifestyle the leads to more happiness, harmony, and satisfaction and less suffering and conflict. We strive for win-win outcomes with our relationships. Ultimately, we feel empowered, curious, and excited about our growing clarity about ourselves and our world. We respond in ways that have us increasingly feeling fulfilled and contributing to others. We are brimming with hope and possibility and the confidence that our path is wise and proper for both ourselves and others. We act in ways that are focused on the long-term success. This is the state of being and living as a Betterist. With our daily accomplishments of daily planned ISTEPs, we travel the trail forward one step at a time toward the grand summit and destination of greater clarity, calmness, conviction, and contribution. We become a trekker who has endless adventures and opportunities for reaching new summits and scaling yet once again another challenging summit.

CHAPTER 5

Making Peace with the Natural Order of Things (NOOT)

"Be Sacagawea"

"Be Michelangelo"

Life is 10 percent what happens to you and 90 percent how you react to it.

–Charles R. Swindoll

It was a warm and sunny spring morning as we stood above the headwaters of the Ohio River on May 21, 1972. There was a gentle breeze and a fishy river scent in the air. With the greenish vibrant Allegheny River to our right and the polluted brownish Monongahela River to our left, I paused for a moment to look downstream at the grand Ohio and ponder the journey ahead. Ron Ree and I had just completed our fall semester at Carnegie Mellon University and were about to embark on an adventure of a lifetime. There, nestled between Pittsburgh's Mount Washington and the Allegheny Mountain foothills, we said our goodbyes to my parents and Ron's girlfriend. We left them standing on the banks as we began paddling our canoe downriver. We had 1800+ miles ahead of us. This odyssey would take fifty-four days before we arrived in New Orleans in our seventeen-foot green fiberglass canoe called "Canoe."

As members of the school's chartered Ukrainian club, Ron Ree and I became good acquaintances. During a 1972 Ukrainian Club News Year's party, after having had a bit too much to drink, we vowed to canoe from Pittsburgh to New Orleans. In the next few days after we had sobered up, we were convinced that the surprising drunken thought was actually a good idea. We soon began our planning and preparations for a spring departure after the semester was completed.

Canoeing 1,850 miles through forty-plus locks and dams on the Ohio and the expanse of the grand Mississippi Rivers was both an amazing adventure as well as a trying interpersonal experience. Imagine being with the same person 24/7 for fifty-four days with personality styles like those from the movie *The Odd Couple* with Walter Matthau and Jack Lemmon. I remember us having a big blowout argument in the middle of the one-mile-wide Mississippi River near Memphis. We were yelling at each other, self-righteously making our case regarding who had been canoeing harder for the last one thousand miles. Very funny to think about this now, but not so humorous in that moment.

ROUTINES FREE US

A number of routines and habits evolved between us during that eight-week period. We developed a rhythm with our paddling with so many strokes done on one side before we switched simultaneously to the other side. I made an oatmeal breakfast each morning while Ron broke down the tent and packed it. We usually had sardines with crackers or peanut butter and bread for lunch as we drifted on the water. In the evening we would find a sandbar, island, or clearing and set up camp with our tent, sleeping bags, and small stove. Duties were clearly divided between us. These routines freed us from having to discuss and decide who did what on any particular day. The people we met along the way were incredibly friendly and supportive.

One evening, we went into a local bar for beers and saw ourselves on the local TV news channel being interviewed along the riverbank earlier that day. Drinks were "on the house" after that. Ron had worked with Carnegie Mellon's PR representative, who in turn contacted numerous newspaper and TV reporters who met us over a dozen times along the way as we camped near their towns. In Natchez, Mississippi, I was rushed to the hospital in a police car, siren blaring, as a result of a snake bite. I remember this mad rush with the flashing lights and all the while I was drinking a Coke and thinking "man, this is cool," It turned out that the bite was not poisonous. There are dozens of other experiences and stories that I will share with you (in my next book, perhaps?).

Sometimes the flow was slow and of little help as on the dammed Ohio River. At times it was a great ally, as on the Mississippi, especially when flood waters from up north helped us achieve a record sixty-mile travel day when the current added to our efforts. Our path was clearly identified and only required the simplest of routines to follow to achieve our destination.

As taxing as that journey was with twelve to thirteen hours a day of paddling through scorching sun and occasional thunderstorms, it was in many ways easy. The path ahead was simple: go downstream on the Ohio River, make a left at the Mississippi River until you reach New Orleans. There were few decisions to make, other than perhaps walking to a town once a week and buying supplies like Dinty Moore Beef Stew, oatmeal, and sardines. We went with the flow downstream.

There were literally no crossroads to come upon to decide which path and direction to take next.

REAL LIFE IS FULL OF CROSSROADS

Real life, on the other hand, is complex and full of many responsibilities and numerous occasions for deciding which way to turn next. Life often requires us to make decisions and answer challenging questions:

"What is the right thing to do here?"

"How do I best respond to this situation?"

"Why me?"

"How can I help?"

"Why don't they see _____?"

We can easily become overwhelmed and lost in the unlimited arena of "what do I do now?" and "what should I do next?" We can have great uncertainty and second guess ourselves no matter what we decide. We can lose our spark for life and become full of anger, frustration, or despondency. Unrealistic expectations and *foolish selfishness* can lead us down paths of misery and self-destruction. This uncertainty and negativity can be remedied, however, with wise empowering language.

Charles Swindoll's quote at the very beginning of this chapter nicely frames the degree of influence we have. He states that life is largely about how we react to occurrences around us; the point being that you and I are NOT victims of circumstance: "I am the master of my fate: I am captain of my soul . . . " William Ernest Henley states in his poem "Invictus" (meaning *unconquered* in Latin), which reminds us that we are empowered to guide ourselves wisely forward. We indeed have tremendous untapped potential to better focus our energies and resources to create more good and less bad (*the path of Betterism*) for ourselves and for others.

Most would agree that spending time, energy, and resources for achieving "the good" and "the better" is wise. The very definition of *progress* implies just that. Likewise, spending an excessive amount of time and energy with suffering, denigrating, anger, conflict, frustration, despair, and regret is undesirable. Languishing and obsessing over these negatives are both harmful and a waste of time. It consumes our precious limited energies and enthusiasm for life, and can leave us feeling depleted and exhausted. Stagnating, dwelling on the negative, and feeling sorry for ourselves kills motivation, desire, and ability for making real meaningful progress. The *opportunity cost* with "X" precludes that same resource from being used for "Y."

NEGATIVE EXPERIENCES ARE
SPRINGBOARDS FOR PROGRESS

However, when these negative experiences and feelings are used as springboards for progress, they are powerful motivators for getting better. These are the 10 percent. We are best served with applying a large preponderance of our efforts learning from the people and world around us to be better and adding to our *book of life* with lessons learned. This, once again, is the path of *Betterism,* the pursuit of more good and less bad. In the context of this book, terms characterizing "good" are: harmony with others, win-win solutions, laughter, vibrant health, financial security, peace of mind, purpose, healing, etc. Likewise, terms related to "bad" are: suffering, despair, frustration, anger, bitterness, conflict, etc.

The use of a better language improves our perception and definition of what the problem is. It helps us to sort out symptoms from root causes. The use of a better language minimizes the waste that results with emotional drama, negative emotions, futile perceptions, and actions that make things worse. With wise language, we empower ourselves and others to focus on common ground and common good. With healthy words and language, we can avoid wasting our time blaming or shaming, but rather spend our time and energies solving and salving.

Central to achieving successful results with this book is your interest and willingness to pursue an unprecedented level of *dispassionate clarity* in seeing all around and within you. This vantage point evaporates the drama and emotion that can distract and derail us from seeing things objectively. It allows us to recognize symptoms as just that; symptoms, not cause. The result: achieving better solutions to any problem we might face and speedier conflict resolutions. It allows us to best decide on future responses and proactive measures, as well. That is the 90 percent that Charles Swindoll addresses in his quote.

The objective with this chapter is to equip and empower you to be a guide for yourself and others, to *be like Sacagawea,* the historic Indian scout on the Lewis and Clark expedition. To assist you with achieving the clarity that results from having a dispassionate view of things, I recommend using the concept of *The Natural Order of Things (NOOT).* Seeing the *NOOT* of it all when something happens will give you the freedom and ability to recognize *Legitimate Empowering Alternate Realities* (LEAR) and *Higher Truths* that will facilitate your personal and leadership progress, as well as your influence on others with making things better.

Guides are essential when traveling in unknown and uncharted territory. They have the expertise with how to find direction that sustains forward progress. They focus on seeing what is actually there as opposed to a distorted view with what they may wish to be there. They help us avoid getting lost, reaching dead ends, or perhaps at times going over a cliff and falling into darkness. Objective observation without preconceived bias is critical. Guides also provide a level of confidence, encouragement, and support for others who also desire to navigate forward with their lives. Guides provide "context to a new destination, they remain encouraging forces, cheering you on to reach the summit, or assuring you . . . They are your friend and a bridge to new worlds and cultures."[12]

LEWIS AND CLARK

In the early 1800s, President Thomas Jefferson tasked expedition leaders Meriwether Lewis and William Clark with exploring new territory associated with the Louisiana Purchase. This North American Territory was west of the Mississippi River and extended to the Pacific Ocean.

When the expedition had reached what is today North Dakota, they set up camp and built a fort called Fort Mandan. Here they enlisted the help of a French trapper Toussaint Charbonneau and his pregnant Shoshone Indian wife Sacagawea. As he was getting ready for the journey, Meriwether Lewis gathered knowledge, tools, and supplies in preparation for this exploration and charting of new lands. Sacagawea added to his team by acting as guide, go between with Indian tribes, and as a medicinal healer for the group.

Like Sacagawea, I will do my best to initially be your guide here. The objective is to equip you with the knowledge and tools to ultimately be your own guide with future journeys and explorations, well after you finish reading this book. The state of being, "Be Sacagawea," is a view you can have to assist you with the journey toward achieving a dispassionate clarity about the concept of *NOOT*. The presumption here is that all that has happened was inevitable. It was the result of DNA, the laws of nature, environmental evolution, and experiences with the events occurring around us that led us to be where we are. It is a *natural* and *neutral* reality, *it is what it is*, and was destined to be as it was. We were destined to be as we have become. People can't help being who they are given their DNA and experiences in life. The inevitability of NOOT means that given the past, the present is understandable, and in fact it could not have happened any other way. Empathy is the understanding that is implied within the famous quote by John Bradford: *"There but for the grace of God go I."* Empathy, in turn, leads to a compassion which promotes kindness.

To achieve real compassion, there are prerequisite actions required. Taking the time to understand why someone became who they became and accepting that they could not help being so. Taking the time to understand human nature as with the *Platinum Rule,* which says to treat others in the manner they wish to be treated (in contrast to the Golden Rule that focuses only on our personal views). Achieving healthy compassion also requires us to have boundaries with consequences, otherwise we cannot feel safe, at ease, or confident in dealing with another. When we see this inevitability with outcomes, we can uncouple ourselves from negative emotions like fear, anger, or despair and be calm, at peace, and wise with our reactions and responses. We can now be optimistic and self-confident with an "I've got this" mentality. Compassion in many ways is the truest of love we can have for others.

Had I been born with their DNA, raised as they were, lived in their environments, and experienced what they did in life, I would be them. Compassion is the love and caring we have for others as a result of our empathy for them; not necessarily agreeing with them but accepting and embracing them as they are. They certainly have the potential to improve, and we may nurture their improvement along. Our success with nurturing them, however, lies with our empathy and compassion for them along with the boundaries we set with our mutual interactions. This is crucial in order for us to have meaningful connection and communication.

A common theme in movies is that of a protagonist who begins life as an innocent, honorable, and well-meaning person, then devolves into a ruthless and brutal perpetrator. The character Michael, played by Al Pacino in the *Godfather* movie series, is an example. If you study some of history's most diabolical tyrants and courageous heroes, you will likewise see how their DNA and experiential evolution propelled them toward the evil or good that they came to be. DNA, our environment, and our experiences bring all of us to where we are at any moment. There is for many a crossroad set of experiences that led them into a mindset of either *wise selfishness* (seeking win-win and improvement for self and others) or *foolish selfishness* (seeking to better one's own position with little regard for the best interests of others). This perspective becomes a compass for making many future decisions with what to do or not do, where to go and where not to go.

NOOT NEUTRALIZES DRAMA AND HELPS US SEE CLEARLY

With our understanding and belief in NOOT, we neutralize regret, anger, hate, and fear. You must learn to discern and be vigilant to avoid becoming a self-righteous revealer looking for the reason of the day to be offended. When you have *objective empowering acceptance* and embrace circumstances for what they are, the likelihood for your success increases. This will allow you to make real, sustainable long-term progress.

Acceptance is not agreement. This is an important discernment. We often don't agree with how things are, but it is folly and futile to resist it. Surrender to the reality of NOOT. Embrace these realities and understand that it had to be the way it had been up to now. It is with this mindset that you will achieve an unencumbered, clear, and holistic perspective with the wise way forward in your pursuit of more good and less bad.

If we label someone with words such as "unfriendly" or "stupid," we have restricted our perception and understanding of them. We have put on blinders and our perceptions of them becomes myopic. Our ability to effectively communicate with them in the future is tainted with a self-fulfilling prophesy woven into the language. We will then reinforce this label easily with many of our future interactions with them, such as asking, "What did I expect?" or taunting, "See, I told you so!"

This is how oppositional identities (or *contra identities*) are created, when a person's worth is being determined by someone else's worthlessness. It is like basing our view and opinion of a house based solely on inspection of its crawl space. There is a subtle nuance between the view of "unfriendly" as opposed to a more meaningful assessment "afraid of rejection." Yet the difference is profound with our connection and communication with others, and in many instances with ourselves, as well.

A view of only the crawl space of a home is but a fraction of what it is. Seeing the neighborhood, curbside view, inside rooms, and backyard gives a much more complete assessment of what it is and is not. As we pursue understanding why another is as they are, we will come to see a higher truth. We will find a much more accurate assessment of them beyond binary views. We will discern LEAR that empower and motivate us. If we see someone as afraid of being rejected, we are likely to temper our body language and words with compassion and are far more likely to promote a healthy relationship and effective communication. Likewise, if we were to come to see that an individual was verbally abused as a youth, or that their self-worth is very fragile and easily threatened, we will interact with them much more effectively. Maybe we come to see that they are just holding on by a thread with keeping their lives together as they may be filled with fear, anxiety, or cynicism. With this view, we can draw from our position of empathy to achieve compassionate, empowering, and effective responses to their behavior. The likelihood and possibility for an improved relationship with them now skyrockets. The chances of us adding value to their lives (as well as our own) increases as, well.

OPPORTUNITY COST

The economic principle of *opportunity cost*, simply stated, is: *specific time, effort, money, and resources spent on "X" cannot also be spent on "Y."* It is important with your Journey into Peace and our efforts for ongoing progress that you are clear with discerning the Xs from the Ys and where you decide to focus your efforts. Some battles should never be fought, while others may be long overdue for engagement. It is critical we can see and differentiate dangerous and useless words from the good, helpful, and healing words that wisely empower us and others. A wise discernment is needed to best identify those things, actions, and behaviors which are described with this principle of NOOT. It is only then that we are ready to begin to react and respond wisely.

Whatever you resist persists.

–Carl Jung

Often, many have a death grip on how things *should* be. Due to unrealistic expectations, they are repeatably disappointed and upset with themselves and others; they resist the reality and actuality of *what is*. Because of this resistance, they persist with their frustrations, anger, disappointment, and conflicts. Therein lies the definition of insanity. When we can stand back and see that all that happened is part of the NOOT and that it was inevitable to have occurred as it has, we are then positioned for success with our communications and actions. As we surrender and then embrace NOOT, we are able to calmly walk out of a prison that chokes off our life with distorted views of "what is" with their *should have beens* and *could have beens*. With this surrender and acceptance, we find new freedom. We begin to limit our exposure to toxins that harm us, many of which are self-administered. We then focus more on the actualities and realities that produce peace, progress, and healing.

The serenity prayer, written by Reinhold Niebuhr, states: *God, grant me the serenity to accept the things I cannot change, courage to change the things I can, and the wisdom to know the difference.* This iconic prayer captures the underlying value of NOOT, which is serenity and clarity. A clarity that points toward harmony, contribution, and construction and away from demolition and destruction with the accompanying animus. You can unshackle yourself from right fights, blame games, and drama dilemmas and go on to build. As we improve our clarity of NOOT with its objective view of *what is*, we grow to accept and embrace the boundaries of our reality and control and our ability to make wise decisions multiples tenfold.

With NOOT we see that detours are the shortest way forward. We view detours and setbacks as opportunities for great adventure, learning, and being better. With NOOT we see setbacks as inevitable and necessary for progress. We are able to pivot away from mistakes and turn on a dime like a school of fish with little hesitation (we go back later with our *Follow-Up Setback System*, FUSS, to add to our lessons learned in life). We see the setbacks as *Learning Experiences for Growth* (LEGs). Lastly, with NOOT we can now identify *Legitimate Empowering Alternate Realities* (LEAR).

You may now say, "Okay, that all sounds great, but I'm still not sure what exactly this Natural Order of Things *is*."

To expand, I give an example from my personal coaching business experiences of the last twenty-plus years with Executive Coaching Services. I have found that one of the top concerns folks have is regarding relationship improvement. In the course of the coaching discussions, we often come to a point where the client states (names and dates here are changed to protect privacy and confidentiality) "Gary/Jane really upset me when he/she did so and so last week . . . I got really angry/frustrated/hurt when they did that. I just hate it when they do that!"

At this point I will ask something like, "Would you say that Gary's/Jane's behavior with that situation is something that they have done before?"

And they will say "Yes, they do it all the time for years now!"

I now step in with this comment, "So let me summarize what I hear you saying . . . " I then pause before next asking, ***"So you were very upset with Gary/Jane for being themselves?"***

At this point, there is often a moment of silence. It is as if a light bulb lights up in a dark room and they are surprised with what they now begin to see and understand. Over time and with our experiences with Gary/Jane, their behavior is largely predictable. Until we can objectively see who others are, we will not be able to significantly improve things for ourselves.

Resistance is Futile.

–The Borg from Star Trek: The Next Generation

This specific situation with relationships is addressed in the chapter on the "EBC Symbiotic 3" (Empathy, Boundaries, Consequences). To begin to make the progress we Must (that's with a capital "M") be willing and able to recognize the objective "what is" with another. We Must come to see that they could not help being who they are, who they became, and who they will be. Given their parents (or lack thereof), social economic status at birth, DNA, height, gender, religious inclinations, education, first lover, siblings, order in family births, country of origin, etc., it was inevitable that they became who they are, both good and bad, with their habits, behavior, values, and principles (or lack thereof). Their trajectory going forward is predictable in many ways.

Our unwillingness or inability to accept and then additionally embrace this dooms us against making things better for ourselves and others. Our ability to see these limits and respect this reality allows us to stay on a path of progress with them as well as ourselves.

The use of the word *natural* is intentional within the NOOT acronym. *Natural* implies things like the laws of nature or the laws of physics, for those with religious beliefs the will of God or for those more secular folks the will of the universe. It is to be expected that if an apple detaches from the tree it falls to the ground below. It is to be expected that the turtle will not climb the tree or fly. If someone unexpectedly experiences a loud noise, they will flinch or jump. These are all *natural*.

The word *Order* likewise is selected for good reason. *Order* here is in the context of cause and effect as with the sequence of experiences and genetics for a person and their resultant behaviors. If I take a fuel like gasoline, blanket it with oxygen, then add heat from a lighted match, it will set afire. Those three components will produce a rather predictable result. Likewise, failure to address a severe oil leak with an automobile's internal combustion engine will eventually cause it to lose lubrication to the crankshaft then seize up and be severely damaged if not destroyed. A neglected slow leak in our lives can lead eventually to a catastrophic crisis if not addressed early enough, as well.

The concept of NOOT allows us to calmly see that all that occurs around us was and is inevitable. These things just had to happen. They happened not because someone deserved it, like some Godly justice, but rather as consequence of all that unfolded beforehand. Now with seeing NOOT and embracing it, we can disentangle ourselves from toxic emotions and blaming, shaming, or denigrating. Instead of responding with vengeance or impulsive anger, we can contemplate the wiser response; the "higher road" that rises above perceived injustices and focuses more on win-win and wise selfishness (as opposed to foolish selfishness). Instead of being misdirected, derailed, or having our view clouded, we can have an objective clarity and confidence with our decisions and responses going forward. We can make wise responses and wise decisions that markedly improve our odds for success. We can now select the best detours which become delightful detours to keep our positive momentum going.

REMOVE THE WASTE TO BRING OUT THE MAGNIFICENCE

When Michelangelo produced the magnificent "David" his genius and masterful skill was not about adding to the marble stone. Rather, his focus was with the intentional removal of waste and unnecessary material that would eventually reveal the masterpiece. To a large degree, with NOOT we can remove wasted time and energy and provide clarity that reveals the essential issues and wisest course of action to achieve the important desires we seek.

CHAPTER 6

Legitimate Empowering Alternate Realities (LEAR)

What qualifies as a LEAR?

"Be the Glass 1/2 Full"

If there are different possible views, it is wise to select the one that is more empowering for oneself. Pick the one that produces a higher likelihood of win-win with others, as well.

–Michael Starr

William Shakespeare's play *King Lear* is a tragic story of love, deception, jealousy, and greed. The king loses faith in his youngest daughter Cordelia, who truly loves him beyond measure or words, and is deceived by his two older daughters who have nothing but disdain for him. As a result of his misguided beliefs about the three daughters, he disinherits Cordelia and places a dangerous amount of power and wealth with the two other daughters. From there, this dark tragic tale unravels to unfortunate calamity. In this play, Shakespeare clearly shows the evil and duplicity with many of the characters. The depiction of the cast of characters and their actions leaves little room for deciding who and what is good or bad. Life, on the other hand, is rarely so polarized and simply compartmentalized into binary realities. Things often can be two things, good or bad, at the same time depending on our vantage point and perspective. This chapter speaks to another concept. It is about *Legitimate Empowering Alternate Realities (LEAR)*.

A definition of the term *duality* is that things can be two things at the same time. In quantum physics, atomic properties can be both a wave and a particle. A glass can be half full and half empty simultaneously. Aboard a ship, one side may be the right side or the left side depending on which way you are facing. History is full of examples where one person's salvation is another's tyranny. The Cherokee Indians' experience with the Trail of Tears and the "Cherokee removal" of 1836 to 1839 is a tragic example of this.

Perhaps the most poignant example of duality is within us. We are often our own best ally as well as our worst enemy. We often create or exacerbate many problems and suffering for ourselves. Yet, we are capable of healing ourselves, as well. By recognizing our culpability with bringing suffering, pain, conflict, and upset into our lives, we reach an optimistic threshold. By crossing over into this new reality, we can begin to heal and to achieve real progress and peace of mind. The key here is to select views that fall best on the side of being *Legitimate Empowering Alternate Realities* (**LEAR**). Given that in many cases there are near equal legitimacies with an experience being empowering, neutral, or disempowering, the wise choice is to select the empowering reality and stay focused on that one.

To be successful with many areas of our lives, there is a need to have a working simplified understanding of things. We need not have a PhD in psychology to be effective communicators or mentors. We need not be a neuroscientist to understand how best to achieve better clarity with our thinking. We may never know the 100 percent truth about why someone acts and feels a certain way (that includes ourselves, as well), yet with empathy, boundaries, and consequences, we can find a workable and successful approach to dealing with them.

GIVING THE BENEFIT OF THE DOUBT

With the concept of LEAR, we seek out views and paradigms that serve us best with win-win perspectives that employ *wise selfishness*. These perspectives may not be absolute truths, but they can be *higher truths*. There are different ways to see many things in life. That being true, why not choose to see people and circumstances in an empowering way?

We must not be Pollyannas, however, naively seeing all things in an optimistic and nice way. Rather, our views need to have a high degree of legitimacy about them to qualify as being probable or likely. This view must be grounded in a reality that can be supported with facts, experience, and probability. In order to say "I am" this and that, or "I will" be accomplishing this or that, those statements must be grounded in reality.

One of the **Golden Keys** terms in an empowering language is the concept of NOOT. As was previously presented, NOOT is crucial for moving forward with our Journey into Peace. This concept of NOOT is in many ways a Legitimate Empowering Alternate Reality, as well. By seeing that *people cannot help being who they are,* we create a calm space for objective observation, assessment, and future planning. This improves our ability to best decide, respond, and interact with that person or situation in the future. Rather than impulsively reacting with anger, self-righteousness, or resentment, we are best to temper our response with empathy and understanding. Rather than doing something to retaliate, which no doubt will magnify the upset and conflict, we can calmly decide on an appropriate response that includes Empathy, Boundaries and Consequences, the *EBC Symbiotic 3*.

LEAR EXAMPLES

Here are three examples with minor, medium, and major scenarios for LEAR:

Minor Example Scenario: *I am at a checkout counter with my grocery purchases for the week. As the checkout person is scanning an item, I may ask them if they could please tell me the price of the eggs before they ring them up." The response I get is, "The prices are marked where you got these eggs, didn't you look first?" said in a very irritated and demeaning tone of voice.*

Two possible realities here are:

1. The checkout person is an employee, and I am a customer who just expressed a fair and reasonable request. It would take no effort whatsoever for them to give me the price of the eggs . . . this is terrible customer service!

2. The checkout person is unhappy about something; this is not about me. Perhaps they are experiencing family, financial, or serious health problems. Perhaps they were raised in a dysfunctional and abusive home.

My responses with these two perspectives can vary significantly.

A. With the first view, I may become self-righteous and snooty with them and say something like, "Your job is to attend to the customers, do you want me talk to your manager about how rude you are being with me?" This possibly will have me leaving the store upset and agitated. My upset may spillover into the hours afterward as I relive the experience later.

B. With the second view, I may respond with having a sense of empathy. My tone of voice and word choice would be kind and respectful. Perhaps I would say, "I am sorry, I should have looked. I'll do so next time. I really would appreciate it if you would help me out this time if possible." I will likely leave the store feeling good about myself and my interest with healing and being a mature individual. Perhaps I give myself a silent "*Bravo*" for deciding not to engage in a "right fight."

Medium Example Scenario: *I am stopped at a red light while driving my car. I look to my right at a garage sale sign placed on the road beside me. While I am reading the address and information on this sign, the light changes from red to green. I am still reading the sign several seconds after the light has turned green. The person behind me honks their horn for an extended time, and as I turn left at the intersection in front of me, they pass me honking and wave their middle finger at me.*

Two possible realities here are:

1. I was two or three seconds late with moving my car after the light turned green. This a very minor thing and the person behind me is rude and disrespectful, making a mountain out of a molehill. I will give them a taste of their own medicine.

2. The driver is unhappy about something; this is not about me. Perhaps they are experiencing family, financial, or serious health problems. Perhaps they are very anxious with getting to a destination and they are already late.

My response/reaction here could go one of several ways based on my view of things.

A. One response is to honk my horn back at them and return the waving middle finger then proceed to tailgate them and flash my lights.

B. A second response would be to feel sorry for them, as their anger and agitation is most likely about some aspect of their life that is going poorly. I just shrug my shoulders in a humble manner and mouth an "I'm sorry" expression as they pass me and carefully move over, getting out of their way and distancing myself from them.

Major Example Scenario: *I am a supervisor at work having a meeting with several other employees. My boss comes into the room and asks in an agitated voice, "Who forgot to turn the safety warning light on near the loading dock?" I speak up and respond, "It is my group's responsibility to do so. I will find out what happened and report back to you with my findings." My boss becomes loud and angry and publicly admonishes me for poor supervision with my group and finishes with saying, "That is F'n not acceptable," using a vulgar term. He then goes on and asks, "You got that mister?"*

Several possible realities here are:

1. I think to myself, "How dare you speak to me that way, you jerk. I can't control what other people do 100 percent of the time, you just embarrassed me in front of people I care about. I hate this job and you. You are such an A-hole!"

2. This is way out of character for the boss to act this way toward anyone . . . something else is going on with him. I wonder what is really bothering him.

3. The boss does this frequently with me and others. He is demeaning, disrespectful, and bullying with others often. I believe he acts this way because he was mistreated when he first joined the company and is very unsatisfied with his life in general. Lately he is even worse after he did not get a promotion he was expecting.

4. The safety light not being turned on when required is a serious company violation and could easily have led to a fatality or serious injury. The boss understandably had good reason to be emotional and upset, as last year an employee had his leg crushed and never returned to work at the loading dock because the warning signal had been left off.

My response/reaction here could go one of several ways based on my view of things:

A. Say, "F you I quit!"

B. I am afraid of losing my job and I will say nothing. I'll just find out what happened and apologetically report back to him later.

C. I will find out what happened, then when he is calmer meet with him in private to explain what had happened along with my action plan for remediation so that it does not happen again. Afterwards, I will then ask why he was so angry in a public place with me and ask him if there is something else going on.

D. I will find out what happened report back with him. I will think through and prepare for a calm way to explain to the boss that I found his behavior inappropriate and disrespectful, and that I would appreciate it if he would refrain from doing so in the future. Later, well after this meeting, I will decide on the consequences for future crossing of this boundary of public berating. Perhaps I will be documenting these instances and report him to the HR department, or perhaps I will update my resume and begin a serious pursuit of looking for another job or transferring somewhere else in the organization, if possible.

> *The Confrontation Principle: Caring for people should precede confronting people.*
>
> -John Maxwell[13]

E. Failure to turn on the warning light could easily have gotten someone killed. I understand why the boss lost his temper, as this could be a life-or-death issue. Last year, Harry James, an employee here, had his leg crushed at the loading dock when the warning light was left off. He never returned to work again and has gone through several operations to repair his leg. I will focus on identifying person(s) responsible and ensure they don't do it again with a documented conference. I will review the seriousness of this violation of company policy with my work group and why it is important to always comply with this policy. Daily at the beginning of the work shift for the next month I will review the whys of the policy, explaining again how important it is. Also, I will remind them failure to adhere to this requirement could lead to a written admonishment on their record or possible termination.

Note in response "D" above that I have empathy and compassion for the boss, yet I have boundaries with his behavior and consequences I will implement if the behavior continues.

With an awareness of the possible existence of LEAR, we can find better ways to see the people and circumstances around us. This vantage point increases the odds and probability for successful outcomes for all involved. If there are different possible views, it is wise to select the one that is more empowering for oneself. Pick the one that produces a higher likelihood of win-win with others, as well.

CHAPTER 7

Setting Effective Boundaries Begins with Empathy

Do I have consequences associated with my boundaries?

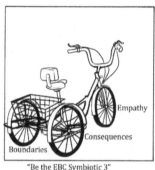

"Be the EBC Symbiotic 3"

Explaining your boundaries to another is secondary; expecting another to respect your boundaries is also secondary.

–Michael Starr

Clearly understood and respected boundaries are at the heart of all civilizations. They replace mayhem and disarray with order and certainty. Without boundaries, anarchy reigns within a society as well as between individuals. Identifying and wisely responding to hurtful or undesired behavior by another is essential for having healthy relationships. When we cooperate and work together for the common good based on mutual expectations, we reduce conflict and increase our peace of mind. These expectations bring a desired level of predictability into our lives.

Boundaries, when defined and enforced, separate a world of laws and teamwork from one of a *Mad Max* madness where anything goes. Without an expectation of compliance to boundaries, fear reigns and a *might makes right* behavior prevails. Without boundaries, disputes flourish, as there are no agreed upon rules of right and wrong, let alone any means to settle disputes and disagreements peacefully. The most feared, loudest, and strongest aggressor wins in a world without laws and limits. Here mob rule reigns.

Documented lines of demarcation are invaluable for promoting harmony, as there is an agreed upon set of rules we can follow, the dos and don'ts of that community. Two keys with an effective boundary are its clear definition and the expected consequences when crossed. Few attempt to cross the DMZ between North Korea and South Korea, as both the boundary and the consequence for crossing it are unequivocally understood by all. The understanding of the limits with behavior and the certainty of a negative consequence is what makes it effective.

Sadly, now in 2023, there is a growing politically correct mindset that conflates civilized order for the common good with the self-righteous moral convenience of the day. Now we often see the victims being treated unfairly and the perpetrators being excused from established laws with their consequences. This is a tyrannical trend that is moving us ever closer toward anarchy and away from civilized behavior. Social media lynch mobs swarm upon those they dislike or disagree with. Political leaders follow the mob and often become part of it. Rules and laws are selectively enforced based on personal agendas and individual beliefs. Ours is a society faced increasingly with a cancel culture mob seeking to silence opposing views. In this atmosphere fascism and tyranny flourish.

BOUNDARIES BEGIN WITH EMPATHY AND COMPASSION

Well-thought-out and enforced boundaries reduce conflict and chaos and promote cooperation and harmony. They are wisely viewed as *Sacred Boundaries*. Boundaries create clarity and certainty with the expectations of what another will do and will not do. In many ways, they are lines that separate right from wrong. Imagine attending a sporting event with no firm rules for what is acceptable or unacceptable; there fun would turn rapidly and predictably into fury. These boundaries promote stability and peace, they minimize disputes and conflicts. In the absence of boundaries, whether they be physical or interpersonal, civilized behavior unravels and conflict is enabled. In this chapter, the concept of the *EBC Symbiotic 3 (Empathy, Boundaries, and Consequences)* is explained and promoted.

When deciding how best to have meaningful boundaries, it must be a symbiotic combination of the three components of empathy, boundaries, and consequences. It's not just the boundary in isolation that allows us to succeed. We must be clear as to what the boundary is and why it is important for us. At its foundation is empathy and compassion toward another. We must start with empathy and understanding before we move next to defining our boundary. In a number of instances, we will find that understanding why others are the way they are (or why we ourselves are as we are) will actually evaporate our upset away, and the need for the boundary my no longer be required or desired. When we have empathy, compassion, and understanding of why things are as they are, we are resolute, unafraid, and calm as we follow-up with our boundary consequece(s).

People can't help being who they are, given their DNA and experiences in life. The inevitability of NOOT says that given the past, the present is understandable and in fact it could not have happened any other way. Empathy is understanding: "There but for the grace of God go I."

Had I been born with their DNA, raised as they were, and experienced what they did in life, I would be them. Compassion is the love and caring we have for others with our empathy for them. Not agreeing with them but accepting and embracing them as they are. Yes, they certainly have the potential to improve, and we may nurture their improvement along. Our success with nurturing them, however, lies in our empathy and compassion for them and the boundaries we set with our mutual interactions.

After building our empathy, next we define our sacred boundary. This sequence of empathy then boundary is crucial. To do so effectively we must have the knowledge of why this boundary is really important for us. Take your time here as this inquiry and contemplation of *"Why do I want this boundary?"* goes to the heart of who we see ourselves to be. Only after empathy and boundaries are clear can we proceed to decide what our consequences will be. We must be committed to responding with these predetermined consequences each and every time encroachment occurs. We must be resolute with this, as it assures our confidence and peace of mind by knowing we can count on ourselves to follow through as planned. *The cooperation or lack of cooperation from the other is secondary. Primary and foremost is our willingness and conviction with enacting a wise, well thought through consequence.*

The three components of Empathy, Boundaries, and Consequences make this concept whole and a strategy for success, when considering our need for boundaries. With the *E.B.C. Symbiotic 3,* the emotion and tendency for revengeful vindictiveness is taken out of the equation. With this trinity we can calmly move forward, confident that "we have this," and diminish if not extinguish fear and anxiety with interactions in the future.

Boundaries can be egregiously crossed, as with borders between countries violated by invasion, grand theft of property, or rape. They can also be of a moderate nature with behavior such as with verbal abuse, failure to deliver expected performance, disrespect, or dishonesty within a relationship. This chapter addresses the latter, the more moderate instances of the day-to-day hurt and suffering that often occurs between individuals and organizations. Many of us suffer from frustrations, hurt, and demeaning behavior from those close to us. We know that their behavior is toxic or hurtful for us, yet we don't know what to do about it. We expect others to change while we continue doing things as we always have. This is an arena where the insanity of doing the same things over and over again and hoping to get different results thrives.

WE DON'T KNOW HOW

One might ask, "If we are suffering and upset with someone else's behavior for months or possibly years, why can't we do something about it?"

The answer, I believe, is that we just don't know how to go about doing something meaningful and lasting to improve the situation. We tend to focus on another changing, but do not improve our responses to unacceptable behavior. There are understandable obstacles that get in our way of achieving peace of mind and calm here. One such obstacle with getting to a much better place for ourselves is that we may have a deeply seated component of resentment or vindictiveness with it all. We may think, "they need to pay with pain" or "they need to understand and admit they are wrong." It is this approach that can eventually erupt like an exploding volcano, spewing hatred and a denigrating attack upon another. This does little to make things better, and in the long run often worsens the situation. Another obstacle is an inability or unwillingness to understand another and having empathy for the Natural Order of Things, as they could not help being who they are. We may also be afraid to confront a person or situation for fear of retaliatory consequences for ourselves.

Lastly, there is the false belief that telling another what your boundaries are will lead or should lead to their changing their behavior. Telling someone what they need to do tends **not** to be an effective means of achieving the results we desire.

Explaining your boundaries to another is a secondary issue. Consistently enacting well-thought-out wise consequences when encroachment occurs is essential. Let me assure you that as you clearly define your boundary and do so in the context of empathy and compassion and then establish a wise consequence, you will find a surprising level of peace of mind and be taking a great step forward for yourself. Your boundary is best viewed as a *Sacred Boundary*, as you will make no exception with following up with your consequence when it is encroached upon. Have faith and courage in knowing that a short-term discomfort with executing your consequence will lead to a long-term improvement.

I share a small and minor personal example of a situation between my wife and myself that illustrates this concept:

I had asked my wife on numerous occasions not to put anything on the laundry room chair. Yet she continued to do so. I often use the laundry room as a "mud room" when coming in from working outside and have a need to sit down to take off my shoes, which are often dirty. If there is something on the seat, I cannot sit down without lifting up the items and getting them dirty with my soiled hands. Then one day I decided to take what was on the seat and put it inside the dryer. When she asked if I had seen the item previously on the seat I said "it's in the dryer" in a calm tone. Then in a respectful manner stated that I would continue to do so in the future. It was important that I was respectful and calm, otherwise a distracting counter argumentative response would likely have occurred. Now, months later, no items have been placed on that seat . . . consequences work!

JUST OPEN YOUR UMBRELLA WHEN IT STARTS TO RAIN

Consequences need not be dire or a huge, big deal. They do need to be consistent and courageously followed though each and every time, however. Having empathy about the situation removes a drama component that tends to lead to defensiveness or offensiveness and a tit for tat or right fight between individuals. Approaching the situation calmly and with respect goes a long way to minimize the expected resistance another has with our changed behavior. Yet be advised it is usually threatening to others when you begin to make firm changes in how you respond to them. Proceed nonetheless and persevere; this is a necessary path for your progress and usually but a short-term condition with you feeling uncomfortable. Do your very best to design and execute your consequence as a **dispassionate consequence**, one which is a matter-of-fact action. Avoid anger or harshness with it, just do it calmly, like opening an umbrella when it starts to rain. **Be the Umbrella Opener** who calmly opens their umbrella when outside and it begins to rain.

I would caution you, though, not to proceed with your consequences with an expectation that the other person will change their behavior. Often, they will not change or improve their habits and predispositions. The real objective here is to respond to the undesirable behavior in a manner that minimizes your suffering and upset. You can't guarantee another will improve their behavior in a manner to your liking. You can guarantee, however, that you can substantially reduce your pain, suffering, and upset with a wise selection of consequences that you courageously and consistency implement each and every time, such as, "I will calmly disengage from any abusive conversation and leave the room."

This approach with the *EBC Symbiotic 3* will bring unprecedented peace and healing for you.

CHAPTER 8

Desire-Power, Yes...Willpower, No

What do you do to create desire power for yourself?

"Be The Self-Motivation Maestro"

It's not my job to hold your hand. It's my job to take motivated people and show them how to become better.

–Chuck Noll

In this chapter, the focus is with providing tools and ideas to help you to become a better *self-motivator.* You are called upon here to be much like an orchestra conductor who leads musicians to play a symphony. During different times in your life, you will call upon different self-motivating instruments and players to inspire you to action.

There are many wondrous symphonies ahead to play and enjoy, each with their own unique destinations and journeys. It is up to you to lead them. The challenge is to become a maestro, with your ability to create and sustain self-motivation. It is you who will motivate yourself through other people and self-chosen experiences. If you are thinking there has got to be a better way to become motivated, this chapter can deliver that way for you. It provides an effective path for sustaining self-motivation.

WE NEED BOTH DIRECTION AND MOTIVATION

To have a meaningful and successful life of peace, progress, and healing, we need both direction and motivation. This book provides the direction, it is up to you to provide the motivation. In this chapter, ideas and tips will be presented that assist with your *self-motivation,* creating it and maintaining it. We will explore the concept and components of the wise empowering language of *desire-power.* In contrast, the idea of *willpower* will be exposed as a *useless word* that serves you poorly. You will be encouraged to strive for an "I want to" mindset as opposed to an obligatory "I need to" one.

Motivation is the rocket fuel that provides the ability for us to accelerate, alter course, and improve ourselves. Without motivation for improvement, we stagnate and drift like space debris circling the planet; moving yet going nowhere. This chapter will present ways for you to become a better self-motivational leader who continually fuels your own rocket engine. With a wise direction and strong motivation, you will maintain and sustain your journeys forward into peace and progress.

To further the analogy, self-motivation is like a rocket engine that is continually fueled with its two-part propellant: fuel and oxidizer. As with specific propellants that use a mixture of liquid hydrogen and liquid oxygen, so it is with our self-motivation having two ingredients. Self-motivation has aspects that draw us toward something as well as move us away from something else.

To review an earlier concept, words and language impact our perceptions and subsequent responses. They fall into three categories:

1. Useless

2. Dangerous/Tyrannical

3. Wisely Empowering

The word *willpower* is a word in the category of *useless,* as it produces little to no benefit as a vehicle for improvement and change. It is a misdirection away from meaningful and real sustainable progress. It tends to lead to feelings of inadequacy, as with, "I just don't have the willpower to get this done."

The term *willpower* also tends to be used in a binary manner, as you either have it or you don't. It leaves little space for gray areas or nuances with this perspective. This willpower approach is often accompanied with thinking "I need to do this" as an obligation.

A far more valuable and useful approach is what I call the *"I want to"* one. It is largely aspirational and far more likely to support you with **Being the Self-Motivation Maestro** as opposed to having *willpower.* Here you bring a particular fuel and oxidizer together as your propellant that keeps your progress burning strong. With motivation, you have the aspirational components that draw you forward towards a desire as well as avoidance ingredients that move you away from a concern or fear. Both aspirational and avoidance self-motivators can be helpful with being the Self-Motivation Maestro.

MOTIVATION CAN BE BOTH A PULL AS WELL A PUSH

Being the Self-Motivation Maestro

Motivation is both a push and a pull desire. We are being pulled or drawn forward when we think about an exciting event or future achievement. We are moving toward something when planning to climb a mountain, publish a book, or perhaps establish a foundation for the needy. Going on vacation and achieving financial independence are two common pull motivations. These future possibilities beckon us forward because they are aspirational in nature. We tend to be excited and enthusiastic with their pursuit.

Yet motivation can also push you. We may decide to move forward to avoid something. We may desire to prevent something we fear happening in the future as with divorce, health problems, or financial calamity. The push motivation is not necessarily an undesirable one. It is only natural that we seek to avoid pain. This desire to avoid pain and suffering is a push motivation that has brought about many great accomplishments throughout history. *"Necessity is the mother of invention."*[14]

Significant Emotion Events often are life-changing ones that have motivated many to take quantum leaps forward. Dramatic life-changing improvements may be the result of having had a heart attack or having lost nearly everything of value in life due to substance abuse. Seek out and create both pull and push reasons that are legitimate and are worth adding to your self-motivation symphony.

When Marianne Noll, the wife and soulmate of legendary Pittsburgh Steelers coach Chuck Noll, was asked about Chuck's style and success as a repeat Super Bowl coach, she stated that he did not see his job as that of a motivator. Chuck felt it was the player's responsibility to be motivated. He expected that players who came to the team would bring their own motivation, as with being self-motivated. Chuck saw himself much more as a teacher of technique and understanding of the game for his inherently motivated and talented players with his Steelers team.

CONSIDER ASPIRATIONAL AND AVOIDANCE ACTIONS

There are thousands of philosophies, opinions, books, videos, and audios relating to motivation. You may ask, "Why is this book with its philosophy any better than those?"

My response is "Because the very premise for the concept of motivation is challenged."

The word *motivation* is ambiguous when used in the context for personal improvement. It is far better to always use the more precise term of ***self-motivation***. Self-motivation is not a binary all or nothing way of being, rather, we all have a degree of self-motivation within us at any instant in time. The secret is to strategically add to the existing ones. Look at self-motivation as being composed of many possibilities that are divided into two categories:

1. Aspirational activities that move you toward a desired result

2. Avoidance actions that move you away from an undesirable outcome

As we improve our language, it will nurture us forward by focusing on our ability and desire to self-improve.

With ***"being the self-motivation maestro,"*** the operative word is the empowering term "maestro," as with mastery of a skill. You are the doer; the action implementer. It is up to you to select and call upon different elements in your orchestra of instruments to play that inspiring masterpiece of music. Different times will require different instruments. The word "being" implies believing, behaving, expecting, and thinking in a specific manner. Here, you are the captain of your ship and master of your fate. Short summary: it is you who makes self-motivation happen! How will you do this? You will do this by making self-motivation a daily habit.

YOUR MORNING ROUTINE AND SELF-MOTIVATION

The following proposed method to bolster and enhance your self-motivation is grounded in a daily morning routine called The *Marvelous Start Morning Routine.*[15]

Your Morning routine is a *sacred habit* that is followed each and every day. It is not negotiable nor subject to being ignored. As with breathing oxygen, it will become the lifeblood of your successful journey to *Betterism*. Each day, as part of your morning routine you select a planned action that supports building or maintaining your self-motivation. Worksheets for creating and maintaining your self-motivation are found at my website, executivecoachingservices.net.

This will be done using the ISTEP concept. The *Intentional Simple Tiny Efforts for Progress (ISTEPs)* process is fully explained in the *Marvelous Start Morning Routine* worksheet.

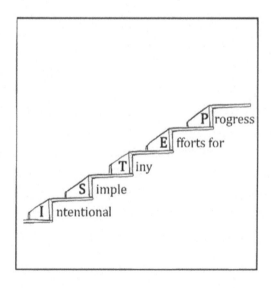

*Self-Motivation begins with self-care ... eat well,
sleep well, exercise, and create a great attitude.*

–Mike Starr

Immerse yourself in positive actions and with experiences that raise your spirits. Surround yourself with those who believe in you. If it applies, nurture your spirituality daily.

CHAPTER 9

Roads of Tyranny, ROT

Do I notice language which divides?

"Be the Bloodhound"

Repeat a lie often enough and it becomes truth.

–Nazi, Joseph Goebbels, known as the law of propaganda

Disclaimer:

In this chapter it may appear that I have disdain for individuals that are in positions of leadership and governing power, but that is not the case. I harbor no ill will toward them. They are part of NOOT. I understand that who they are is a result of environmental, experiential, and DNA factors. I have compassion and empathy for them. I am alarmed, however, with many of their actions (and inactions), and see a compelling need to expose the dangerous language many use.

There is much good within each of us, yet there is a language currently being used that is bringing out the worst in many of us. Many are unaware of the damage they do with the perpetuation of this dangerous language. They are like the doctors delivering babies in the 1800s who did not realize that their failure to use proper sanitizing and sterilizing protocols was substantially contributing to the infant mortality rate of the times. Good people can be led to do bad things if they are not aware and vigilant in recognizing dangerous tyranny and maliciousness in language. It is extremely important that we can recognize this danger; a danger that has become woven within our common everyday language.

The tragic death of George Floyd led to riots, looting, and killings and cost billions of dollars in damage to private property and government buildings. The narrative that triggered this was that it was an act of racism. The circumstantial evidence was ginned up and a lynch mob response occurred. Now, in retrospect, many have made the case that his death was due to several root causes that had little to do with a "racist" policeman. Perhaps a correct assessment of the factors that led to this tragedy includes police accountability for engaging in unnecessary force, training with proper ways to detain/restrain resisting suspects, Floyd being high on fentanyl, his aggressively resisting arrest and forcing his way out of the police car, his education and social economic status and limited opportunities available to him to be a productive member of his community. Nonetheless, the first lie stuck and led to great harm to many innocent people. Many of the contributing factors to this tragedy have yet to be addressed because they don't fit the initial political narrative. This is one of many consequences with the use of the language of tyranny today that demonizes and distracts from meaningful solutions.

Today, in 2023, we are facing monumental crises which grow worse by the day. Record fentanyl and other drug related deaths. Economic unraveling with self-induced inflation and reckless spending and printing of government-controlled money. Unsustainable fantasy idealistic notions are diverting focus and resources away from identifying and mitigating crises in the here and now. A federal governement policy is encouraging an unsustainable and dangerous invasion of illegal immigrants crossing the southern border that threatens our economic stability, community safety, infrastructure with schools, hospitals and housing. Weather change realities are exaggerated into apocalyptic doomsday scenerios that focus on paper straws and avoid efforts to manage our forests better. Meanwhile, Hamas terrorists and Russian leadership are emboldened to attack Israel and invade Ukraine leading to thousands of deaths and unimaginable suffering. Criminal activity with murder, assault, and theft are on an alarming trajectory to reach levels not seen before. Healthy personal identity and foundational concepts of right and wrong, good and bad, are murkier now that ever. Children are encouraged to question their gender and sexuality at young ages. Children are enabled to identify, act and dress as "furries' in school. The very fabric of our civilization is being unraveled with governing that is anything but wise or working for the common good. It has become much like the fantasy idealism of the multitude of communist and fascist regimes that enviably lead to the death of millions and untold suffering of hundreds of millions. The Holodomor man-made famine in Ukraine in 1933, the Nazi Holocaust, and unraveling of Venezuelan society are but a few of many examples.

LIKE AN ARSONIST FIREMAN WHO RETURNS TO BE A HERO

Today, anarchy is growing while civilized behavior is shrinking. Sadly and tragically, solvable challenges are not improving. Real solutions are ignored. Our home is on fire, and we are focusing on the need to clean the windows. These problems are actually being exacerbated by our leaders at international, national, institutional, community, and family levels. Leaders too often focus their efforts on promoting intentional internal conflicts to distract from their incompetence, corruption, and at times sinister agendas. They are ship captains running their vessels aground and into collisions. They then blame others for the very problems they have created. They are like the arsonist fireman who sets a building on fire and returns shortly later to be a hero who comes to the rescue. Rather than rallying their citizens and promoting teamwork by emphasizing our many areas of common ground, many leaders plan and implement ways to divide us and confuse us. Rather than encouraging civil debate to ferret out the best truth that serves the common good, they encourage and lead mobs to shout over their opposition and seek to censure and cancel those with opposing views. Elitist malcontents promote the tearing down of protective barriers, boundaries, and laws that protect citizens while they live in gated communities with security guards around them. Erecting a fence with thousands of troops around our capital after the trespassing on January 6, is the height of this irony.

The level of legitimate checks and balances we once had with objective reporting by media is at an all-time low. Mainstream corporate media and social media are often not part of the solution, but an integral part of the problem. We are inundated by multimedia narratives that repeat malicious catch phrases. They announce and advertise slanderous, divisive, and distracting stories that spring up simultaneously like tornadoes springing up from out of nowhere. This triggers a lynch mob following, who are quick to jump to conclusions and judgments that support their bias and agenda. This mob is a modern day KKK focused on harming and discrediting its political opposition and eager to execute mob justice upon their perceived and often ginned up adversaries. The current news medias and social medias are at the forefront of the smoke screens masking truth and the common ground and the good we have between each other. They promote alarmist exaggerations of devils and demons amongst us. Bad news sells news.

At the heart of much of this is a tyrannical use of words and language. Language is increasing being weaponized to distract and divide. Sadly, this destructive and dangerous use of language is often intentional, designed by a few and promoted by many. It is like some diabolical movie plot which has a virus designed, created, and unleashed upon an unknowing population to create chaos and death. Like King Herod, they seek to figuratively kill the baby in the crib with those who have threatening oppositional views.

This chapter's intent is to assist you with seeing this dangerous use of words. You will be encouraged to *"Be the Bloodhound"* and notice the scent and stench of this tyrannical language and the roads they lead us down. These are Roads of Tyranny (ROT). By seeing this dangerous language for what it is, you can avoid becoming part of the harm it does. Hopefully, you will help with a much-needed healing at a time when civil discourse, tolerance, and empathy wane. You can then point out this danger to others, like pointing out a rattlesnake ahead on a hiking path to your fellow hikers behind you. You can become part of the vanguard for peace, progress, and healing within your communities.

Dog whistle catch phrases surface overnight on multiple media platforms within hours of their introduction in the news narratives. Many news media outlets coincidentally use this overnight tempest terminology to slander, malign, and alarm. The simultaneity and parroting of identical language calls into question their independence and whether this be coincidence or collusion. This has become increasingly Orwellian, as with the book *1984*, where the very definition of blue and red changes overnight and a "double think" dysfunctional thinking takes place. In his book *1984*, George Orwell uses the word "doublethink" as a description of how people accept what the ruling party tells them even when it contradicts something they already know to be different. Unlike the concept of a LEAR, this view often is not legitimate and contrary to the facts. Unlike LEAR, it is neither empowering nor inclined to promote win-win. This view demonizes and divides. It supports self-righteous *contra identities* where people feel important through a view of others as inferior.

WITHOUT WISE BOUNDARIES AND RULES, ANARCHY FLOURISHES

Many of todays "leaders" are ignorant with understanding the basics of economics such as supply and demand, opportunity costs, or living within your means. The negative impact of inflation that results from printing large amounts paper money is lost upon them. One need but look at Venezuela to see the tragic consequences of incompetent and corrupt leadership. The belief that printing more money is the answer for funding a plethora of "desirable" programs is clear evidence of their dangerous, incompetent, and misguided leadership.

During decades of working with and facilitating problem solving teams, I learned that in order to be effective with solving problems and achieving sustainable results, there are two important prerequisite steps necessary to take before delving into any action items. These first two steps with problem solving are:

1. Decide which problem(s) to focus on. There are limits with our time, energy, money, and resources with what can be worked on at any one time to achieve real results and improvements. Work on the important first and set aside the less important.

2. Define the problem. Recognize symptoms apart from root causes and don't embed solutions within the problem definition.

As a short summary with achieving real and lasting results, here is a brief explanation of the concepts of *opportunity costs* and proper *problem definition* ("problem solving" will be discussed in more detail in Chapter 16).

Opportunity Cost

Clearly the same time, effort, and resources used in dealing with issue "X" cannot also be used with issue "Y" as well. The use of a dollar or labor hour spent on one problem precludes the use of that same dollar and labor hour being used for another issue, so with that, a choice to work on one thing impacts the opportunity to work on other things.

Problem Definition

As for proper problem definition, it is important to see symptoms as just that, symptoms. The problem statement should not jump to conclusions and embed a solution within it. It is essential that it be objective with what is known, as opposed to what is speculation. An example of a poor problem statement would be to say, "The patient is ill because their body temperature is too high."

A better definition would be, "The patient has a high body temperature, feels weak, and disoriented. The cause that brought this on is unknown at this time. Let us continue to look for the real cause while we lower their body temperature".

Tyrannical language is moving us away from both of these prerequisite problem-solving imperatives. First with identifying and focusing on priorities with what to address as opposed to what to pass on. Priorities are being driven by their political voter impact and hidden agendas, not by the degree of pain and suffering they cause within our communities. Problem statements are embedded with politically motivated conclusions and solutions that steer us away from the real root causes of that problem. This is a means of using money and resources to essentially bribe and influence voters and achieve hidden agendas such as the redistribution of wealth. At least the communists are forthright with their agenda of redistributing wealth.

Recently, I met an employee at a local auto parts store who had moved to the United States from Venezuela. I asked him "How are things back home?"

He responded, "I spoke to a friend from my hometown on the phone a few weeks ago and he said people are eating dogs because of the scarcity of food there."

In but a few decades, Venezuela devolved from the most prosperous country in South America to a country with rampant hyperinflation, food, medicine, and supply shortages, and tyrannical governing.

Today's failure to make substantial progress goes beyond

incompetence and corruption, which is largely the case with Venezuela. It has moved to a malevolent level intended to divide and confuse as well as undermine the very fabric of a civilized population. Rather than heal, the theme has become to increasing divide, distract, and exacerbate problems. Tyrannical language is causing confusion and creating misdirection away from the root causes of problems and away from true crises. It poisons certainty with what is right and what is wrong. Criminals become the victims and the victims are the perpetrators. As with the Netflix series *Stranger Things*, the gates of hell to the "Upside Down World" have been opened. Leaders are acting like pied pipers, leading us over a cliff into a chasm of division, distraction, intolerance, and the suppression of civil debate.

Unproductive and token actions which contribute little to the community are elevated as examples of meaningful efforts. Banning plastic straws is one of many examples here. Give away programs are focused upon and shifting people from being productive with a sense of personal pride of accomplishment to being dependent on government handouts. Healthy and capable people are being guided and pushed toward dependence with an economic umbilical cord attached to their government host body. Their pride, self-worth, and sense of contribution is being suffocated. The merit of personal skill and ability take a back seat to a philosophy of identity politics that emboldens entitlement and demonizes "the opposition." There is an unprecedent level of defiant and combative behavior taking place that is increasingly leading to physical assaults.

BUREAUCRATS ARE OFTEN REWARDED FOR INCOMPETENCE

Bureaucrats and institutional leaders are often rewarded for their incompetence and lack of interest or ability with fixing things. A government department wastes time, money, and resources and is rewarded with a larger budget and the hiring of more employees next year. Universities raise tuition at alarming rates without accountability for their effectiveness in education. They waste money on landscaping, building elaborate structures, and creating politically correct departments of study that border on the absurd. These institutions become consumed with self-preservation at the expense of the population they purport to help live better lives.

Professional politicians and bureaucrats have a dominant priority which is to continue to get reelected and stay in power, often with little regard for the common good. This is a clear example of what I call foolish selfishness as opposed to wise selfishness that seeks win-win outcomes. They join and lead the mobs who are screaming for a perverted execution of instant social justice. They distract us with unrelenting investigation of others they oppose. Not able or willing to solve the real, in your face problems we face today, they become masters of telling us what we can't do, obsessed with regulatory power that gives them a sense of control. They squander money through not-so-subtle programs and policies to influence a voter base. They sow the seeds for future vote harvesting with transparent counterproductive give away programs. Their attitude is that the best defense is to shine the light away from their mismanagement and toward putting others on the defense. They initiate avalanches of waste and destruction that grow each year taking away the money, time, and resources needed to fix important areas of suffering, all the while making hurt and distraction a priority over harmony, healing, and clarity. In some cases, legitimate medical alternatives have been suppressed from public view to further their diabolical agendas. Recently in California (October 2022), Assembly Bill 2098 would give power to the Medical Board of California to take away the licenses of physicians who disseminate "misinformation" or "disinformation" regarding COVID-19. Doctors are being threatened with losing their licenses if they oppose involvement in children's sexual reassignment surgery and treatments with puberty blockers. Terms such as "gender-affirming care" are used as Trojan horses that promote potentially dangerous confusion for children.

This is beyond Orwellian and more closely aligned to fascism where the government decides what is truth and real.

So called "scientists" seeking grant monies and wishing to avoid public criticism have now joined the mob. Rather than encouraging open debate, they tacitly approve of stifling it (see Robert F. Kennedy's book "The Real Anthony Fauci"). Many look away from seeing and finding objective statistics in their efforts to avoid having the mob turn on them. Hitler did not come into power because of his universal appeal, but much more so through the fear he and his brown shirt supporters perpetrated upon the German peoples. The "Night of the Long Knives," or Operation Hummingbird, took place from June 30 to July 2 of 1934, when political opponents were executed essentially overnight. Estimates are that hundreds of political opponents and perceived threats were killed in less than forty-eight hours. Thousands more were arrested. This brutality and tyranny were not lost on the German populace and the remaining surviving government leaders. They quickly fell in line out of fear for their lives and the lives of their families. *Might makes right* in the absence of fair and enforced laws. Today many cower and remain silent. They are afraid to speak out for fear of being persecuted by the social justice warrior mobs or prosecuted by a politicized justice department.

Recently, incompetent and corrupt bureaucrats have taken an ominous dark turn toward harm. They are likely aided by astute linguists and wordsmiths who "design" tyrannical language. These behind-the-scenes engineers of division and diversion feed a waiting media like a mother who offers her breast to a child. They standby eagerly, to pivot on a dime if necessary, and in lockstep recite the tyrannical word or concept of the day.

I believe many see our universities and the teachers' unions as institutions that are infecting young minds with personal agendas directed at dividing us by diminishing the good and accentuating the shortcomings with our country and history. They are the Henny

Pennies who seek obfuscation of their own shortcomings and self-serving agendas. They have created the breeding grounds and planted the seeds of tyranny with language that divides and promotes hate and intolerance. They have infected our language with the seeds of tyranny, much like fascist regimes of years past. Words and phrases are designed much like a deadly infectious virus that is introduced into the general population for nefarious reasons and spreads often unchallenged as it divides, distorts, dehumanizes, and destroys those in its path.

Examples of tyranny being used with words that have been weaponized to divide and distract follow:

"Libtard"—this term is used to denigrate those who promote the progressive left's policies and ideologies

"Anti-Vaxxer"—this term categories those who have concerns with the side effects of vaccinations as hysterical extremists or kooks

"Racist"—this term is thrown about recklessly and generally goes undefined. Today it is used in vague and ambiguous ways. Its overuse diminishes the real problematic behavior of those treating people differently and unfairly because of their race. It has come to be diluted and lost in a flood of false and exaggerated slanderous accusations. Accusations meant to discredit and silence opposing views. Ironically real reverse racism is growing and often goes unchallenged.

Snowflake—this term is used to diminish the views and feelings of those who align themselves as political liberals

"Cultural appropriation"—a term which arbitrarily is used to create a sense of self-righteousness in previous areas of little concern such as children's Halloween costumes.

"Believe in the science"—which is actually being used in the context of "believe in the sciences" that I believe in. Real science encourages questions, embraces challenges, and promotes civil open debate.

"Gender-affirming care"—promotes premature and potentially dangerous treatment and surgeries on children.

"Gender Neutral or Non-Binary"—this denies the biology of animal species and promotes confusion and uncertainty, especially with adolescents. It conflates gender with sexual preference.

"Misinformation" or "Disinformation"—this has been used to discredit oppositonal views. One egregious example of this was with the Medical Board of California that sought to take away the licenses of physicians who disseminate "misinformation" or "disinformation" regarding COVID-19.

"Black and White"—this binary view lumps Italians, Ukrainians, Spaniards, Portuguese, Germans, English, Norwegian, etc., into an over-generalized and exceedingly simplistic category. It ignores the heritages and strengths of their diverse cultures. More often than not it is used to promote a truly racist agenda that treats people differently because of their race. A politician whose mother was Caucasian, was raised by Caucasian grandparents, and whose father was born in Africa is called a "Black man."

"Insurrection"—trespassing by a small group of angry people becomes a monumental smokescreen to persecute, silence, and instill fear in those who disagree with them.

"White supremacist"—a term that is designed to put others in a binary box like those who ask the question "when did you stop beating your wife?" At times it comes down to the following definition, "If you are Caucasian and disagree with my social agenda then you must be a white supremacist because you disagree with my belief."

"Institutional and Systemic Racism"—this term is being used in a grossly exaggerated manner. It promotes and enables people to see themselves as victims. Now more than ever, the policies and rules governing companies and institutions are more vigilant and clearer with the importance of making decisions and treating others fairly and independent of their race, religion, or sexual preference. Not a perfect state, but certainly one that has made great strides and continues to make progress with equality of opportunity.

"The Definition of National Borders"—is being characterized as hindrances to the good of humanity when in fact it is the very foundation for what a civilized country is and is not. They are a logical conclusion to sovereignty and protection of citizens. Borders clearly delineate sovereign territory where resources can be accessed and laws enforced. Basically, borders define the area where money, rules, taxes, and benefits apply to citizens.

"Black Lives Matter (BLM)"—the term has nice words in it and an intentionality in the definition which is true. Unfortunately, this movement has been rife with corruption and used to blackmail, slander, and spread both hate and divisiveness and facilitate reverse racism.

"Gun control" as opposed to violence control, is being touted as the only real answer to perpetrators killing innocents. It is used to distract away from the other two important components to crime, those being the individual's behavior and the environment that enabled this behavior to take place.

"Russian Collusion"—a political strategy of accusation that was untrue when it came to any area of real substance , yet it was perpetuated and ginned up well in advance of having all the pertinent facts.

"Manufactured Crisis"—a term used to discredit serious problems we are facing.

"Mostly Peaceful" use to distract away from mayhem, arson, assault, murder, and crimes committed in dozens of US cities.

"Deplorables"—demonizing people with opposing views.

"White Privilege"—begins with the presumption that Caucasians are "white" and diverts focus toward victimization and away from self-reliance and personal ability. Enables people to believe their happiness is contingent on others' behavior change. It negates views of an abundance mentality which promotes merit based efforts to develop our own personal skill sets. It marginalizes the differences of various European cultures into a binary view.

"Nuclear Family"—often used in a context that disparages the value of a two-parent family to justify an unhealthy and serious trend with illegitimacy which is brought on by reckless sexual activity, government entitlement programs, and the irresponsibility of male sexual partners.

"Equity"—a Trojan horse for retribution of wealth away from those who earned it to those who did not, based on a distorted view of social justice. Eventually it can lead to discouraging entrepreneurship and innovation.

Crybaby, whiny—term used to generalize those with an opposing view as weak and fragile

"Fake News" —overused term that discredits opposing views. Rather than take on detailed misreporting and countering with facts, it often just becomes a generalized binary view that they are all bad.

"Climate Deniers"—term used to stifle debate on the extent and real severity of the weather changing in the years and centuries ahead.

"Existential Threat"—an esoteric term often used to promote a political agenda by appealing to lofty, self-important views of eminent apocalypse.

"Hate Speech"—a gateway to censorship and cancel culture as it is undefined, and as such is subject to an arbitrary standard of application.

"Toxic Masculinity"—a term which denigrates and negatively exaggerates inherent male characteristics.

This dangerous language constrains and diverts efforts from meaningful actions needed to solve real problems and reduce suffering. This failure of leadership and use of tyrannical language has led to growing frustration, hate, pent up anger and an inner sense of emptiness many have today. We are living in a time where many are being misguided toward having *contra identities* built primarily upon oppositional views. Anger, frustration, hate, and bold defiance are reaching a critical mass. Societal mental health is in decline. Instead of "working on me" and my talents, skills, and personal challenges and character defects, people are sidelined into finding fault with others and institutions. Merit is taking a back seat to focus on feeling victimized, blaming others, and feelings of entitlement. This perspective with an emphasis on the exaggerated dark side of humanity appears to be growing at an alarming rate. It is fueled by political vote harvesting motives seeking to hold on to power and influence by those outside our country. There are also intentional strategies to divide and weaken our country's economic and military world influence by those who reside outside our borders. Entitlement and indignant self-righteousness are promoted while at the same time commitment to merit-based talent is being marginalized. This is a time when many subconsciously look each day for another reason to be triggered into "being offended" by yet another confirmation that "I am good because you are bad" example.

CHALLENGE TYRANTICAL LANGUAGE
BEFORE IT METASTASIZES

I call this tyranny of words and concepts *Roads of Tyranny (ROT)*. These roads are tempting pathways that provide an immediate sense of purpose, importance, and thrill. They are easily taken with their tempting entry ramps, beckoning us with the allure of thrilling indignation and a sense of self-importance when we ride upon them. As with the immediate *high* one gets from riding a roller coaster or taking an addictive drug, people can immediately feel good and forget their personal problems. Like young teenagers joining inner city gangs, they now become part of club with fellow members to commiserate with. Their self-identity is bolstered by promoting *fantasy idealism* as it gives them a sense of moral superiority, as well. Another dysfunctional advantage is that they can also raise self-indignant outrage and offense at being victimized by the *Bad People*. No wonder this group can be easily mobilized into a lynch mob to descend on individuals and organizations. It is hard to resist the Henny Penny (the sky is falling chicken) attraction of being a clairvoyant Nostradamus combined with the self-righteous anger with "those fools" around them. Statistical probability and objective data are irrelevant when the so-called unsubstantiated "emotional real truth is known." They then move on to censure and disparage those with opposing views like a nihilist who is hell bent on destruction and obstruction. It is important to quicky notice and call out this infection for what it is to minimize its deleterious impact on our communities, families, and the population at large before it metastasizes.

There is a tragic absence of dialogue that sincerely and competently is looking for common ground and meaningful solutions to our real problems. Rather, *binary language* enables divisive views. Examples of these binary all good or all bad views are:

Pro-Life vs. Pro-Choice

Racist vs. Unprejudiced

No Guns vs. Any and All Guns

Fantasy Idealism vs. Anything-Goes Capitalism

Prolific Injustice vs. Rare Injustice

Climate Change Apocalypse vs. "No Problems Here" Weather Change

Helping the Needy vs. Total Self-Reliance

Borders vs. No Borders

Tyrannical language is being used to denigrate the value of two parent households. The term "Nuclear Family" is disparaged and trivialized. This misdirection diverts attention away from the well-documented good that two parent families provide.

> *"If we have learned any policy lesson well over the past twenty-five years, it is that for children living in single-parent homes, the odds of living in poverty are great. The policy implications of the increase in out-of-wedlock births are staggering."*[16]

We are living in a time when the illegitimacy rates have skyrocketed. (For period 1965 to 2018, Whites 3.1 percent to 28 percent, Hispanics 12 percent to 52 percent, Blacks 24 percent to 69 percent).[17]

Imagine if instead of these divisive, binary conversations, we began talking about working together to:

- *Reduce unwanted pregnancy brought about irresponsible sex* (which account for over 90 percent of abortions).

- *Debate the definition of what racism is and is not,* so as not dilute the serious with the trivial.

- *Discuss root causes of deaths caused by firearms* as a result of the person, the environment, as well as the weapon.

- *Provide healing communities for the homeless* where they could be triaged into categories as with mental illness, substance abuse, or need for training and education so as to become self-sufficient.

- *Establish guidelines for civil debate* and actually promote civil discourse in educational institutions and media outlets to seek out best practices and real continuous improvement initiatives.

ABILITY AND WILLINGNESS TO SOLVE REAL PROBLEMS IS MARGINAL

Many discuss the causes of these trends of divisiveness, disenfranchise-ment, victimhood, entitlement, and bold defiance. They may discount my belief that tyrannical and dangerous language used by bureaucratic leaders and institutions are at its center, intentionally fanning the flames of discord and upset. Not so debatable, however, is the reality that our ability and willingness to solve compelling problems at a level that makes significant improvement and healing is marginal at best. Perhaps a much-needed shift in our paradigms of cause and effect here is well overdue. Let's give the "Language of Peace and Progress" a chance, please.

Parts of our common language have been kidnapped and its words manipulated to form a nightmare orchestra. A harmful symphony is played each day through a media lacking in objective reporting, corrupt and incompetent political leaders, and self-serving educational institutions. This ensemble is likely being encouraged and orchestrated by domestic and foreign political operatives who are incompetent, corrupt, and/or duplicitous. Many people have been unknowingly hoodwinked into a "Henny Penny" persona which makes them feel important with their cries of "The sky is falling!"

They feel they have an enlightened knowledge not known by the masses. It gives people a sense of inflated importance by crying wolf at every turn. We are in the midst of modern-day Salem witch hunts and Mayan sacrifices to the climate gods. There are few leaders who are both courageous and wise enough to stand as bulwarks against the anarchy, incompetence, and divisiveness with the use of tyrannical dangerous language; Dr. Jordan B. Peterson is a rare example of one who is willing to do so.

Words can empower us and promote harmony. Likewise, they can divide us against one another or distract us from a healthy path forward. Toxic language infects our views, thinking, and exacerbates division and animosity toward one another. This negative language is at the root of what stifles progress. It enables our problems to dig themselves in deeper and moves us ever closer to the abyss of anarchy and tyranny. Tyranny with language can be either unintended or designed. Some language evolved haphazardly and contributes to confusion and our inability to solve real problems. Yet an ever-increasing amount of our public efforts to improve are being derailed by puppet masters who have been duplicitious with the designing and promotion of words for harm and interpersonal conflict. As opposed to empathetic views of others where we seek common ground and compassion, tyrannical language dehumanizes our perspective. It serves us well to avoid incorporating this language into our conversations and thinking.

Who we see ourselves as (our identity), as well as who we see others to be, can have a profound impact on our self-communication as well as interpersonal communications. The adage of believing in yourself and believing in others' ability to succeed and make progress is an essential component of promoting inspiration and motivation. Do we see that our identity is about being empowered to be all that we can be, or do we put on the cloak of victimhood as a means to avoid personal responsibility? I have long contended that embedded in the definition of *victim* was the belief that *no action is required*. How convenient to believe that it is up to others to change in order for me to be better. With this view people become spectators of their own life, far from an attitude of self-reliance and empowerment summarized nicely in the saying *"if it's to be its up to me."* Am I the person who sees the need for focused effort on my part to make improvements?

By being vigilant and on the lookout, we can see the tyrannical language for what it is. It is the enemy of peace, progress, and healing. It is a perpetrator which perpetuates suffering and conflict. *Be the Bloodhound* and sniff out this dark and harmful path, warn others to move away from it and not become unknowing accomplices to its damage. Quickly identify words and language that plant the seeds of tyranny. Be a healer who reveals this danger and provides the antidote of self-reliance, common ground, empathy, empowerment, and harmony to counteract its evil.

I have an inexhaustible faith in people and their potential to achieve better. I also believe people are inherently good and have great compassion and love for all of humanity. There is much common ground that we can build on together. I see exciting opportunities for us to be better with both increasing the good and decreasing the bad as dedicated *Betterists* who pursue more positives and less negatives for ourselves and others with our path of *Betterism*. There is little I desire more than to see each of us focused on learning from each other and getting along civilly. At worst, let us agree to disagree and have clarity with prioritizing our efforts to work on our real significant problems and challenges. I believe that by using a wise empowering language and working together we can solve and improve issues that contribute to much of the suffering and conflict many are experiencing today.

CHAPTER 10

Put it on Autopilot . . . Habits, Routines, Results

Do I make my habits or do my habits make me?

"Be on Autopilot"

Few skills are as valuable as knowing how to design and implement wise habits for ourselves.

—Michael Starr

A few days before her death on October 4, 1970, Janis Joplin recorded her only number one single, "Me and Bobby McGee." The song had been originally written by Kris Kristoffferson and was inspired by his reflection on the failures in his own life. This song provided a mantra for the free-spirited generation of the time with its iconic chorus line defining "freedom" as having nothing left to lose. At the time of the song's release, I was an idealistic twenty-year-old, long-haired hippie with aspirations of joining the Peace Corps. I loved that song. Janis's authentic raw energy and raspy desperate tone in her voice resonated with many of us back then. I was not quite sure what the chorus meant, but it sure sounded "cool." A few years later, while in the jungles of the Yucatan, I came to understand that meaning of freedom.

In December of 1972, I completed my studies at Carnegie Mellon University in Pittsburgh and received a Bachelor of Science degree in electrical engineering. In that very same month, I was one of the last people drafted into the military, and as a result joined the Navy as an enlisted sailor. My draft number was seventy-three. I was allowed to postpone arrival at boot camp by six months and decided to take some time to hitchhike and travel with my backpack and sleeping bag.

What followed was a four-month adventure that started with driving a retired couple's black Fleetwood Cadillac from Pittsburgh to Fort Lauderdale. I spent a few days there with a high school friend named Ron. From Fort Lauderdale I hitched a ride in a small red Fiat Triumph convertible to New Orleans. I was able to be part of the Mardi Gras madness. I slept under the bleachers in Tulane stadium in my sleeping bag. I will never forget taking a shower in the stadium and the regret I felt for having taken off my glasses before stepping into that large, tiled room. There were more than twenty guys and girls inside showering. There are some sights and experiences once missed that we may never have an opportunity to have again. I have rather poor vision without my eyeglasses, so it was an opportunity lost in a blur.

I later hitchhiked to Houston, where I got a "walk on" job with a construction crew. One day while working, I found myself buried underground inside a large concrete drainage pipe. I had been working a jackhammer suspended overhead by a chain. While breaking through the side of that tunnel pipe with the jackhammer, the ground collapsed above me. I was rescued by the crew above as they dug frantically to remove the collapsed ground around me.

While in Houston, I slept in a real flea bag hotel where cockroaches roamed free and sheets were not provided. Why were several girls usually sitting in the crude lobby every day, wearing their short skirts? Later, after leaving Houston, I eventually made my way to Brownsville, Texas, and into Mexico on my way to Guatemala.

As I journeyed south through Mexico toward Guatemala, I met a number of English-speaking travelers. One fellow I met, who had quit his job as an aeronautical engineer in Southern California, mentioned a town he enjoyed. It was a lovely, quaint southern Mexican town called San Cristobal, located near the border with Guatemala. I stayed there for nearly a week and befriend several fellow adventures there. One remarkable lady I met was an Australian nurse. She had years earlier shipped her Volkswagen from Australia to India. From there, she and a friend had driven to France, later traveling to Nigeria and working there as a nurse. I met her as she was making her way north from South America toward the United States. She was tall and stately looking with a kind, reassuring smile. She had a wrinkled and weathered complexion that had seen plenty of sunny days. I remember that she was gracious and gave me some money to help me with living costs (which at the time were about $1 to $2 per day).

As I traveled onto and through Guatemala, I saw the towering volcanic mountain at Lake Atitlan and spent a few days in Antigua during Easter celebrations with magnificently decorated floats carried by robed participants and parades through the streets. Antigua is a centuries-old city founded by the conquistadors in 1543, where later Franciscan friars would build a chapel.

LOSING MY FEAR OF DEATH

Later, while staying in Guatemala City, I bought a ticket for $25 to fly on board an old freight plane to the ancient Mayan capital of Tikal. I sat in that plane on a wooden seat with a clasped rope as my safety belt and a cargo net directly in front of me. I distinctly remember looking out at the endless sea of the Yucatan jungle and having an intense crescendo of unbearable fear build within me. I felt terrified. I was flying above the jungle, thousands of miles from home. If we crashed in that World War II relic of a plane, any quick rescue would be impossible. No one would know I perished there. At that very moment, something profound and unforgettable happed to me. It was like a stretched rubber band had reached its limit with my fear when something released inside me. Something snapped. An immediate wave of calm and peace enveloped me. From that moment on, to this very day, I no longer fear death. I had an emotional epiphany that swept over me. I realized in that moment that nearly everything around me was out of my control. This was not a cognitive conclusion, but an emotional surrender to *what is*. This is where the beginning of my understanding of NOOT started.

We landed on a dirt airfield near the ruins of the Tikal pyramids. The runway was guarded by several soldiers holding submachine guns. One night while camping there, I snuck into the main courtyard between the two major Tikal pyramids. The midnight experience standing under a full moon in the center of the Tikal court with its opposing ancient tower pyramids, was awesome and chilling. This was a place where centuries ago human sacrifices had once been made. Perhaps those offerings to the gods were their response to fears of military attack or climate change? I was living Jack Kerouac's book, *Lonesome Traveler*. This experience was the ultimate in freedom to do whatever and whenever I wanted. Yet, in spite of the adventure and marvelous places experienced, I grew uneasy with this freedom and felt lost within its aimlessness. The meaning of freedom was just as Kris Kristofferson had written and as Janis Joplin had sung; that when we have no structure, obligations, or commitment, we have total freedom.

Shortly after returning home from this adventure, I reported to the Naval base in Great Lakes, Illinois. I went from absolutely no structure or schedule with my life to the highly regimented ways of military boot camp. Strangely and unexpectedly, I felt relieved with this routine and its certainty. I felt a comfort with this training and my belief that I was making progress toward a meaningful destination. The routine and regimen freed me of the angst and listlessness I had felt during my previous months of hitchhiking, with its impromptu travels and meandering directions. I could then think on a higher plane, as I was no longer consumed with the thoughts of what I needed to do next to find a place to sleep, eat, or be safe. This routine at the Great Lakes Naval base was an autopilot that took over the menial parts of my life and gave me the opportunity to think beyond the basics of existence.

While in boot camp, I applied for the Navy's nuclear power program. I had the prerequisite education to qualify as an officer on board a nuclear submarine. Several months after finishing boot camp while stationed in Little Creek, Virginia, I had an interview with Admiral Rickover and his staff near Washington, D.C. The interview was with several technical experts, and then finally ended with the Admiral. I actually had two separate meetings with him that day. The first meeting resulting in Admiral Rickover turning to the officer who had accompanied me into the room and saying "get this horse's ass out of here!" Oops! That was a result of my answer to why I wanted to be in the nuclear power program. My answer had been, "So I can get a good job when I leave the Navy."

Afterwards, I was escorted out to sit alone in a small, windowless room by a uniformed Naval officer. The officer turned to me before leaving and asked, "Are there any other reasons you would have for getting in this program?"

I sat alone in that tiny room for what seemed like an eternity (but probably closer to an hour or two). Later, I returned to the admiral once more. He asked again for reasons why I wanted to be in the program. After sitting alone in that room, with its solitude of uncertainty, I had reached a much more fundamental conclusion. I said, "Because I enjoy hard work and the satisfaction and purpose it brings me."

That was true then and is still true today. It proved to be a successful interview and I was selected into the Navy's nuclear power program training and later became a naval officer aboard a nuclear submarine.

My next level of training was to attend Officer Candidate School (OCS) in Newport, Rhode Island, which was a cake walk and lots of fun. Afterward, I was required to successfully complete nuclear power theory study at the training center near San Francisco in Vallejo, California. This six-month program was the first half of a one-year demanding program for future Naval Officers aboard nuclear-powered vessels. This was a no nonsense, highly accelerated learning requirement that would provide the understanding and knowledge that might someday be needed to make life or death decisions. A submarine is a highly complex and sophisticated machine. It could house multiple intercontinental missiles with over one hundred hydrogen bombs. This was more potential destructive force than all of the armaments and bombs in World War II. While it is being powered by its nuclear reactor and is submerged continuously for months at a time, it sustains the crew with electrified refrigeration and the oxygen and water it produces through the electrolysis and distillation of seawater.

ELEVATING PROCESS OVER OUTCOME

This training school and these studies were no esoteric exercise in intellectual curiosities, but rather a "real deal" education for technical competency which provided a basis for future need to make critical decisions. We were continually evaluated through testing for our understating of subjects like chemistry, physics, thermodynamics, fluid mechanics, and nuclear theory. These studies were grueling. It was during the course of this experience at the Vallejo Naval Base training center that I came to have a life-changing view that elevated process over outcome. This view reinforced the value of having wise routines in my life.

After several weeks of this theory training, I found myself floundering and ranked near bottom of the class of seventy-plus Naval officers.

I was both mentally and physically exhausted. I distinctly remember that one Saturday morning (we did have weekends off) when I sat down with myself and decided I needed to do something different. Working harder, which had always been my "go to" process for achievement, was not working here. The harder I worked, the less sleep I received, and the more difficult the studies became for me. I decided to design and implement a routine with a few habits and to stick to it no matter what. I brainstormed some ideas on paper and decided on a few *sacred habits* to weave into each day. The previous routine I had in place was there by default and not by design. The intentional new routine, with a few habits within it, definitely required faith and commitment. I decided to stop studying each night at a specific time then unwind with some fun activity like reading, playing guitar, or listening to music, and then prepare for the next morning by setting out my uniform and study material for class. Sleep time became a sacred habit and commitment. I was always in bed by a specific time and no later. Added to this was a specific waking time that gave me about an hour to study and review before bicycling off to classes on the base each morning.

A NEW FREEDOM— WISE ROUTINE

As a result of my focus on this new approach, my anxiety dropped and I started to have some fun with the experience. I certainly had far more peace of mind. I took horseback riding lessons on the weekends, went on a few dates, and bicycled through the hills in the area. After a few months, when others were frantically cramming for exams, I was lighthearted and joking with my classmates. At times, I would go off to the movies the night before a big exam. One weekend, I set off with two instructors and climbed Half Dome, where we spent the night on top that granite dome in Yosemite National Park. The process, this new routine, worked. I ended up near the top of the class at the end of the six months of training. This new freedom was a result of my sacred rules and routines. Not a freedom to do whatever I felt like at the moment, but rather a freedom from anxiety, fear, and suffering by surrendering to structure and commitment.

The clarity, certainty, and commitment we discover when we identity what is truly important with our lives is a breakthrough for our personal peace. Surrendering and aligning with sacred rules is a new healthy freedom. Discerning what is truly valuable for us on a fundamental level as with health, relationships, and contribution gives us purpose and meaning. After clarifying which area(s) you wish to improve upon, next create habits and routines to support progress there. In boot camp, the routine was designed for me, afterward the routines became my personal responsibility. *Few skills are as valuable as knowing how to design and implement wise habits for ourselves.*

The focus on habit is a two-sided coin. One side is *what* habit, the other side is *how* you put this habit in place. Routines are groupings of habits, as with a morning routine that includes several habits such as meditation, review of personal boundaries, review of our ten convictions, exercise, and daily planning. A philosophy I call MISS (Making it Simple and Streamlined) is excellent for helping design habits for a better life. With the vitality in *Being the Stream*, by being alive and thriving through forward movement, we are confident that our actions and direction are indeed the best choice for now. Having wise habits and routines is an excellent way of increasing our peace of mind, sense of progress, and meaning in our day to day lives.

WISE HABITS INCREASE OUR PEACE OF MIND

To achieve this better place for ourselves, we must identify, implement, and maintain high leverage habits and routines.

Four steps with creating habits:

Step 1 (The Foundation): Decide what area(s) in your life is truly important and in need for improvement

Step 2: Identify what habits and routines will support this improvement

Step 3: Implement the habit

Step 4: Maintain the new habit

Step 1. The Foundation — What is really important?

In our personal lives, as in business, it is important that time, effort, money, and resources are not squandered. It essential that our efforts, time, and money are optimized to get the best results possible. With the knowledge of the economic principle of opportunity costs, we understand that what is invested into "X" cannot also be invested into "Y." There are limitations and a mutual exclusivity, as the use of one resource precludes its use elsewhere. Before we embark upon a significant initiative, let us choose wisely. "I've climbed the ladder of success and reached the top only to find it was leaning against the wrong wall" is a tragic commentary for many. People often come to realize that after spending years with dedicated and imbalanced efforts pursuing short-sighted goals, they have missed out on close relationships and their personal health.

It is important to remember that how we live with integrity in the NOW is what is ultimately important. The wise lifestyle of *Betterism* (more good/less bad, more happiness/less suffering) rules here. The journey is without meaning if there are not destinations being pursued. The destination gives the journey context and meaning. The journey, on the other hand, is life with its actions and inactions. There is a plethora of destinations we can pursue, so let us choose wisely. It is best that they both have integrity and address real concerns in our lives. Be wise with your introspection and assessment of which destination you seek today. Make the journey fun, full of adventure, and harmonious.

Step 2. Identify which habits and routines will support the foundational improvement.

The Pareto Principle was developed by Italian economist Vilfredo Pareto in 1898, at the University of Lausanne in Switzerland. This principles states that for many outcomes, approximately 80 percent of results come from about 20 percent of the efforts. These are the high leverage actions that give us the easiest and fasted desired results. It basically states that for many situations, a few strategic efforts can give as a large return with achieving what we seek.

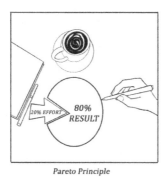

Pareto Principle

Determining these critical few habits is very important to your success in any one area. Choose a select few and make them as simple as possible (please see attached MISS article at end of this chapter).

Step 3. Implement the new habit.

Be realistic with who you are and who you are not. Be honest and clear about what time of day, what amount of time, and what your rhythms and lifestyle are before scheduling habit type and times. Accept and embrace your limitations as well as your strengths. Use your strengths as foundations to build upon. Quarterbacks don't spend much time practicing and honing their ability to block a player but do look for better ways to make successful completions with their passes.

I am a morning person who wakes up full of energy and enthusiasm. It is a time that serves me best for creativity. Evenings just don't work for me with learning or creating. With my writing, I do that early in the morning usually between 5:00 a.m. and 8:00 a.m.

Having a morning routine is extremely valuable with the creation of a new habit. Renew and review daily what you will do that day within your morning routine to progress a new habit and continue your self-motivation.

One step at a time with ISTEP (Intentional Simple Tiny Efforts for Progress)

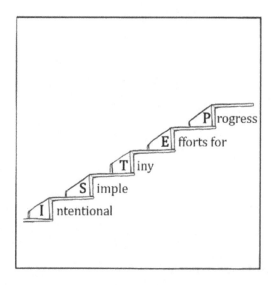

Consider linking your new desired habit to a habit that exists now and is solidity in place (one you do 99.9 percent of the time). An example here would be to plan and write down an ISTEP small activity you commit to that day to support a particular destination and journey and do so before having your morning coffee. Post your commitment somewhere as a reminder. It can also be helpful to share this commitment with a trusted friend or coach, as well, to hold you accountable and be mindfully reminded of your commitment.

A great example of this can be found in James Clear's book Atomic Habits, chapter 5, "The Best Way to Start a New Habit—Habit Stacking."

Step 4. Maintain the new habit.

You wisely selected a focus for improvement as a *Betterist*, where the journey and the destination are symbiotic. You next determined which habits would nurture your progress there. After implementing this strategy, it is important to maintain your progress with your new habits.

The maintenance phase is often neglected, as it is largely proactive and comes with little fanfare or excitement. It is not nearly as compelling as a crisis that motivates our desire to respond and improve. Nonetheless it is essential, just as much as replacing your vehicle's tires when the tread is low. Waiting for a blowout to occur is not the prudent time to do maintenance for obvious reasons. In the next chapter, a detailed strategy for maintaining your forward progress will be presented. I published the following article a number of years ago and am reprinting it here. It speaks to the value of designed elegant simplicity.

"Far Better to MISS than Kiss"

MICHAEL STARR

LISTENING FROM THE HEART

Mancos Times
April 11, 2012

In my listening to others, and to myself as well, I often hear how life has gotten "complicated," "cluttered," and "busy." I hear how we have become inundated with all that "stuff" around us as, seeing our closets, yards, and garages overflowing, feeling our minds overflowing with all that we "need" to do and "want" to do, anxious and frustrated that we don't have enough time, energy, or money to do it all. Having too many "to dos" and so many possessions, that they seem to own us with their demands for maintenance and attention. Our cup does indeed runneth over, and yet we still acquire and commit to ever more! Does not this state of overload with possessions, commitments, and expenditures promote an atmosphere of uneasiness and dissonance around us and within us?

One of my favorite quotes is: "If you can't explain it simply, you don't understand it well enough"— Albert Einstein.

As I have reminded my daughters, perhaps too many times, one must work hard to master a subject or talent and finally understand the simplicity about it, WORKING HARD TO MAKE IT SIMPLE. Often, I have heard the term KISS "Keep It Simple Stupid" in business and have come to believe that this phrase is very much off target. Ideas, concepts, and lives do start out simple, yes, but they nearly always must have some essential refinements and additions to make them truly effective. It starts out a as a simple concept but usually is incomplete. Unfortunately, as we refine and add to it, much unnecessary complexity is added as well, much like earmarks added to federal legislative bills. As a result, often life and processes become difficult to sustain at this level. All those obligations and maintenance of possessions such as autos, boats, gardens, yards, relationships, work, social commitments, etc., become a saturated whirlwind, perhaps even a tempest about us. We begin to lose sight of key life values such as taking care of our physical and mental well-being, nurturing important relationships, or fortifying our self-esteem by being our word with others, being our word with ourselves as well, or living financially in the "black."

I have found that there does come a time to stand back, reassess, and develop a streamlined strategy for our lives. A time does arrive to herald us to distill our lives into the essentials and basics, re-engineer our lives, so to speak, in an intentional manner, focused on the critical few. I must admit that it does take a certain level of maturity and life experience, however, to achieve clarity with what the really valuable things that matter. It is difficult to do so without setbacks, successes, and the life experiences that put things in a mature perspective. It is difficult to have clarity and confidence about what it is we truly need to feel fulfilled, such as our health, an attitude of gratitude, empathy in our relationships, and streamlined spending, to name a few. Frankly, it does not take much money or many possessions to have a true sense of serenity, joy, harmony, and contribution when we do get honest about our lives and what truly matters.

So, I have coined the phrase MISS—Make It Streamlined and Simple. Is it time for you to stand back and re-engineer your life and discover and commit to the essential elements for yourself, time to be the master of your ship and navigate a new course ahead, time to shed some possessions, some commitments, perhaps even some relationships as well? Is it time for you to MISS your life, to get your life?

CHAPTER 11

Maintaining Peace With the Past and Progress With the Future

Do I take proactive daily action(s) to prevent backsliding with my progress?

"Be the Wise Frog"

Find a way.

–Diana Nyad

As your Journey into Peace moves ahead with the use of wise empowering language, you will make satisfying and substantial progress. By choosing and then pursuing meaningful goals (goal = destination + journey toward it), you will build a strong sense of purpose and accomplishment. The path of *Betterism* will reduce the duration, intensity, and frequency (*durinfre*) spent with past hate, anger, frustration, or despair.

This is a wonderful freedom to experience. This direction will also grow the intensity, duration, and frequency of your inner peace, progress, and optimism. There will be times, however, when you may have setbacks and begin to move away from some of the accomplishments previously gained. Sliding backwards toward previous unhealthy past views and behaviors can easily occur. This chapter equips you with tools to help you avoid regression as well as how best to handle the early stages of backsliding when it does occur.

Ice cleats are traction devices with small, short spikes attached to your footwear to prevent slipping on ice and snow. Crampons are much more substantive devices with large, jagged teeth for traction in the most hazardous of ice and snow conditions. In this chapter, *ice cleats* are proactive measures you take to maintain progress. Your *crampons* will be reactive responses that address an ensuing backward slippage.

ICE CLEATS ARE PROACTIVE TOOLS
THAT MAINTAIN PROGRESS

Ice Cleats: Proactive Action

Preparation is indeed an important key to most successes. As we journey ahead, it is wise to prepare for the times when we might lose our forward momentum. Ice cleats are habits and routines you will design, implement, and sustain to support you in your daily journeys. These are a proactive set of tools you will hone and be mindful of each day. They do require a bit of daily and weekly attention so that they will keep your traction in place. Time spent with these daily and weekly routines will be an excellent investment for your future successes as a *Betterist*. These ice cleats include a personal mantra plus three sacred habits:

(1) Have an empowering prayer/mantra/affirmation

(2) Sacred Habit: *Marvelous Start Morning Routine*

(3) Sacred Habit: Week in review session

(4) Sacred Habit: Follow-Up Setback System (FUSS)

Have an empowering prayer/mantra/affirmation

Negative thoughts are going to happen. An elixir for dark thinking is to counteract it with convincing language that leads us back to thoughts of empowerment and optimism. I believe you will find having an empowering prayer/mantra/affirmation will be most helpful to use as a countermeasure with that "stinking thinking." The objective is to keep you on track with making continued progress. The traction of the ice cleats ensures firm forward movement. Develop and then often repeat your empowering mantra motto to yourself. Alcoholics Anonymous does this with the "Serenity Prayer." Your mantra should be a motivating reminder of who you are and your faith in your ability to accomplish the important objectives you deserve and desire. As with prayer, it can also remind us that there are things out of our control and that it is best to surrender to a level of uncertainty with the future.

After turning sixty years old and having failed four times previously with her attempts to swim from Cuba to Florida, Diana Nyad set out once again to establish a world record with her swim in 2013. This arduous swim from Havana to Key West was rife with challenges with the extreme distance, waters filled with aggressive oceanic white tip sharks, and box jellyfish with their deadly venom. She suffered a serious sting by a jelly fish during her fourth attempt that kept her from finishing.

In her preparations for attempting yet a fifth effort to make this swim, she had a specially designed suit and mask made. Perhaps just as important, if not more so, she developed a mantra that resonated self-motivation and confidence within her during her next phase of preparation. She did indeed complete that final fifty-three-hour world record swim at the age of sixty-four on September 2, 2013. Her mantra motto was *"Find a Way."*

MANTRAS ARE POWERFUL

Can a mantra be that powerful and important with achieving "success"? The answer is, yes it can! Perhaps the largest obstacle, the greatest enemy we face with our ability to make progress, is ourselves. It is negative self-talk inside our head that more often than not sabotages our ability to move forward and live a life of *Betterism*.

Examples of Prayers/Mantras/ Affirmations:

- *Find a way.*

- *If it's to be its up to me.*

- *Lord, I am your servant and vessel for good and healing, give me the strength and courage to be wise with my thoughts and actions.*

- *I am making progress, setbacks are but detours along my journey, I will continue my forward movement.*

- *My physical health, healthy relationship, personal meaning, and attitude of excitement for today and tomorrow are my life . . . I am on a quest to pursue this every day.*

- *God grant me the serenity to accept the things I cannot change, the courage to change the things I can, and the wisdom to know the difference.*

- *Mistakes are my friends, they are my teachers, I embrace them as opportunities and steppingstones for becoming a better me.*

- *Interruptions to my plans and expectations are opportunities for me to contribute to another.*

Marvelous Start Morning Routine, a strong and healthy start for your day

See Worksheet "Marvelous Start Morning Routine"
(go to www.executivecoachingservices.net)

Our day begins with waking and putting our feet on the ground. The first fifteen to thirty minutes afterward can be a valuable launch for our day ahead. I strongly encourage you to have a well-thought-out and simplified morning routine in order to leverage a marvelous start to your day.

Automatic repeated behavior falls into the categories of reactions, habits, and routines. A reaction is an immediate feeling we have and the action we take as a result of something happening around us. Reactions can be the result of well-thought-out views. Reactions, however, are often an unconscious fight or flight response to a perceived threat. A habit is one specific behavior, such as taking a shower immediately after waking up. A routine is a group of habits such as waking in the morning then taking a shower, dressing, having a cup of coffee with breakfast, and then walking the dog. It is important that you have a wisely designed morning routine to sustaining your peace and progress.

For the longest time, I kept saying to my wife (and myself), "I really need to get to a point where I am writing daily with my book," . . . but this just didn't happen. My writing was sporadic at best. I contend that *willpower* is not enough when it comes to achieving long-term progress. Forward progress requires well-designed and wisely implemented automatic habits and routines. When an activity becomes automatic and routine, there is no need to decide or choose. The activity becomes effortless, like putting on a seatbelt when sitting in your car. You just do it. After listening to an audio book called *Atomic Habits* by James Clear (which I highly recommend), I was reminded of the concept of linkage; i.e., linking the creation of a new habit with a firmly established existing habit. I decided I would not drink my sacrosanct morning coffee until I was sitting at my computer cued up to write. This small change worked fabulously, and I am now writing seven days a week for two or more hours each day.

Week in Review Session–Reflection and Correction[18]

The weekly interval is frequently used as a time for reflection and improvement. Religious services are scheduled on a certain day of the week. AA and NA meeting are scheduled at least weekly, as well. With NFL football teams, Mondays after the Sunday games are a time to review the film of the previous day's game to see what went right and what went wrong. The Bible speaks to the importance of the seventh day as a time to rest. There is great value for you with scheduling a certain day and time for assessing your week to learn, improve, and celebrate. For most of us, this will be a one-person meeting with me, myself, and I. For some, having a weekly meeting with a therapist, counselor, or coach may be an option, as well.

Be consistent with attending your week in review session and limit its length to a sustainable interval. Start on time, as if you were attending a sporting event or religious service. It is wise to view both your morning routine and weekly session as sacred routines that must happen. They are as important as refueling or recharging your automobile.

During the course of your week in review session, you may wish to jot down notes as to what went well and what seemed to go awry. Review your Follow-Up Setback System record with its recorded mistakes/setbacks during the week. While listing the good, bad, and ugly, be mindful to note the scorpions you allowed to ride on your back.

The definition of insanity is doing the same thing over and over again but expecting different results.

–Albert Einstein

It will be helpful to have an agenda for your weekly assessment, planning, and celebration session.

Follow-Up Setback System (FUSS)[19]

When we are faced with setbacks, it is important to pivot past the problem with a quick turn and *"be like a school of fish."* Too often, a setback derails us and we waste valuable time and energy before we get back on track. It can also lead to even bigger problems as a result of our emotions, reactions, and decisions afterward. It is wise to see that detours are the shortest path forward, as when the mountain stream runs up against a boulder that is in its path and immediately diverts to the next easiest route. In that moment when we are facing a mistake or setback, we will pause, note the issue in the FUSS log record, then continue our forward progress and move on with constructive activity. We will avoid getting derailed or stalled by emotion or confusion in that moment of now. If immediate damage control actions are necessary, we will take them. During these times, we will be confident that this experience may later become an excellent LEG. We will avoid the temptation to become enraged, frustrated with others, or beat ourselves up.

The FUSS log is a place we record the concerning setback/mistake. We will review this log during our scheduled week in review session. At that time, we look to best understand why it happened and determine if it is something worthy of our follow up for improvement. Not all upsets are worth following up, as they may be rare or have little to do with us and be another's personal problem.

Example: I am working on a project at home painting a room. I find myself in the middle of working when I realize that I don't have spare paint rollers for a second color being used. I had asked my son to buy them, and he did not. He is not home right now. I make a note in my phone under the category FUSS, then I go and buy the necessary material and return to my work. Rather than going into a rage or getting angry, I record the issue for later handling to determine possible ways of preventing it from happening again the future (writing out a checklist, double checking material on hand before beginning work, setting accountabilities with son, etc.) This avoids working or driving while angry or upset, which is not a good idea as it often can lead to additional problems.

This method for recording an upset/mistake can be with the use of a notepad, planner, phone, voicemail left to self, etc. These setbacks do need to be recorded and there does need to be some scheduled time to review the list to determine subsequent action, if any.

Knowing you have this system in place and that it is a sacred habit of yours will provide you peace of mind and circumvent drama and emotions. It will limit the degree of upset with unmet expectations and be a process that will help you prevent reoccurrence of that same upset.

The four proactive activities that make up your ice cleats will serve you well. They will prevent or at least minimize losing ground with hard earned progress.

SERIOUS SETBACKS REQUIRE DAMAGE CONTROL FIRST

Crampons: Reactive Response

Unlike the four aspects of ice cleats which are proactive, crampons are reactive and put in place after the fact. There will come a time when we are standing on a slippery slope and find ourselves slipping backward and losing ground. Losing ground is okay as long as it is kept to a minimum and we quickly regain our footing. It is only human for us to occasionally slip. Temptations, second guessing, and regression are an aspect of NOOT—they are inevitable. With wise advanced preparation, we will promptly notice the slippage, open our backpack, and put on our crampons. With this we will soon be back on track and moving forward again.

We want our crampons to be quickly available, sharp, and fit properly, as it is with all important tools. Whether it be a first aid kit, spare tire, or our ability to do the Heimlich maneuver or provide CPR, it is wise to have these aides and skills readily available to us during an emergency. There are two phases in dealing with circumstances where we find ourselves regressing away from our progress:

First Phase: Damage control

Second Phase: Step back, regroup, and assess

When a serious setback or upset is in progress, it is wise to recognize it is happening and immediately go into action to minimize damage. Like having a kitchen fire, the first order of business is to put out the fire by calling 911 and/or using a fire extinguisher in the kitchen. Having a phone and a fire extinguisher readily available is a crucial preparation done in advance. In the damage control phase (especially with relationships) it is crucial that we have practiced a way to quickly bring calm into our thinking and feelings beforehand. Sometimes, the best thing to do is to politely extricate ourselves from the situation. Where this is not possible, we then focus on remaining calm, cool, and respectful. Practice this in advance with a mantra, saying, or prayer such as "this too shall pass" or "while they are just being themselves (NOOT), I myself can rise above this and take the high road."

AFTER DAMAGE CONTROL, STEP BACK AND ASSESS

After the damage control phase, the next step is to step back, regroup, and assess. Perhaps one of the best actions we can take in this second phase is to use our FUSS process, with its log record, to schedule a time later to review what happened and decide what, if anything, you will do about it. You can then, as part of your week in review session, decide whether this is a Learning Experience for Growth and worthy of inclusion into your morning routine with its ISTEPs.

With knowing when and how to put our ice crampons on, we will keep a firm grip on our advancements both present and future.

Be the Wise Frog

With our practicing and honing our habits for wearing ice cleats and knowing when to put on our crampons, we become the wise frog who refuses to let the scorpion get on our back again.

CHAPTER 12

Healthy Relationships Enhance

"Am I okay with this person being who they are, can I accept them for themselves and not expect them to change? Does their good outweigh their shortcomings?"

"Be the Good Poppy"

The perfect is the enemy of the good.

–Voltaire

For thousands of years poppies have had a fascinating history. They were found in ancient Egyptian tombs. They express diverse symbolism for different cultures. In Ukrainian culture, they are seen as symbols for beauty and youth as well as symbolizing the blood shed by the Cossack warriors who historically defended Ukraine. For Ukrainians, they also are an important ingredient in a number of foods such as poppy seed rolls, breads, and Kutia, a traditionally non-meat dish served during

Christmas time, made with boiled wheat, honey, and poppy seeds.

Poppies easily flourish naturally in the wild. They thrive in some of the most grueling conditions, especially where lime deposits exist in the soil, as it was around the limestone rubble from World War I battles. It was one of the first plants to grow in destroyed fields in the aftermath of conflicts on the battlefields of Western Europe during World War I. This quality of resilience led to their being memorialized in Canadian physician Lieutenant-Colonel John McCrae's famous poem "In Flanders Field." Flanders Field was a war zone in Belgium and France during World War I. During and after battles, poppies would grow in the fields being used for conflict, and at times they grew around the bodies of fallen soldiers and on their graves. After World War I, the poppy came to be a flower symbolizing peace and the remembrance of fallen soldiers.

Poppies are grown and harvested for their beauty, cooking ingredients, or opium production around the world. This beautiful and tenacious flower can be a symbol for good or harm. So it is for each of us as we grow in our lives. We can be a source for healing and peace or contribute to conflict and hurt. By taking the path that pursues more good and less bad with *Betterism,* we will be healers and happier. With wise empowering language, we too, like the poppy, can prosper in many different and difficult circumstances by ***"Being Like Betty"*** and seeking the better and not the perfect.

I have had over forty-five years of professional interactions. During that time, I have been a Naval submarine officer, corporate manager, and coach for hundreds of clients. With these experiences, I have seen that my coworkers' and clients' top desire for improvement is most often with their relationships. Unhealthy relationships and unhealthy expectations cause them frustration, disappointment, anger, and fear. These unhealthy relationships often are a mental prison that restrains their ability to have peace of mind and make desired progress in other important areas in their lives. In a number of circumstances, it can become an obsessive downward spiral that weakens and debilitates them.

HEALTHY RELATIONSHIPS ENHANCE US, NOT DEFINE US

Healthy relationships and healthy expectations, on the other hand, enhance us as well as another. These relationships prosper in a win–win environment. A healthy relationship requires both a need to be nurtured as well as a desire to nurture, as with the flower and the gardener. A healthy relationship does not define us, but rather enhances the good within us; not doing so is unhealthy.

It is important to define and objectively view what a *relationship* is and is not so as to facilitate making it better. It is helpful to see that a relationship with another consists of three components. I call this view of relationships the **Relationship Trinity**. I believe you will find that using this language will aid you with making progress in your relationships. Wise empowering language guides us toward healing and *Betterism* by facilitating progress and peace.

Relationship Trinity

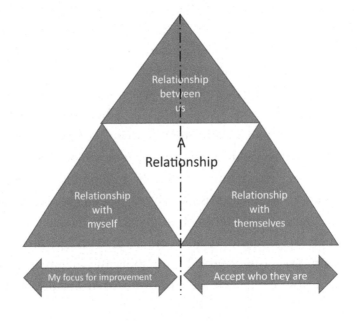

The *Relationship Trinity* recognizes that in a relationship with another there are three components:

1. The relationship with oneself, where my responsibility = 100 percent.

2. The other person's relationship with themselves, where my responsibility = 0 percent.

3. The interactions between us, where my responsibility = 50 percent, limited to how I respond, react. and interact with them.

More detail and a worksheet on the Relationship Trinity is provided in the Worksheet "The Relationship Trinity" (go to www.executive-coachingservices.net).

With the *Relationship Trinity* view, we focus our expectations, efforts, and energy in an empowering and wise manner to improve ourselves. We accept the *Natural Order of Things* with another. With this perspective, we avoid frustration and avoid wasting our time with dead end carousel thinking that makes no real progress. The *Relationship Trinity* perspective puts us in a mind set of "what will I do to make myself better" as opposed to "what they should/need to do is . . . "

Hoping and expecting someone else to change is folly. Working to improve yourself, on the other hand, is a far better investment of time and energy with relationship improvement. It is possible to have relationships shift from unhealthy to healthy through our use of wise empowering language. Yes, in many cases (not all), we ourselves, all by ourselves, can make the difference with whether a relationship is nurturing, healthy, and rewarding or not by improving our perspective.

Our first order of business is to look to see what we, ourselves, can do to become better. Learn what your needs and desires are, and then examine them to see if they are realistic and empowering. At the core of your relationship with another is your relationship with yourself. Your expectations and boundaries will determine the health of a relationship in many ways (see Worksheet "Who Am I?" at www. executivecoachingservices.net).

SURRENDER TO REALITY . . . WHAT WE RESIST WILL PERSIST

It is also important to understand who the other person is, as inevitably they will continue to be themselves (see Worksheet "Be the Archaeologist" at www.executivecoachingservices.net). Often in coaching sessions, I hear clients angry and disappointed with another in a relationship for being themselves. In most circumstances, it should be no surprise to us that another responds, reacts, or interacts as they do, for that is who they are. Often there is resistance to accepting people for who they are, especially in close relationships with significant others, family, and friends. This, in turn, leads to a damaging disconnect between our expectations and the reality of what is. It is best to take an attitude of "let them be themselves," because frankly you have no choice. You may as well surrender to that reality. Surrender can be a very good thing in certain circumstances; this happens to be one of them. For example, surrendering to the laws of gravity is always a good idea. With surrender and acceptance of another also comes a need to occasionally establish boundaries with consequences as with the concept of the *EBC Symbiotic 3* (Empathy, Boundaries, Consequences). Strong fences do make good neighbors, and good lovers as well.

As we are actively working to be more comfortable and at peace within our own skins, we become more mindful and engaged with our responses to another. Our interactions must be kind, respectful, and empowering for the other, as well as with ourselves. We seek win-win circumstances where possible and avoid the temptation to try and change them. We are realistic and objective with seeing the other for who they are, both positive and negative. It is wise to accept them as they are and restrict our focus on how we respond and interact with them. The *EBC Symbiotic 3* are crucial components here with behaviors and circumstances we find unpalatable or toxic for us. Begin with the focus on empathy for the other, through understanding who they are and why they became this way. See the NOOT with them and that it was inevitable that they became who they are. Identify boundaries with any toxic behaviors and think through the consequences you will enact if the boundary is encroached upon or crossed. *It is much more important that you enact the consequence calmly than to remind the other of the boundary.* Execute the consequence each and every time.

When it comes to how best to interact with another in a relationship, here are some key considerations:

- Have empathy and compassion through understanding why they are who they are.

- Be mindful of your personal unhappiness being projected onto them. Be objective with yourself and have a plan to address important concerns with yourself.

- Remember the platinum rule, treat others as they wish to be treated, by working to best understand their dreams, desires, fears, and insecurities.

- Where possible, achieve win-win solutions and interactions. When someone else causes us to modify our agenda, consider framing this as an "Opportunity for Contribution."

- Be kind, respectful, and a safe haven for others.

- Improve your Relationship Listening (See chapter 15).

- Take the time to understand what realistic expectations you have in the relationship.

Do not lose sight of the *Relationship Trinity*. Be mindful, through daily renewal and review, to stay clear headed here. There will be setbacks; apologize, make amends, and reset yourself where appropriate. Remember, with having a healthy relationship our energies focus on the portions of the *Relationship Trinity* where we have real influence. The other portions are not ours to control. We will optimize and prosper only if we focus and restrict our actions within the boundaries of the half of the trinity that we have control over. It is important to see and stay in bounds here. It is also crucial to see and be mindful of the *Natural Order of Things* with why people are as they are. The foundation for success with a relationship begins with being okay with ourselves; having a healthy self-relationship.

Some of the components within this the area of being okay with ourselves lie with our having a positive self-image and using constructive self-talk with our language. It is also important to align our beliefs with our actions, keeping our ten convictions at the forefront, having realistic healthy expectations, and being in an ongoing flow of personal improvement as a *Betterist*. The language we use will either enhance the good or detract from it. It is best to choose wise empowering language.

DECIDE IF YOU ARE OKAY WITH THE OVERALL REALTIONSHIP

Now the BIG decision comes, but only:

- After you are on a path of being at peace with yourself
- After you are doing well with being nurturing, kind, and respectful toward another
- After seeing clearly and dispassionately who they are in the context of NOOT
- After being realistic with your expectations
- After you are clear with your boundaries and consequences

After progress in all these areas, there is a major decision to make. Drum roll please!

Am I okay with this person being who they are, can I accept them for themselves and not expect them to change? Does their good outweigh their shortcomings?

Some of the reasons why relationships fail are:

1. People are not happy within themselves. Because of their internal unhappiness, they project this unhappiness on another. They are not committed to owning and living the concept of *Betterism,* which is an ongoing pursuit through actions for finding and creating more good and less bad in their lives.

2. Absence of empathy and a resistance to accepting (and surrendering) to *what is* because there is little depth with understanding why "they" and why "I" have come to be as we are

3. Failure to set wise boundaries with calm, consistent consequences

4. Unrealistic or unhealthy expectations

5. Loss of trust with dishonesty or not being one's word

6. People don't feel safe to make a mistake or express their concerns.

HURTING PEOPLE HURT OTHER PEOPLE

Have you noticed when someone close to you is feeling good about themselves how easy it is to communicate and get along with them? On the contrary, when folks are not doing well it can be a real challenge to interact with them. This concept is nicely covered in John Maxwell's book *Winning with People* in the chapter titled "The Pain Principle: Hurting People Hurt People and Are Easily Hurt by Them." Are you, yourself "hurting?" If you are in pain, anguished, frustrated, angry, or despondent, the foundation for a healthy relationship is likely to be unstable. On the other hand, if you feel optimistic and confident about having a better today and tomorrow, you are on solid ground to further your progress with a better relationship. You, yourself are the gateway to heaven on Earth, especially with relationships.

When your trajectory forward on the playing field of life is imbued with *Betterism,* it sets in motion a growing level of self-efficacy that is both comforting and rewarding. It gives you courage, strength, and optimism. A belief of "I will find a way" that emboldens you with an attitude of "bring it on, I will handle it, I've got this!"

The clarity of your beliefs with *The 10 Convictions,* coupled with the ability to discern the "important" and follow up with focused daily simple actions (ISTEPs), is the foundation for your progress. Your view of the *Natural Order of Things* frees you from the prisons of resentment, anger, self-doubt, and despair. With wise language that empowers us and focuses us with being a better version of ourselves, there is no need to have yourself defined with a "contra identity" that requires self-righteousness, animosity, or denigration of another as a lifeline for meaning.

> ### When the student is ready the teacher will appear.
>
> –Lao Tzu

When we are ready and open for improvement, people, ideas, and resources just seem to crop up and appear to support us. As with the *Law of Attraction*, explained in Rhonda Byrne's book *The Secret,* the right mindset attracts good to us. That said, many are not ready for improvement, at least for now. I have seen a number of coworkers and clients who are not ready to take personal responsibility for their lives. They often are comfortable with playing the victim or with an outright surrender to despondency and complacency. They see paths of action for forward progress as arduous, threatening, or unacceptable. For them, actual doing is not doable. It is far easier to default to a "no action required" state of mind. They are often resigned to talking and complaining to whoever will listen.

For folks who are averse to taking action for self-improvement, they likely have little or no interest with the effort needed to perform and do. They would rather be spectators, becoming impassioned critics of those who actually do take action, yet fall short. Do not write them off, however. I do believe that with those resigned to inaction, it is important that we find a view that allows us to believe in them and their future potential for self-help and progress. It is important to be respectful and empowering yet maintain certain boundaries for our own self-care, as well. Let us always have the inner belief that they can do it, if not today, perhaps some time in the future. Today they are not ready, tomorrow they may be.

My Naval career in the submarine force ended with a sense of accomplishment and self-satisfaction; however, it did not begin that way. For a variety of reasons, I initially had difficulty keeping up and fitting in with the team on our submarine. It was primarily through the nurturing leadership and encouragement of both the captain and especially the executive officer (XO) that I was able to eventually succeed. There were times I was on the verge of becoming a pariah on fleet ballistic submarine SSBN642 Kamehameha. It is a very small world on a submerged nuclear submarine, isolated at times for months. Our crew's ability to interact with family, friends, and the outside world was not possible. There was no escaping the society, culture, and judgment of over 100 men. Nicknamed "Big Al," the executive officer (second in command on a naval ship) clearly projected his belief in me. Though the XO had a commanding physical presence and booming voice, he was a funny and exceptionally self-deprecating man. He also had been nicknamed "Zero" in his freshman year at the Naval Academy because of a small incident on his first day there when his pencil broke while filling out a form. His remarkable kindness, empathy, and compassion for others no doubt had roots in his own experience with being labeled and called "Zero" while at the academy. Rather than having it be a curse that haunted him, he had turned it into a teaching experience and often shared the story with others. This label and humiliation became a "push" motivation. As a result, he was self-motivated to both personally succeed with his personal performance and lift others around him up with encouragement. He is the quintessential example of a person with wise selfishness in constant pursuit of win-win conditions. Where some might see inadequacy and victimization, he found a *Legitimate Empowering Alternate Reality* with a profound level of empathy and kindness toward others and healing for himself.

BELIEVE IN YOURSELF FIRST, BELIEVE IN OTHERS NEXT

The XO came to believe in himself and his ability to overcome adversity and humiliation. Perhaps because he so believed in himself, he was more than capable and willing to believe in me. There were times I did not believe in myself, questioning my ability to succeed in that foreign new world of submarine life. The few people who believed in me sustained me and kept me motivated to continue to improve until I later became a proficient and valued member of the team. In your relationships, I do believe it is important that you believe in the good of both yourself and the other, even when they don't believe in you or themselves. Like in the story *The Little Engine That Could*, there will come a time when everyone likely will be capable and self-motivated enough to climb the hill forward. They will crest the hill and begin an automatic journey of coasting downhill and become self-reliant and self-sustaining.

Perhaps you, yourself may not be ready. Perhaps you are currently making little or no progress with challenging concerns. Maybe you see that you are losing ground, getting worse and becoming discouraged. Take heart! It does not have to be this way. If nothing else right now, remember this quote with your journey toward better days ahead:

> *If you find yourself in a hole,*
> *the first thing to do is to stop digging.*
>
> -Will Rogers

This book is about improving ourselves with the wise use of our language and the subsequent clarity it provides us with the view of the world around us. As with having a compassionate and objective understanding of ourselves, it is also important that we develop an empathetic view of the other. Two books most helpful here are *The Platinum Rule* by Tony Alessandra and Michael J. Conner, and *The 5 Love Languages* by Gary Chapman. These two books stress the importance of going beyond the "Golden Rule" (which focuses on understanding ourselves and treating others as we would wish to be treated) but moving to a more valuable paradigm (treat others as they wish to be treated) of seeking to understand who another is and why they are as they are. Working to understand both our own as well as another's desires, hopes, and fears is an honorable path. Seeking to see and understand why things are as they became is how empathy is created. Compassion is the warm, loving understanding that comes from empathy; it is the foundation for our efforts toward building better relationships. Our dispassionate view of the why, with a belief in NOOT, will lead to healthy and realistic expectations. Expecting that a turtle will someday be able to climb a tree with the right training and encouragement is a formula for frustration and disappointment. Expecting a pet turtle to live a long life with the proper care and feeding is likely. Having "healthy expectations" is key to success.

UNDERSTAND AND SURRENDER TO OTHERS' LIMITATIONS

Not all relationships are healthy today; and some may never be so in the future. It is important that we can discern first what we are providing in the relationship for the other person. Next, we must understand the other in terms of their limitations and what they bring to the table. Most relationships can be fruitful and healthy by firmly establishing *The EBC Symbiotic 3* with empathy, boundaries, and consequences. Some relationships may never be healthy given the baggage another may have from their past. There are some circumstances when it is best that we move on and past a toxic or abusive relationship. In the case where disengaging may not be possible, firm boundaries with consistent consequences are even more important.

Examples of healthy expectations with a healthy relationship:

- Believing in each other's honesty and ability to be their word.

- Respect and accept each other for who they are and understanding why they became as they are. We act kindly toward one another and focus on their strengths, gifts, and talents.

- Believing in the other's ability to achieve what's important for themselves.

- Mutual Reliability—You can count on one another to do what they say they will do.

- Feeling safe with one another—Is the relationship a safe haven to retreat to or a hell to avoid?

- Approachability—Can each person speak their mind without being judged or admonished?

- Mutual nurturing—Bringing out the better in each other; enhancing each other.

- Sincere listening—Listening to understand both what is being said as well as what may be going on behind the obvious words. Listening from the heart for their heart and respectfully acknowledging what you hear.

Examples of unhealthy expectations and relationship behaviors:

- Co-dependency—Each partner is defined by the relationship and need it to feel important or complete.

- Expecting another to change their core beliefs and values.

- Right fights—Making being right more important than nurturing a respectful and healthy relationship.

- Blame games—Badgering another for causing a particular problem.

- Physical or verbal abuse.

- Substance and alcohol abuse.

- Contra Identities focused on pointing out the flaws and short-comings of the other to bolster one's self-worth.

- Easily offended—Lacking in a solid personal identity based on merit and ability, and as a result easily upset.

- Habitual deceit or lies.

- Lacking in empathy and understanding of the other.

- Self-righteousness—Needing to have the moral high ground or position of eminence.

- Superficial listening—"Listening is what I do while I am waiting to talk." Listening to respond rather than listening to understand.

- Unreliablilty—Failing to follow through and do what they said they would do.

Relationships are imperfect, as are we ourselves. Healthy relationships are vital to a balanced and meaningful life. I do believe that most relationships can be rewarding and healthy. To have this be so, we must take ownership and the initiative with improving ourselves and having realistic healthy expectations within that relationship. Most relationships can become healthy even if they do not appear to be so today. "Be the good poppy," focusing on your part of the *Relationship Trinity*. Be resilient, empowered, and continue to work for good, even when the world around you may be in chaos. Be okay by designing and living an aligned life that is continually making progress and is grounded in integrity, empathy, and kindness. You can do it!!

CHAPTER 13

Forget Forgiving,
Go for Self-Exorcism

Am I harboring upset over a past experience?

"Be the Exorcist"

"Be the Archaeologist"

Reject your sense of injury and the injury itself disappears.

–Marcus Aurelius

In 1995, I was assigned to the Houston Locomotive Repair Facility as its plant manager. There I was responsible for 200+ employees and a budget of over $25 million. This facility was one of the oldest on the Southern Pacific Railroad system, designed and built in the early steam locomotive days. Here, locomotives were repaired and maintained so they could operate reliably over deserts of the Southwestern United States as well as the Sierra Nevada Mountains. The quality of work done by the skilled craft workers there was excellent. Their safety record, however, was the worst on the system. A history of adversarial labor management relations had left many there with a confrontational and suspicious attitude toward management. To a large degree, things were done more by compliance than commitment. My challenge was to work with the in-place team to build trust and reduce the number of injuries occurring there.

The craft personnel, supervisors, labor union leaders, and middle management assigned to me proved to be honorable and honest. In contrast, my boss, headquartered in Denver, was a tyrant who publicly demeaned his subordinates and was ruthless with his expectations. He would demand a relentless amount of after-the-fact explanations for any miscues, mistakes, or problems which occurred in my area of responsibility. To say he was a Monday morning quarterback would be an extreme understatement. Once, during a so-called team meeting conducted in an offsite hotel conference room, he stood up on a line of tables walking back and forth in his socks, raising his voice and threatening us with being fired over failure to perform and achieve certain goals he expected.

During my time living in Houston, I was also dealing with some substantial family problems. I was fearful of the potential economic and geographic relocation impact on my family if I were to lose my job. One of my peer managers, who worked in yet another city, resigned over this manager's excessively harsh treatment. It was not unusual after one of our daily conference calls with him, to find my hands shaking. My sleep became increasingly restless. He demanded I spend more and more arbitrary and unnecessary hours at work. This unneeded time at work took away from time with my family when they needed me most.

Eventually, his superiors at headquarters became painstakingly aware of his behavior and had him terminated and escorted off the company property. For years afterward, any reminder or thought of him evoked a deep hatred and anger. Though I had worked for him for only two years, the pain and suffering over my hurtful treatment lasted far longer than that. I am now embarrassed to share the following conversation I had long after he had been terminated. During a phone call with another manager in our company, this former boss's name came up and I stated, "I won't be happy until I am standing over his grave urinating on it."

That was how full of rage and anger I was toward him, even years after he was long gone.

Many of us have had experiences where we were treated terribly or unfairly. Some of us may be in a battle with a past or current abuse today. These experiences can be traumatizing and cause us to be consumed with anger, resentment, fear, or despair. The ensuing upset compromises our peace of mind, frequently leaving us feeling anxious or unnerved. It can seriously damage our physical and mental health as we obsessively relive the experience over and over again. We may find it difficult to have hope and enthusiasm because of the hostility and hurt we harbor within ourselves toward a past perpetrator. We may even fantasize about taking actions of revenge to make them pay for what they did or are doing. With this chapter, I am excited to share with you a simple and speedy way to get past this upset.

FORGIVENESS IS NOT THE WAY

There is a process to help you let go and disengage with this tug-of-war battle with the past. *Forgiveness,* however, is **not** the way. The way to do so is through *understanding* the why of what is and what was. Afterward, the way to sustain forward progress lies with the *EBC Symbiotic 3* (Empathy, Boundaries, Consequences).

Anger is an acid that can do more harm to the vessel in which it is stored than to anything on which it is poured.

–Mark Twain

I believe one of the main intents with the concept of forgiveness is to get from "A" to "B", where:

"A" = our current state of mind where we harbor animosity, fear, or despair with a past negative experience.

"B" = is a future state of mind where the animosity, fear, or despair is gone.

The A to B process takes us from a place of imprisoned suffering to a place of empowered peaceful freedom. The B destination is a place where those negative feelings have evaporated away. It is where we have an enlightened view to see that there was really nothing to "forgive" in the first place. This process for getting from A to B is an example of finding a *Legitimate Empowering Alternate Reality* (LEAR). I contend that forgiveness is not a doable action, it is not a verb, it is not the path for getting from A to B. Rather, understanding is the achievable effective elixir here. Success is achieved through understanding and empathy.

During my forty-three-plus-year working career, over forty years of marriage, and more than thirty years with children, our family circle, like many, has had their share of ups and downs. Like many of you, we have had to face and deal with death, financial crisis, relocations, suicide, verbal abuse, drug and alcohol abuse, breakdowns, and estrangements. It was easy and tempting at times for me to demonize someone in our circle of relatives and immediate family and see them as the culprits to my problems. There were times that I felt intense anger and resentment with some of them. At times I had a loathing for myself, as well. It is an easy path to take, being in that role of the victim, perhaps obsessively replaying the injustice and unfairness of it all. It was tempting to blame *them* and how they should be shamed into being better, how they *should* know better. "They could have done more," I thought.

One of the important motivations for this book occurred as a result of my observation that many people strongly desire (if not desperately desire) to get over and let go of past injustices and hurts.

I have been a manager, leader, and servant to hundreds of people. With my experiences, I saw that I was not alone with my struggle with harboring negativity toward another and the ensuing suffering that resulted. I came to a view of myself and others in the handling of a particular challenge as having a choice to be a *winner* or a *whiner.* Depending on the circumstances, we can be winners in one arena and whiners in yet another, as with work and family. Winners constantly look for ways to be better and seek to *Be Like Betty;* they are natural survivors (in that specific area). They are *Betterists* in continual pursuit of more good and less bad for themselves as well as for others.

Whiners, however, should not be disparaged. They are stuck, if not doomed, to complain and blame. When we are acting as whiners, we are deserving of compassion and empathy. When we are whiners, finding a way to be better is often short circuited with inclinations toward defensiveness, victimhood, insecurity, and a history lacking in self-efficacy with achieving desired outcomes. We are stuck because we don't know any other way to be (once again in that specific arena). For us there is only this one reality, to be victims and be bogged down in that quicksand view of the past. Take heart and comfort: there is a way out of this mental prison.

I believe I have found a way out; an escape plan if you will. I hope to convince you that as you improve your language, you will change your thinking, views, and responses. In turn, you will make decisions that produce many more win-win long-term desirable outcomes for yourself and others.

THE VERB "FORGIVING" IS A USELESS WORD

Seeing "forgiveness" as a real action verb is a futile view. It is akin to considering teleportation as a means of taking us from point A to point B. As if the verb "Madriding" was a method of transport to take us to the Spanish city of Madrid. What is crucial, however, is to purge ourselves of the toxic negativity that infects us when we hold on to ill will toward another. When we believe *forgiveness* is something we can do, this has us going round and round on a musical carousel, distracted for the moment but back to where we started when the music stops. Forgiveness is a **useless word** when used as a verb, as a word for action. The concept of forgiveness is also a condescending one. It obstructs true empathy because it places us on a pedestal where we look down on another, much like a judge ruling on the misbehavior of another.

An effective and lasting way of healing with an ongoing upset over past experiences is explained in this chapter. It is important that before this healing process begins, however, we first recognize the magnitude of its severe harm and suffering. This realization can produce a compelling self-motivation for change. When we see the pervasive impact that the harboring of ill feelings has, there will be a call to arms within us to find a way to unshackle ourselves from this ASAP. Unfortunately, desire is not enough, we also require wise direction and guidance. We can easily become exhausted and discouraged trying to find our way off that carousel to nowhere. We need a viable process to do so; one that works and is easily doable. A process that empowers and enlightens us to soar and move forward to explore ever greater heights. This process is revealed in the pages ahead.

As we proceed further along the path of understanding why, we will draw ever closer to true compassion and empathy towards one another.

–Mike Starr

As a gardener recognizes the danger of weeds in their soil, so must we see the danger of our ongoing conflict(s) with the past. It needs immediate attention, as it is a threat to our inner peace, future growth, and ability to have healthy relationships. It threatens our ability to prosper. Now is the time to begin the process of rolling up our sleeves, getting down on our knees, and humbly and meticulously beginning to pull out those toxic weeds from our garden of life.

THE REAL PROBLEM LIES WITH OUR VIEW OF IT

After seeing and acknowledging how dangerous this conflict with the past is, we next clarify what the problem is and what it isn't. The problem is not about "them" and their need to change. The problem lies with and within ourselves. We own this problem and give it fuel. This deep-rooted toxic negativity within us is like some demonic possession inside us. We are haunted by a past injustice or upset and in need of a *secular self-exorcism.*

Rather than taking exhausting years of suffering to get to point "B," there is a quick way to do so. There is a path to get you there expeditiously. This specific *Trail of Progress (TOP)* process has been blazed ahead for you.

The path leading to "B" has two parts:

1. *Understanding and Empathy*

    Here we achieve a deep understanding of NOOT as relates to the past abuse or injustice. Understanding why things were as they were; why another became as they are; seeing that people cannot but help but be who they are. Here we clearly discern that acceptance is not agreement. Here we move above and beyond *resigned acceptance* to an **objective empowering acceptance** with a heightened enlightenment and an embracing of *what is.*

2. *Boundaries with Consequences*

    In the case where it may happen again (as opposed to a situation where a person who abused us is deceased or completely out of our lives), we put in place the *EBC Symbiotic 3*; Empathy,

Boundaries and Consequences. After achieving real empathy, we then set clear, wise boundaries for ourselves in dealing with future potential repeat occurrences. When these boundaries are crossed, we then respond with a clearly selected set of *dispassionate consequences*. We will be resolute with following through with these each and every time our boundaries are encroached upon.

Getting from "A" to "B"

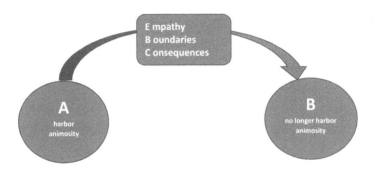

I don't like that man. I must get to know him better.

–Abraham Lincoln

I believe you will find that this journey from A to B will produce the successful outcome you desire. The strategy with the *EBC Symbiotic 3* for getting there is a simple and elegant process. It does require effort and a willingness to discover new views of how sustainable improvement occurs. This path empowers you with the courage to face and embrace your own shortcomings as well as calmly and dispassionately seeing others' imperfections and shortcomings.

Your willingness to learn and practice a new way of thinking about forgiveness will get you to the summit of your desires. Using the referenced worksheets at the end of this chapter (located on my website www.executivecoachingservices.net), you will arrive at a place akin to being in a mountain meadow clearing, with a new-found serenity and enlightened understanding. You will find peace of mind, having shed some serious baggage from the past. Within this calm, you will clearly see your next step and goal with advancing your journey with peace, progress, and healing with your life. You will then be ready to move on.

FOREGIVENESS IS NOT AN ACTIONABLE VERB

Forgiveness is not an actionable verb, rather it is a romanticized concept of something doable when it actually is not doable. It could be seen as a noun, as a resultant place of peace, however. Actionable activities are things we can observe or measure, such as we can run, we can sing, we can make breakfast, we can meditate, or we can even study a book. Many of us have eventually arrived at "B" (no longer having a consuming obsession over some past injustice). When we did get to "B," it likely happened for a number of reasons such as:

- We became more interested in other things and the result was that previous consuming negative influence diminished for us, as in "time heals."

- We came to have empathy for another person and understand his or her behavior, and this led to us having compassion for them.

- We just became numb and callous to the past injustice.

Often people will say they *"forgave"* as if some single activity occurred that they called forgiveness when that was not the case. It did not happen because we took an action of forgiveness, but rather for reasons such as those previously mentioned, which they inaccurately called an act of forgiveness.

Using wise empowering words and concepts can help us make real progress, as we will see reality in a truer way as we discover a *higher truth,* as with the discovery of the concept of bacteria and the subsequent prevention and treatment of infections. With the knowledge and understanding of the existence of bacteria, we were then capable of seeing the need for sterilization and sanitizing techniques with medical procedures in hospitals and with health workers. In turn, the energy was then focused toward a wiser area for investigation and research that led to the development of pharmaceutical treatments such as antibiotics. By clarifying our understanding of *what is,* we are empowered and equipped to think and act better. We have wiser responses and make better decisions.

SOME WORDS CAN CONSISTENTLY DERAIL OUR PROGRESS

Some words, however, derail our progress by dis-empowering us. They cause us to blame others. We then become consumed with upset and anger toward another, this makes us victims, and in turn imprisons us. They can actually make things worse, as with victimhood and entitlement mindsets, causing hate and denigration of others. Identity politics is one example of this. With this, many see others through a binary lens where they are either (1) good and approved or (0) bad and disapproved. As a result of this view, they are then doomed to poison meaningful communications and cooperation in the future. This clouds their ability to actually see what is really going on around them. With identity politics, many are unconsciously pursuing reasons to be offended and demonize others. Their "positive" self-identity then becomes conflated and codependent with a negative view and/or outrage toward another. They have made their happiness prisoners of other people's behavior where only others can set them free. Wrong diagnosis . . . wrong remediation. This enrollment in the arena of self-importance, with putting other people down, is a *Faustian bargain* with the devil. It becomes a short-term feeling of significance and purpose with long term toxic results for ourselves and many around us. I call this a *contra identity,* as it is oppositional with its definition.

Some words just take us nowhere, stall us, going round and round like some musical carousel that might feel good at the moment but really make no forward progress . . . "a different day . . . same problem."

When we see a spouse as "mean" or a coworker as "stupid," we are using terms that obfuscate the real issues and create a self-fulfilling prophecy that precludes resolution or improvement. Often, "stupid" may be better seen as *ignorant* or *having learning distractions.* "Mean" may be better characterized as *insecure* or *previously abused.* These alternative terms at least begin to allow us to see a better way to interact with them.

ANGER, RESENTMENT, AND ANXIETY BLOCK OUT SUNSHINE

Fear and animosity toward another can consume us. It can cause us to see the world through smeared, darkened eyeglasses obscuring our clarity with what is going on around us. We, in turn, make poor choices and decisions that unnecessarily harm others as well as ourselves and make matters worse. It can destroy our peace of mind and lead to severe anxiety and physical maladies as a result of improper rest and hormone imbalances. Being in a frequent state of "fight or flight" for long periods of time is an example of chronic stress. This can cause physiological damage and disease due to adrenaline and cortisol overstimulation.

The long-term activation of the stress response system and the overexposure to cortisol and other stress hormones that follows can disrupt almost all your body's processes.[20]

Persistent surges of adrenaline can damage your blood vessels, increase your blood pressure, and elevate your risk for heart attack or stroke. It can also result in anxiety, weight gain/loss, headache, and insomnia that compromise our immune system. We become victims who are drowning in a cycle of blame and shame, in many ways at war with ourselves. Our ability to make long-term wise decisions is restricted. We are derailed from being on track with *Betterism* and cease to pursue the ongoing noble quest of adding more good and diminishing the bad in our lives. We become continually distracted with "blame games" and "right fights."

Consider hostility and despair as hand puppets. Only through us do they come to life and exist. We have the ability to remove our hand from within and remove the fuel that feeds so much of the fiery drama within us. The important question to ask is, "am I willing to disengage?"

We are both the protagonists and antagonists in our own dramas and dilemmas. We are our best allies and our worst enemies, as well.

> *The mind is its own place and in itself, can make a heaven of hell, a hell of heaven.*
>
> –John Milton, *Paradise Lost*

Are you ready to pull the weeds of anger, resentment, and frustration from your garden of life? How can you *be the gardener* with pulling out these toxic weeds that are restricting your joy and peace of mind? Let us begin a path toward success by conceding and committing to the importance of doing so. We must admit that this upset with the past has a very serious negative impact on us. We then will muster the courage and determination to confront it through love, kindness, empathy, and wise boundaries with consequences. Then we will begin to proceed to pull out those rascals one at a time.

Are you at a place where you do recognize and admit how toxic and destructive this resentment/anger/anxiety is? Anger/resentment can come to define us and make us codependent on it for our very identity. Are you getting your meaning and purpose from a dysfunctional crusade of anger, being offended, and victimhood, frustrated because "they won't change?" Let me warn you in advance, the process of evaporating away a current hostility or resentment toward another may lead you to a vacuum. At first, this clearing out of harmful baggage may leave you feeling empty. You may feel lost, like a military warrior after the battle is over and feeling no purpose. Only through this catharsis, though, can you be in the place to grow and prosper, much like a freshly tilled garden.

BE THE ARCHAELOGIST AND UNDERSTAND WHY

If you are tired of the negativity of past memories wreaking havoc with your peace of mind and eager to get past this, then the way forward is the process of *understanding what is.* To do so you must *be the archaeologist!* You must dig into the past to seek to understand first what is going on within yourself and the impact it is having on you. Next, you will then work on your perceived *perpetrator* to uncover who they are and why they became that way. Doing the best you can, dig into their past and find the roots and genesis of the behavior(s). There are reasons why we are who we are and why we act as we do, which include environmental, experiential, and genetic conditions.

As the "archaeologist," when we make a sincere effort to dig into their past and best understand and know them, we will find that their behavior in a particular set of circumstances is often predictable and not a surprise at all. That is who they are, that is who they became. We will come to the conclusion that this is *the Natural Order of Things.* We can then become free of the hold this negativity toward them has had on us, because we are in a place of kind compassion, empathy, and understanding.

After an enlightened and empathetic understanding of them, the focus shifts from "what they need to do" and how they need to change to "how am I going to interact or not interact with them in the future?"

Our next action is to set boundaries with consequences for likely future interactions and incorporate a daily mindfulness practice such as a prayer, mantra reminder, or affirmation. An example of a boundary with consequence might be related to a certain political or religious topic and our polite refusal to engage in that conversation. An extreme example might be physical or verbal abuse within a marriage or work environment where the consequence is to seek divorce or find another job. A mantra or prayer may be:

People cannot help being who they are given their history and genetics, I must be mindful to honor my own boundaries with them. When _____ happens, I am resolved to always do _____.

KNOW NOOT ... UNDERSTAND NOOT ... BE FREE

The Natural Order of Things (NOOT) highlights the inevitability and neutrality of events, neither good nor bad, it *just is, just was,* and *just will be* that way. Stripped of emotion and drama, it is equivalent to accepting the laws of physics such as gravitational attraction, "what goes up must come down." NOOT is the predictability of water's boiling and freezing points at a particular pressure. However, within our daily lives and our interpersonal relationships, NOOT is often obscured and most elusive. Why is it difficult to see NOOT and wisely prepare to best anticipate that predictable future? Perhaps it is because we are so completely enrolled in our stories and narratives of what is and what is not. Perhaps we are compelled and driven by unrealistic expectations of what "we" want. We can't even imagine that there is a Legitimate Empowering Alternate Reality (LEAR), let alone find one. It may be near incomprehensible that there is indeed a *Higher Truth.* Opening ourselves to a higher truth may undermine and collapse a house of cards reality we currently believe and perceive. Any hint of challenge to our views puts us on the attack or defense. It can be profoundly complex on one level and unseeable to us on another, limited by our current thinking and paradigms of *what is.* We are blind to it on one level and averse to considering an alternative view on another, as it undermines our certainty and personal values. It may threaten a strongly held personal belief as well as our current identity view of self.

The Golden Rule vs. The Platinum Rule

It is a huge challenge for many of us to objectively see and understand ourselves. There were about 1.2 million behavioral health providers in 2020 in the United States.[21] In 2020, there was an estimated 53 million adults in the U.S. who had a mental illness.[21] I believe a large number of people who are suffering from conditions from depression, anger, anxiety, fear, etc. are looking to understand why they feel as they do and what they can do about it. That said, one can see that to go beyond self-awareness and self-acceptance, to then move on to seek to understand others can be a rather daunting challenge. When we are consumed with ourselves, our ability to understand others is short circuited. Ironically if we were to flip the script and spend far more time thinking how to respond to others in an empowering way, our own problems would substantially subside.

In Tony Alessandra's and Michael J. O'Connor's book *The Platinum Rule*, this rule is stated as: "Treat people the way they wish to be treated."

This is a stark contrast to the Golden Rule, which states: "Treat people the way you wish to be treated."

It is a challenge in and of itself to understand ourselves and how we wish to be treated. Understanding self is but child's play as compared to taking the time to pursue understanding of the people important to us, each different than the other. The book *The Platinum Rule* goes on further to elaborate on four basic personality traits as a means of better understanding others (there are many other proposed models for understanding personality traits, one such being the famous "Myers-Briggs Type Indicator").

*When I get ready to talk to people, I spend two thirds
of the time thinking what they want to hear and
one third thinking about what I want to say.*

–Abraham Lincoln

If we begin with the premise that people's behavior was inevitable and indeed the Natural Order of Things, we see that they can't help but being who they are.

JESUS ADDED A PLEA TO UNDERSTAND THEM

*Father, forgive them, **for they do
not know what they are doing.***

–Luke 23:24 New International Version

While crucified on the cross, Jesus did not just say "forgive them," but added a plea for understanding them.

In his book *The Seven Habits of Highly Effective People*, Stephen Covey shares a story about an experience he had on the subway. A man with his children came onto the subway car. The children were acting wildly and disruptive toward other passengers. Covey approached the man and told him the children's behavior was bothersome, and asked if he could do something about it. The man apologized, saying they just came from the hospital where their mother and his wife just died a few hours ago. Covey went from A to B not through forgiveness, but through empathy and understanding. Empathy is the gateway to our inner peace. Empathy not only for others but for ourselves as well.

The *EBC Symbiotic 3* is the process for progress. It is the vehicle that gets us from "A" where we are, to "B" where we desire to be. Worksheets referenced at the end of this chapter and posted on my website will assist you with taking the path for pursuing and seeking to understand another. Like the balloon once tethered to the ground, we are set free to soar, explore, and move on forward on the path of *Betterism*. In the worksheet exercises, a listing of a number of factors impacting others' behavior are presented to assist you with understanding why they are as they are. I contend that when we calmly and objectively study the background of another, we see that they are in sync with NOOT. It may be a synchronization that we object to, but like the weather, it is what it is. Given all those factors of birth order, age, gender, socioeconomic upbringing, geographical home(s), height, stature, appearance, ethnicity, race, culture, etc., of course, they had to become exactly who they are; it was inevitable. Here we come to a state of *objective empowered acceptance*.

Once at B, we no longer harbor fear, anger, resentment, or frustration. We will have ascended and transcended from being in a dark valley harboring ill feelings, to now having an enlightened view devoid of that prior negativity. It will be like standing on the summit of a mountain with a breathtaking view, seeing, appreciating, and making peace with the past to make progress with the future. This is a view of what is and not what we want it to be, and we are okay with that.

Five Steps for Conducting a Self-Exorcism

Resentment/Anger/Despair ———> Absence of Resentment/ Anger/Despair

1. Use worksheet "A to B" to define the problem and the desired outcome. Courageously confront the full negative impact that harboring ill feelings toward another is having on you.

2. Use worksheet "Who Am I?" to improve your self-awareness.

3. Use worksheet "Be the Archaeologist" to discover who and why others are as they are to build your empathy for them.

4. If applicable (where you continue to interact with this person or organization), complete Worksheet "EBC Symbiotic 3" to move forward with empathy, boundaries, and consequences.

5. Use Worksheet "Prevent and Minimize Regression" to prevent or minimize backsliding.

Note: All worksheets can be found at www.executivecoachingservices.net.

CHAPTER 14

The Ten Convictions, Your GPS for Peace and Progress

Are my responses and decisions aligned with my values and convictions?

"Be Like Moses"

It took a long time to settle on a title: '12 Rules for Life: An Antidote to Chaos.' Why did that one rise up above all others? First and foremost, because of its simplicity. It indicates clearly that people need ordering principles, and that chaos otherwise beckons. We require rules, standards, values — alone and together.

– Dr. Jordan B. Peterson, from *12 Rules for Life*

There is a compelling need today to be clear about who we are and who we are not as individuals and as a society. In a growing secular world, largely devoid of spiritual and religious beliefs, our convictions of what is right and wrong, and what is true or not true often are being determined by media and political biases. Fundamental certainty is being eroded by popular trends as with gender identity confusion and a permissive outlook toward theft. Unfortunately, many seek their identity and convictions in the arena of toxic self-righteousness that denigrates others. The selective enforcing of the laws of the land, gender identity distortion, and economically unsustainable government policies makes our confusion ever worse. There is a trend toward a fantasy idealism that discounts the realities of an imperfect world. It creates great harm and frustration for many by enabling them to pursue unsustainable and unattainable *panacea for all* goals. Basic human needs for safety, self-reliance, and personal pride are lost in a frenzy that seeks idealistic and unsustainable change. These efforts drain valuable resources away from meaningful improvement initiatives.

This is a time when many have developed a propensity for *contra identities,* focused more on the deficiencies of others and less on their own merits and possibilities. These oppositional identities are dysfunctional and are based on the concept of, "I'm right, you are wrong," and as a result they feel instantly important. This trend is moving us away from meritorious identity defined by ability, talent, and accomplishment. It is leading us in an unhealthy direction, one that focuses on disparaging others. This condition promotes entitlement as opposed to empowerment. It also promotes victimhood as opposed to self-reliance. It is producing a generation of emotional weaklings with an embedded ticking time bomb for serious mental health problems in the years ahead.

Accompanying this contra identity is another impulsive, immediate feel good and feel important mindset I call the *Henny Penny Syndrome.* This state of mind derives a sense of importance by announcing imminent disaster, as with "the sky is falling," and therefore they see themselves as wise sages. Now is a time when we desperately need to find results-oriented solutions for important problems, a time for conflict resolution and remediation focused on achieving win-win solutions. Achieving sustainable progress and finding inner peace amongst the societal confusion of our times can be difficult. Harmony with self and those around us is increasingly unraveling and moving downward in a near death spiral. Symptoms of this demise show up with the increases in substance abuse, frustration, hostility, anger, hopelessness, violence, suicide, and interpersonal conflict.

As we mature and enlighten our self-talk and thinking, we will reduce conflict. This will produce a strong sense of self-confidence with our personal meaning, purpose, and progress. I find it excitingly hopeful to see that with a wise choice of empowering language, we can positively impact our thinking, perception, and behavior. While alive, people deserve to live their best lives possible, both individually and collectively. Ethical rules that nurture the common good are our allies and are essential for health, harmony, and happiness. Anarchy, with its accompanying chaos, on the other hand, is the enemy. Agreeing to disagree and respecting opposing views and ideas is part of healthy coexistence. Having a commonly accepted and enforced set of ethical boundaries is the very definition of civilization. My hope with this book, is to contribute to the next level of enlightenment by guiding our communities and the individuals within them onto a path toward unprecedented harmony, health, and progress.

THE FOUNDTION FOR A HEALTHY LIFE

Moses's presenting of the Ten Commandments spelled out a moral and behavioral code to guide against the anarchy and impulsiveness of his time. In my experience with coaching clients, I have come to have the following conviction: *a healthy life begins with a well- thought-out set of written ethical principles.* I work with clients to develop what I call **The Ten Convictions.** We go through several iterations of these values to refine them into a set of elegantly simple foundational principles.

These principles assist them in closing the gap between what they believe in their heart of hearts and what they actually do. We call these ten statements their *sacred convictions*. The process for identifying and developing them often takes several months. It evolves from a vague first draft to a refined polished living document they firmly and unequivocally believe in. These values can be posted and reviewed each and every day. With these distinct convictions, the batting average for achieving timely and meaningful outcomes skyrockets. As a result we confidently know who we are and what we stand for and make daily decisions and responses in alignment with our convictions. With this certainty, we take automatic relevant action that sustains our progress. Our inner peace, self-efficacy, and serenity grow and blossom like never before. We have few regrets and no need to denigrate others. These *Ten Convictions* are a navigational compass, a GPS that steers us wisely forward. They become us and we become them. Decisions and responses become more automatic and decisive. There is little need to second guess ourselves or have regrets. Actions taken are the best possible at the time with our destinations, journeys, and responses to what is. They accompany us daily as a friend and adviser with our daily pursuit of *Betterism*.

A wisely thought out set of written values and convictions leads us to observe the world around and within us more clearly and calmly. We make wiser decisions while at the same time have an unprecedented and profound peace of mind. Coupled with our enlightened perspective of NOOT, we proceed with empathy, compassion, and certainty with our efforts and enforcement of personal boundaries. Our reactions and responses to the reality of what is and is not in the world leaves us with a sense of "Hey, I did the best I could at the time."

With our use of a FUSS, we believe in our ability to advance and do even better next time. The important few take precedence over the minor many. We live each day with a calm certainty and understanding of what is.

ADVANTAGES OF A WRITTEN LIST
OF YOUR CONVICTIONS

Some of the advantages of developing a written clear set of sound personal convictions are:

Better Decisions

Decisions come easily, as they are grounded in well-thought-out convictions with what is right and wrong. These decisions are more likely to lead to satisfying long term outcomes, as well.

Avoid Second Guessing

Often, we make a decision for action and then when things don't turn out as well as we wish they had, we beat ourselves up over the could-have, should-haves. When a decision and action is wisely considered and acted upon, we know that is the best we can do given our current experience, education, and understanding. Our actions and decisions are grounded in our principles, as opposed to some impulsive knee jerk reaction or a desire for retribution that we come to later regret.

Conservation of Energy

We are far more inclined to say "no" with the minor and not so important issues. We are also far less inclined to be people pleasers and worry about being liked. As a result, our commitments for future action are wisely considered. When we do decide and agree to take a future action, it is in everyone's long term interest. By limiting commitments, we have more energy, time, and resources to dedicate to important issues that further our peace, health, purpose, and fun.

Improved Self Efficacy

When we develop a track record for achieving wise results, our self-confidence grows. We will continue to be successful with our choices for action on our path of improvement. We remember that detours, mistakes, and setbacks are the shortest paths forward. These setbacks are seen as LEGs and the places where great learning and improvement occur. Today's success breeds tomorrow's success.

Interpersonal Relationship Harmony

With the perspective of NOOT, we realize that the world with its many uncertainties and countless souls is largely out of our realm of control and the best action is to focus on our wise response to it. We avoid the drama and wasted energy associated with resisting reality. When we are committed to act within our moral framework, we are prepared for nearly any eventuality, especially with relationships. As with my trip to Africa to climb Mount Kilimanjaro in Tanzania, my preparations were spot on, yet the certainty of summiting the mountain was not guaranteed. The outcome may be uncertain, but the process for acting and preparing was absolutely on target. When we are satisfied with our own behavior and decisions, we are prone to be more empathetic and supportive of others without a need for anger, blaming, or disparaging.

Purpose and Meaning

The act of determining what will constitute our *Ten Convictions* will compel us to assess and contemplate what is truly important in and with our life, be it fame, fortune, contribution, health, relationships, etc.

Reassurance

Who amongst us does not seek some level reassurance that we are okay with what we have done? We often need outside validation in being told what we did was appropriate or not. Our creed limits this need to seek out others' to help us determine if what we did was right or wrong. We are more self-reliant and confident.

Peace of Mind With Knowing We Did the Right Thing

By uncoupling ourselves from the outcome, we instead commit to the process. By acting within the integrity of our credo, we increase the odds of making meaningful progress. By focusing on living within our philosophy, we lose the co-dependence on having a continual need for successful outcomes. At times, early success can become additive and cause us to lose our way with being true to ourselves. When we focus on the process of doing the right things and living a balanced life, we limit compromises to our integrity and identity.

Integrity as Our Compass in Our Journey

More and more these days, there is a view of circumstantial morality and correctness in our current culture. It has infected people's ability to predict and feel confident that things are on track. We can withstand the temptation of expedient action that feels good in the moment, as opposed to acting and doing what we know from deep within us is the right thing to do.

Avoid Cognitive Dissonance

A common place for frustration and angst is with the disconnect between what we know in our gut is the right thing to do as opposed to what we actually do. By investing time and contemplation with developing this creed, we solidify our inner conviction with who we are and who we are aspiring to become. When we pursue wise processes over results, we embed our convictions within our psyches and behavior. We then find that there is little need to do anything other than to have wise routines and ethical conduct for ourselves. It becomes increasingly automatic. With daily review and reinforcement of who we are and what we stand for, only minor directional adjustments are necessary, as with driving a car with minor changes to the steering along the way, as opposed to drastic turns to avert ensuing calamity. We are able to achieve alignment and calmness with knowing that what we are doing is what we are supposed to be doing and where we are is exactly where we are supposed to be.

Wise and Healthy Expectations

With our creed and focus on the process of seeing things with compassion and empathy, we can better avoid unhealthy and unrealistic expectations. Unrealistic and unhealthy expectations lead to resentment and disappointment. With smart expectations, we do our best and move on and let the outcome be what it may. We focus on doing the best possible and learning from setbacks to be even better the next time. We are far more likely to minimize disappointment, conflict, and the squandering of our time energy and resources.

Reduce Fear and Anxiety

As we develop boundaries with consequences and stay committed to clarity and resolve, we empower ourselves. We are able to wisely respond to undesirable behavior and setbacks with our preplanned responses and attitude. Likewise, the uncertainty and confusion of what to do and where to turn is replaced with courage and confidence. We have an "I have got this" mentality.

EXAMPLES OF WISE WIN-WIN CONVICTIONS

Remember to keep your *Ten Convictions* simple, elegant, and descriptive. Make it a living document which you refine over time. The following are some examples of values within the *Ten Convictions* statements that have been developed by several of my coaching clients:

- Commitment—My word is my bond. I'm discerning about which new commitment I make.

- Confidence—I have great peace of mind because I'm certain that my values guide my decisions.

- Empathy and Compassion—I seek to understand why people are the way they are, including myself.

- Curiosity—I am excited to learn, grow, and share ideas. I am not afraid to explore the unknown or areas that challenge my current beliefs.

- Gratitude—I count my blessings and appreciate that there is good in the world.

- Fun—I seek adventures, big or small, planned or spontaneous.

- Trustworthiness—I remain honest, kind, and *reliable*, and do so with impeccable integrity.

- Relationships—I cultivate mutually rewarding healthy relationships.

- Contribution—I serve and empower others, and myself.

- Nutrition—I select food that provides the energy and nutrients I need to be healthy.

- Fitness—I optimize my physical, emotional, and mental health through regular exercise and rest.

- Financial Stewardship—I live within my means and save over the long-term. My money grows and works for me.

- Boundaries—I have boundaries with clear consequences that are built upon empathy.

- Learning from mistakes—I see detours/setbacks are inevitable and are indeed the shortest way forward ... they are adventures and opportunities for learning I will use them to make me a better person.

- Language—I strive to use empowering and healthy language always.

I strongly encourage you to develop you own personal set of wisely thought out *Ten Convictions* over the next several weeks or months. Look deep within your heart of hearts as to what is important and ethical. I also suggest that your number one conviction be "My word is my bond," and shortly thereafter add one rooted in empathy for others. These convictions will come to define you and guide you away from chaos, anxiety, and uncertainty toward a much more civilized life with the peace, progress, and the healing you deserve.

CHAPTER 15

Relationship Listening Heals

How do I care about another?

"Be the Student Listener"

"Be the Empowering Mirror"

When we listen with our hearts, we respect the diversity of others. When we listen with our hearts, we seek to understand and be empathetic to the need by all to be acknowledged. When we listen with our hearts, we do not judge the logic behind someone's emotions. When we listen with our hearts, we open the door for meaningful communication.

–Michael Starr

Effective listening is one of most valuable talents we can have to empower others, nurture healthy relationships, and improve our lives. With wise listening, we reduce misunderstandings and strengthen our connections with others. Our ability to master this skill depends on both our desire and our strategy for making progress. In this chapter, I will make the case for why *relationship listening* is such a crucial interpersonal skill. I will also provide a model and method that will guide you to improve your communications with family, friends, and associates.

As you practice improving your *relationship listening,* you will realize that as your interest in another increases, your preoccupation with yourself decreases, and anxieties with self-consuming thoughts diminish. Effective listening requires you to:

- Seek to better understand another and why they are as they are
- Take the time, make the time to learn from them
- Care about their fears, anxieties, or confusion
- Care about their insecurities and imperfections
- Care about their talents and successes
- Care about their times for celebration and pride
- Love them, validate them, and acknowledge them to their satisfaction so they are convinced they are heard and worthy
- Respect their right to believe as they do

My wife Karen and I have a sincere interest in people and enjoy socializing with others. We often invite folks over for meals at our home. My wife does all the real work with the food preparation, and I do the simple part of cooking on our gray outdoor Blackstone griddle. Most of these meals include our specially seasoned grilled jumbo shrimp. I get more credit than I deserve for these meals, as the preparation is 90 percent of the work. Our friends and acquaintances who visit often bring picture books or digital photos to share with us. We truly enjoy hearing about their hobbies, careers, families, pets, and travels. It is always fun to see their eyes light up as they proudly speak of their experiences and accomplishments. They all have fascinating lives, with their own unique adventures and challenges.

In addition to our core group of friends, we have chats with quite a few strangers each month. Karen and I love to hike with our rescue dogs Rippy and Lola. Several times each week, we walk anywhere from two to six miles in the woods, where we surround ourselves with nature's beauty. On the trail, we often run across friendly folks and strike up conversations with them in the middle of the forest. It is fascinating to learn a bit about them and where there are in their lives. Some of the people we meet are retired, most have jobs, others are students, many work from home, some are from out of state, some are couples in love with plans for marriage. Most of the fellow hikers we meet are enthusiastic and energized. Occasionally, some are dealing with a family tragedy. These conversations ground us and strengthen our compassion and appreciation for others and with each other, as well.

We also bump into folks at the RV parks we visit. We have a modest RV used for camping with our two dogs. After setting up camp with the RV, which includes a portable fence enclosure for Rippy and Lola, I often wander around the park and strike up a conversation with the folks camping near us. RV parks are a great place to meet people from many diverse locations and with fascinating backgrounds. Talking with folks at a RV park is like sitting next to someone on an airplane flight; it is understood you will likely not meet them again. In this setting, folks tend to let their guard down as there is minimal concern with trust or being judged. Most people have little fear or inhibition with being vulnerable in this atmosphere and with this one-time meeting. Camping fosters relaxed and authentic communications.

Both my wife and I have a keen interest in learning from others. We see this as a win-win. We help people to feel good about themselves, and they in turn ground us and educate us, as well. We are reminded that our concerns are not unique and that there is much to be grateful for. Karen and I are retired, reasonably healthy, have largely made peace with the past, and have excitement about the future ahead of us. We understand that this may not be the case for everyone. We are grateful for these blessings and have compassion for others with the suffering or upsets they may be facing. Some of their challenges go unspoken. Based on our own personal heartbreaks, we understand how this can be. One may not fully realize the struggle others are engaged with at any moment in time. We do our best to give others the benefit of the doubt.

Learning about people's lives is like reading a book or watching a movie. There is adventure, adversity, disappointment, and hope within their stories. This goes for both new acquaintances as well as established friends.

One of the things I have noticed with all these communications is a compelling desire to be heard, a desire to be understood, a desire to be appreciated and acknowledged. Karen and I get this and make it a point to show them we are interested in them, because we are. Our interest in them is authentic and unconditional. We expect nothing in return other than knowing we may have lifted them up with our interest and our sincere compliments regarding their accomplishments and knowledge.

I have noticed in my own unscientific poll that about 10 percent of the people we talk with have a sincere interest in us. I do find that refreshing. I approach communications, and especially listening, as an unconditional act of caring for others. I must admit, however, that I, too, have a desire to be understood and acknowledged. I am honored with this occasional bonus. Those 10 percent are especially important to us. We go out of our way to nurture those relationships for future connection.

TWO COMPETING INTERESTS

Our ability to listen effectively at any point in time is a consequence of a balance between two competing interests. One is our interest and caring for another person versus our preoccupation with personal concerns. This balance varies over time, as well as with individuals. We may have a patronizing interest in a coworker or friend that is outweighed by a concern for our financial problems or work deadlines. In the same instance, if we receive a call from a distraught child or visit by an upset boss, we may become instantly attentive, receptive, and interested in their message. If you have an interest in being a better listener, it is valuable to discern these two counterweights. Be mindful about recognizing your interest in others versus your preoccupation with personal concerns. Do strive to develop a sincere interest in hearing what the other person has to say while keeping your agenda in check. *Wise selfishness* supports healthy relationship listening, as it seeks a win–win outcome.

Relationship Listening vs Competing Interests

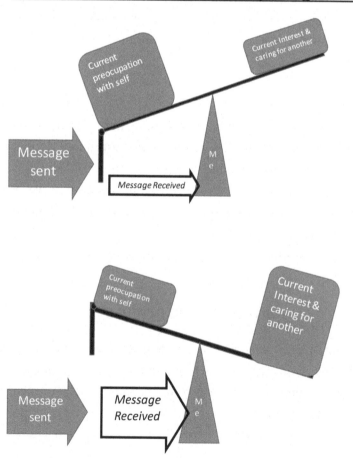

It is important to stop and listen to others, especially when they are distraught, angry, or reaching out for help and comfort. Once again, as with opportunity costs, time and resources spent on "X" cannot also be spent on "Y." It is wise to decide which conversations and listenings we wish to and can engage with. If we are in a hurry, it may be wise to respectfully say, "This is not a good time for me right now. May we speak later this evening or tomorrow afternoon? I will call you then."

It is critical that you absolutely be your word here. Sadly, we often are overcommitted and anxious with being some place other than where we are. Many rush through a yellow traffic light acting as if they are an ambulance driver transporting a dying person for life-saving medical help. Our lifestyles are often a rush of activities. Perhaps this rush of going from one activity to the next is a means of running away or avoiding something? We can become "Human Doings" versus "Human Beings." Whatever the reason for this hectic lifestyle, it causes us to miss smelling the flowers along the way and neglect relationships and people who matter.

My observations with both my coaching business and personal experience are that there is a dire need for improvement in many people's ability and interest in listening to others. Improvement here will go a long way in reducing suffering, conflict, and failure for many. Perhaps at the center of the issue with shortcomings in the area of listening is having an understanding of what listening is and what it is not.

Listening is what I do while I am waiting to talk.

−Author unknown

Listening is often about getting data and factual information, such as with directions for where to go or how to do something. Accurate, unambiguous speech and listening can be the difference between life and death in military combat and operating a nuclear submarine in emergency conditions. Listening for information can be educational, such as with learning at a lecture, seminar, or in a classroom. This chapter is not about these types of listening. The listening being addressed in this chapter addresses *relationship listening*. It is about being clear with both our role and method with interacting with another when discussing concerns or interests. I encourage you to pursue advancing your skills with *relationship listening*. You will find it both an honorable and rewarding quest.

Ask and it will be given to you; seek and you will find; knock and the door will be opened to you.

–Matthew 7:7 (NIV)

RELATIONSHIP LISTENING IS IMPORTANT

As a result of my experiences in life, I find it rather easy to strike up a conversation over some points of commonality when talking with others. There is much opportunity for finding common ground for all of us; we need only to seek it, look for it, and nurture this path forward. Common ground is always there between people, look for it and you will find it; I do, and you will as well.

When we increase our focus on others and less on ourselves, neurotic tendencies diminish. Now more than ever there is a need to reduce the emptiness, frustration, and suffering created by preoccupation with self. It saddens me to see the current trend toward divisiveness and denigration being promoted and growing within our country. As we improve our interpersonal connections with empathy and love, we will find more peace of mind. My experience is that someone needs to be the initiator with the connection. I often choose it to be me. Whether it is at an airport, grocery store, or hiking in the forest, I start with a smile and a sincere hello. I do my best to be a bit self-deprecating and make a short humorous comment about the current circumstance. If there is something I admire about them, I will say so . . . "I really admire your use of hiking poles, that's a great practice for personal safety," or "That's a really cool looking green hat, where did you get it?"

It is no surprise to me that many people are pleased to be acknowledged and are often eager to begin a conversation.

I believe most people have a need to connect with others. They wish to be acknowledged, valued, and appreciated. They wish to transcend a sense of loneliness deep down within them, especially those without a strong leaning toward spirituality or religion. Ultimately, we ourselves are alone, and are but one mind and one body. We naturally seek the comfort of a connection with others. We seek relationships as a means to rise above this reality of being a solitary one. Within a healthy relationship we feel loved, cared about, and no longer alone. Within a healthy relationship we feel important and heard. *Relationship listening* is a powerful elixir for many maladies we often face such as loneliness, insecurity, anger, and hopelessness. Perhaps the greatest opportunity for love and harmony lies with our ability to be caring *relationship listeners*? This skill has the potential to heal psychological wounds and reveal healthy paths forward for others as well as ourselves. When facing extreme stress and difficulty, where do many turn? Some turn to God through prayer, while others may turn to a professional such as a therapist. Both are the ultimate listeners.

Be the Student Listener, Be the Empowering Mirror

This book is built on the premise that suffering, conflict, and despair can often be mitigated if not eliminated through the use of wise empowering language. Likewise, harmony, peace of mind, success, and healing can also be advanced with wise empowering language. In that spirit, I introduce two terms to use with your efforts to improve *relationship listening*. These two terms are states of being: **Be the Student Listener** and **Be the Empowering Mirror**. With *Being the Student Listener*, we seek to understand what and why. With *Being the Empowering Mirror*, we reflect back to others their point of view and our understanding of it. With *Being the Empowering Mirror*, we help them further clarify their perspective as well as acknowledge and validate them. The presumption here with *relationship listening* is that we do actually care about another's well-being and we sincerely desire to improve our relationship with them. The following is a proposed model for *relationship listening:*

Relationship Listening Model

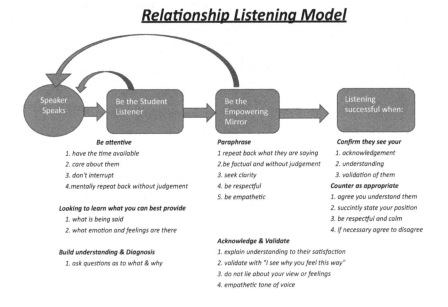

Be attentive
1. have the time available
2. care about them
3. don't interrupt
4. mentally repeat back without judgement

Looking to learn what you can best provide
1. what is being said
2. what emotion and feelings are there

Build understanding & Diagnosis
1. ask questions as to what & why

Paraphrase
1 repeat back what they are saying
2. be factual and without judgement
3. seek clarity
4. be respectful
5. be empathetic

Acknowledge & Validate
1. explain understanding to their satisfaction
2. validate with "I see why you feel this way"
3. do not lie about your view or feelings
4. empathetic tone of voice

Confirm they see your
1. acknowledgement
2. understanding
3. validation of them

Counter as appropriate
1. agree you understand them
2. succintly state your position
3. be respectful and calm
4. if necessary agree to disagree

I suggest these four steps for effective relationship listening:

1. Select a Goldilocks Time
2. Be the Student Listener
3. Be the Empowering Mirror
4. Convince them we respect and care about them

1. Select a Goldilocks Time—*not too little, not too much, just right*
One group stands out for their skill with being excellent listeners. These professional listeners are called therapists. Essential to the role of a therapist is their ability to fully focus on hearing the what and why of their clients' comments. There is a scheduled start time and finish time with their planned sessions. They get paid to listen and it is their job to do it well; they are experts. We can learn from their process to better our relationship listening. Like a sports player, they must keep their eye on the ball, which in this case is listening effectively, so they

avoid being preoccupied or distracted with anything other than the focus on their client and what they are saying. While in session, they are not feeling imposed upon, nor do they feel anxious with a distracting need to be somewhere else. In those moments, they know that they are where they are supposed to be. Their strict boundaries with start time and the length of the meeting frees them to listen keenly.

What we learn from this example is that it is important to avoid having *time* become a distraction. With therapists, time is a non-issue as the boundaries are clearly understood by both parties. Our ability to be fully attentive begins with making the time to listen. *Relationship listening* is usually an impromptu experience without an agreed upon start and stop time. Yet, like a therapist who is ready and fully available to listen, we should listen only at a time when we are able to *be there*. Occasionally, our listening will fall into the category of *drop everything now,* "I am fully here for you." Emergency listening is not the usual case with our *relationship listening*, however.

It is wise to think through ahead of time to be prepared to decide when and if you will engage in a *relationship listening* opportunity. When another begins to communicate a concern, decide quickly if now, later, or never is the best time to listen. Respond respectfully and accordingly here. Often, you may feel that now is the best time to listen. Do so if you can be focused on the what and why of what they are saying. However, if you feel imposed upon or preoccupied with another agenda, it is better to reschedule than to be inattentive and distracted.

2. Be the Student Listener

When we are *Being the Student Listener,* **we listen not to learn what others can provide for us, but rather we listen to learn what we can provide for them**. The subtle shift here is to move from a rather ambiguous and vague notion of "listening" to one focused on motive. That motive is to learn from another so that we can best support them.

When engaged in *relationship listening*, it is helpful to see our role as that of a student. In contrast, it is unwise to see our role as being that of a teacher. As pointed out in the chapter on willpower versus desire-power there is subtle but profound difference in the term *motivation* versus *self-motivation,* as one is ambiguous while the other places emphasis on self-reliance and personal responsibility. Likewise with the terms *listener* versus *student listener,* the motive for listening moves from a vague generality to a more focused motive of learning. This learning is to discover and understand how we can best provide what another seeks from us. They are customers and clients coming to us, and we are charged to deliver for them our understanding, caring, acknowledgment, and questions that facilitate clarity.

> *People don't care how much you know*
> *until they know how much you care.*
>
> —Theodore Roosevelt

Most of us say we "care" about another, yet often we are unclear about what that really means. This can be akin to saying we love someone (that is yet another discussion) while we live in a cognitive dissonance mismatch between our unloving actions and our loving words. The term caring is perhaps as vague and ambiguous as the word happiness. As a *student listener,* we see our role as one where we seek to understand both the words spoken as well as the emotions and feelings behind them. Often, the words others speak within relationship communication do not align with their feelings. Often, they themselves are unclear and unsure what is going on other than they have a need to speak. Strive to understand and diagnose the totality of the communication. We listen to understand the words, we listen to understand concerns and fears, we listen to determine the totality of the entire picture. We ask questions to build our understanding and ask questions to help them clarify what is going on within themselves.

This stage of communications is to receive the best information we can gather on what's being said as well as why. Along this learning path as a student listener, we must exercise the greatest of respect and humility: "I'm sorry, I am not sure I understand that last point, would you mind expanding on it a bit more please?"

Remember, your motive here is to learn to understand and diagnose what is going on . . . you are the student learning from them; not just passively but also with kind calm questioning for building clarity. Care to know not just the what and why, but how you can provide what it is they seek. Help them to best see what it is they seek, as well.

3. Be the Empowering Mirror

With *being the empowering mirror,* our motive and intent is to reflect back to them our understanding, acknowledgement, and compassion for them. We reflect back our belief in them and their ability to make things better for themselves. Some parts of that might include:

- Validate them: "You have good reason to have this concern." (It may be an unjustified concern, but it is still their concern.)

- Acknowledge your understanding of the words: "This is my understanding of what I hear, am I correct?" (This can also help with their improving their own clarity, as well.)

- Acknowledge their feelings, pain, frustration, anger, despondency, etc.: "I see you are upset . . . what can I do?"

- Show kindness, respect and caring: "I respect you and your life experiences. I can see how painful this is for you. I truly desire to know what I can do to make things better, if possible."

- Apologize (but only if it is justified): "I see I owe you an apology here. I am so sorry that . . . "

- Convince them of your empathy and compassion: "Any one of us in those circumstances would feel the same way."

- Empower them: "You are a smart person with a lot of life experience. I know you will find a way to deal with this challenge. What do you think are your options here?"

- If they are uncomfortable with your questions or comments, ask them: "What is it you hear me saying?"

- Provide your view of their position and what you heard them say to help advance their own clarity.

4. Sell, Don't Tell . . . Convince, Don't Impose

Take the time to use the Platinum Rule, treating others as they wish to be treated and spoken to. Convince them why you feel your view might be helpful, then move on, as in the state of being called **Be the Waiter (make your case succinctly then move on).** Often, asking an empowering question can be useful with guiding others to help them guide themselves to make forward progress.

The objective with relationship communications is threefold:

1. First, it is to understand what is going on with another.

2. Second, it is to convince them that we understand their message and do so to their satisfaction.

3. Third, it is to decide what we can do to help and support another. There may be times that all that we can do is to be a relationship listener who cares, acknowledges, and shows respect.

The "talking stick" was a method used to make tribal decisions by North American Indian Chiefs. When someone holds the talking stick, they will continue to do so until they feel fully understood by everyone else around them. While they hold that talking stick, no one is permitted to state their views or opinions. They must focus their attention toward understanding what is being said and ask appropriate questions to completely build their understanding. They must convince the stick holder they fully understand him (not necessarily agree with him, though). This communication technique is profoundly effective with having people becoming open to understanding one another.

I suggest in *relationship listening* that you consider that the person speaking to you is holding the talking stick, and you withhold commentary and your counter views until they feel fully understood, as is done with this Native American tradition. I believe as you practice and hone the skills associated with *relationship listening*, you will be rewarded with not only improved relationships, but more inner peace and less conflict in your own life.

> *Listening is often the only thing*
> *necessary to help someone.*
>
> –Author Unknown

CHAPTER 16

Do the Right Thing and Stop Second Guessing Yourself

What is my process for making important decisions?

"Be the Scout ... Be prepared"

Think things through before acting. If the outcome is not what you hoped for, do it better the next time. Mistakes are my teachers.

–Michael Starr

I was walking on campus to my next class at Carnegie Mellon University (CMU) when Sam (not his real name) stopped to talk. Sam was an upperclassman studying mechanical engineering, I was studying electrical engineering. We had worked together the previous summer in a local steel mill. During this summer job, we found a common ground with being CMU students and having a keen interest in muscle cars. We met socially several times at his home in the Pittsburgh area because of our mutual interest in auto mechanics. During my visits, I had an opportunity to meet his girlfriend, an attractive, kind, and charming young lady.

Sam was an intense, high energy, and fast thinking fellow. Occasionally, his intensity and desire for perfection resulted in an angry outburst. He was a bit of a hot head. His girlfriend, on the other hand, was a gentle, lighthearted, and relaxed soul. I felt she was a good balance for Sam. The three of us socialized three or four times that summer.

When Sam stopped me on campus, I could sense a subdued sadness within him, very much out of character with his typical energetic enthusiasm. He explained that he and his girlfriend had broken up. He was deeply upset and despondent. As I was in a hurry to get to my class, I cut our conversation short and suggested we get together sometime soon. I wished him well and went on to my next class.

A few weeks later, I was listening to the radio while driving, when I heard a radio report of a tragic murder in the Pittsburgh area. A young woman had been killed by her ex-boyfriend with a hatchet in her bedroom. He was waiting near her house at night when he saw her come home from a date. The ex-boyfriend climbed into her bedroom and killed her in a violent rage. It was Sam. I was stunned. I had not reached out to contact Sam after our brief conversation on campus when he first informed me of his breakup with his girlfriend.

Nearly twenty years later, I was a locomotive plant manager responsible for over 400 folks with a dozen managers, more than forty supervisors, and a budget of over $30 million. This was a hectic time for me. I frequently needed to juggle work priorities to deal with the crises of the moment. During my work at that facility, I met with the managers frequently. One manager, who I will call Frank (not his real name), often interacted with me and was constantly coming up with plans to make things better. Frank was a gem with his performance and dedication. In time, however, I came to be concerned for Frank as I was smelling alcohol on his breath and was concerned that he may have a drinking problem. Following company policy, I confronted Frank in private with another manager present. The company protocol was that in the absence of a behavioral reason, two managers must agree to smelling alcohol on an employee's breath before a urinalysis test could be authorized and required. Contrary to my determination that it was alcohol I smelled on his breath, the other manager stated he thought it was mouthwash. As a result of conflicting assessments, the issue was dropped. Shortly after this, I was transferred from that facility to another city 1,500 miles away. Several years later, I was informed that Frank had died . . . from liver failure.

Now moving forward yet five more years, I was in Houston attending a communication training program. I had graduated from this program a few weeks earlier and returned with a few others to serve as class coaches for the next class. I had five folks in this class assigned to me. I was responsible for assisting them with their progress. I would check in with them during the week by phone, and occasionally had lunch with them. I would ask how their homework was coming along and see if there were any concerns I could help with. Mary (not her real name) was one of the class members assigned to me. Mary was a sweet, timid, somewhat self-conscious young lady in her early twenties. She was having difficulty following through with homework assignments and indecisive with decisions for taking future action to better herself. I remember the person who oversaw the class telling me in private that I should be more direct and tough with Mary, and told me to "hold her accountable." I decided not to be firm with her, but to the contrary I was gentler and kinder with her than I was with the other four. I sensed a deep-seated unhappiness and insecurity within her. Everyone in this class was required to select a project and develop it throughout the class program. At the end of the class, each student would give a report on their project. As we neared the end of the class program, everyone in my group was on track with their project except for Mary. She had great difficulty choosing one improvement area and waffled between several ideas. I remember my last phone call with her when I tried to reassure and encourage her by saying it was not critical what she selected, but just to pick one project area and try to stick with it. I emphasized I knew she would make a good decision with whatever she chose. Several days later, I called her in the afternoon on the day of our evening class. I was checking in with her to make sure she was on track with her project and would be attending class that night. When I called Mary's phone, a man answered, it was her father. I introduced myself and explained my reason for calling. He then said that his daughter had shot herself and taken her life that morning.

Clearly, there is much more to these three tragic stories than revealed here. I know but a sliver of the events and history that led Sam, Frank, and Mary to do what they did. In the years that followed, I have reflected on each of them many, many times. I asked myself, "How did it come to that? Could I have done more? Could I have prevented any of this? *Did I do the right thing?*"

Even today as I write, I see their faces. Regret and second guessing can come to haunt us for years, if not the rest of our lives. If you can avoid serious regret, I urge you to do so, make this a priority in your life ... please. This chapter speaks of when and how to make decisions that minimize regret; how to make decisions that keep you from second guessing yourself into a suffering quagmire. This chapter addresses how to decide what the right thing to do is, and then do it. It also addresses the importance of decoupling wise preparation and execution from undesirable outcomes that may follow. Outcomes are often outside your control; your preparation is very much within your control.

MAKING PEACE WITH THE PAST

After years of grappling with these three (plus a few more) devastating experiences, I came to have a clarity and a peace with the past. The seeds of tragedy can become the genesis for future wisdom. These experiences have led me to the following conclusions:

- Have my act together, have my house in order

- Everyone deserves kindness, empathy, and compassion ... always

- Do the right thing ... know who I am and what I believe in, then live and act in alignment with that

This is a chapter about *doing the right thing without regret or second guessing.* My hope for this chapter is to provide a strategy, a Trail of Progress (TOP), that helps others reduce suffering and increase peace of mind by being intentionally wise with both their decisions and their reflections about those decisions they acted upon.

Daily we are faced with dozens if not hundreds of options for what we can do or cannot do. Most daily actions taken are automatic; they result from our biases, values, habits, and experience. These behaviors are not the result of a thought-through decision, as they require little to no consideration; we just do them. When we put on a seat belt, stop at a red light, or drink a cup of morning coffee, these are habits with no decision required. When a fourteen-year-old son asks his father if he can stay out past curfew with his friends and the father says "no," that is what some may call a "no-brainer" automatic response. No contemplation goes into many of the routine things we say or do. Most of these responses and actions are benign. These interactions usually cause little or no harm and *get the job done.* Habitual behavior frees us from the need to take time and energy to think through what to do. Life would be exhausting and exceptionally complex if every option required the effort of deciding which direction to take next as we move through our daily lives.

Occasionally, this automatic way of being is counterproductive and works against us. It can perpetuate or exacerbate a problem. Our hardwired automatic self may be the reason we engaged in an argument or why we forgot to do something important. In these cases, we may see ourselves responsible for the "mistake" because we made "the wrong choice," but these were not really choices but rather habit and our predispositions. These are situations where an action or lack of action led to an undesired outcome. The subject of learning from past upsets and setbacks is addressed in the next chapter titled *Evolutionary Learning*. This chapter, however, is focused on being proactive with a process and preparation we can make with a future decision to minimize regret. This process is called: "One, Two, Three—Decide, Do, Applaud." This method will go a long way toward eliminating regret and second guessing.

Some routine decisions are a big deal and are best approached as not being routine. They can make the difference between suffering and progress, between harmony and conflict. In these instances, it is wise to discern when to stand back and pause before we act. This is especially true when these actions involve others. Poorly worded communications can damage a relationship or lead to serious misunderstandings. It is important to be mindful of *what* we say, *when* we say it, and *how* we say it. This chapter addresses decisions that require preparation before doing, such as dealing with a concern for or with another. This also applies with future plans on how we use our time, money, and energy.

DETERMINED DECISIONS

There are times when it is prudent to intervene with our automatic self and say, "Stop! I need to think this through before proceeding any further."

The next step after seeing a need for this pause is to use a process I call the "One, Two, Three of a Determined Decision." In order to facilitate your success in doing the right thing without regret, I introduce the term **Determined Decisions**. This distinction will serve as a tool to enhance your focus and clarity. *Determined Decisions* are proactive, as they are well-thought-out prior to doing something or saying something. They are the result of thinking before doing. Our ability to distinguish this need for a *Determined Decision* is crucial to our ability to achieve influence and improve our odds for having desirable outcomes.

When we see the need for a *determined decision,* we must stop and take the time to think through what the best and right thing is to do. Deciding to make a *determined decision* is the beginning of the process. After we see the need for a *determined decision,* there are three steps to take. I call these steps the *One, Two, Three*—Decide, Do, Applaud. First, we decide what is the right thing to do. Second, we do that right thing. Third we applaud ourselves for following through with doing step two. This process will profoundly impact our ability to make wise choices and further promote our personal progress.

1, 2, 3's of a Determined Decision - Decide, Do, Applaud

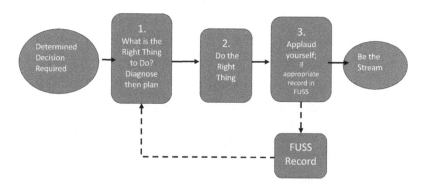

DECIDE WHEN A DETERMINED DECISION IS NEEDED

Automatic responses can be reactionary (reflexive) knee-jerk reactions, more in line with our primitive *fight or flight* wiring, and they can occasionally bring about much regret later. Automatic responses may fail to focus on win-win solutions, or they may have long-term negative consequences.

Determined decisions require pause for contemplation. *Determined Decisions* are required prior to confronting another with a concern we may have. It is wise to take the time to prepare for these communications to minimize misunderstanding or defensiveness. *Determined decisions* are also needed when we wish to influence another in some way, selling them on the value of doing something for themselves or with others. *Determined decisions* are often important with choosing how we spend our discretionary time, money, and energy. If the issue is important and out of our normal routine, it will likely fall into the category of a need for a Determined Decision.

John C. Maxwell makes the case well for preparing before doing in his book *Winning with People* in the chapter titled "The Confrontation Principle: Caring for People Should Precede Confronting People."

The *Follow-Up Setback System* captures concerns and setbacks in a record which we review weekly. It keeps opportunities for improvement on the radar for us. This is another source for selecting which *determined decision* we next wish to make.

STEP #1: DECIDE WHAT IS THE RIGHT THING TO DO

Two key considerations in deciding what the right thing to do are:

1. Integrity

2. Probability

Integrity

Integrity is an essential component with what we say or do and how we say or do it. Doing things with integrity increases our odds for long term success with desirable outcomes. Acting with integrity will minimize if not eliminate guilt. When we reduce guilt, we reduce the negative impact of lost time and energy that results from "beating ourselves up" and obsessing over the *could have* and *should have*. This second guessing can greatly undermine our self-confidence and cause us to be reluctant with making future decisions. It can lead to non-decisions, which then become decisions by default. This is usually not a good thing for us or others.

Integrity ultimately results when our actions align with our wise intentional beliefs, values, and principles. The *Ten Convictions* speak to the importance of knowing who we are through a set of written convictions that we have clarified for ourselves. The *Ten Convictions* document is a personal creed for our actions and views of right and wrong. Principles such as being our word, being honest, living within our means, being empathetic, and focusing on the wise selfishness of win-win outcomes are examples here. For our identity to be a healthy one and have integrity, we must be intentional and positive with our awareness of our talents and skills, as well. This is in contrast with *contra identities,* which are built upon a self-righteous moral high ground created by putting others down.

Some considerations with integrity:

—Know yourself and what you stand for, frequently review your personal *Ten Convictions*, acting in ways that are aligned with your beliefs.

—Be mindful of NOOT, the Natural Order of Things, to keep yourself focused on empathy and compassion. People can't help being who they are given their DNA, environment, and past experiences.

- Be a respectful relationship listener.

- Go beyond forgiveness to understanding. Harbor no animosity or ill will toward another.

- Strive for healthy relationships.

- Care about others.

- Avoid vindictive or justice-seeking actions.

PROBABILITY–PLAYING THE ODDS, *"BE THE BOOKIE"*

We are more likely to roll a seven with a pair of dice than any other number, as the odds favor this. Wearing a seatbelt improves the likelihood for reducing injury and surviving an automobile accident.

A lifestyle with a proper diet and periodic exercise improves our possibility for living a long, healthy life. Some probabilities are exact, as with rolling dice with seven occurring more frequently than any other number. National statistics with seatbelt use clearly show the benefit of wearing seatbelts with reducing injury and deaths. Other probabilities are subjective and not exact. Many of these subjective areas, however, are generally accepted as being successful strategies for achieving desired outcomes. Below are some ideas to consider with improving your odds for success with achieving a desired outcome that also maintains your integrity, as well:

- Do not be hasty with deciding. Sleep on it to give your thoughts time to mature.

- Make the achievement of win-win solutions a key part of your preparations. Our interactions with others can produce allies or enemies. These allies or enemies will be around for a long time and will impact your ability with achieving future successes and progress.

- Take time to understand another's language and points of view speak with them using language they are comfortable with.

- Be kind, calm and respectful. Remember the Platinum Rule: "Treat people the way they wish to be treated."

- Understand who they are and have empathy for them.

- Rehearse or role play before a potential confronting meeting or conversation, anticipate possible responses.

- Do research through reading, YouTube, subject matter experts, and mentors to see what has worked for others.

- Review any boundaries you have and how you will handle the broaching of any boundary in a calm, kind, but firm manner.

- Be mindful to avoid the *blame game* or having a *right fight*.

- After your respectful listening, make your point succinctly, calmly, and respectfully then move on . . . don't badger them. *Be the Waiter* who presents the special of the day; make your case clearly and as convincingly as you can, then move on.

- Anticipate that others may not agree with you, and where appropriate agree to disagree.

- Listen and ensure they feel heard, acknowledged, and validated.

- Be mindful to do all you can to maintain a healthy relationship. When talking about undesirable issues, focus on the behavior and not the person. Focus on how it makes you feel when an undesirable behavior occurs.

- When you believe you are not understood ask, *"What do you hear me saying?"*

- Be mindful of being more of a seller than a teller in order to improve the odds of your effectiveness with influencing another.

STEP #2: DO THE RIGHT THING

After you have taken the time to determine what the right thing to do is, find an appropriate time to follow through and do it. Pick a time when you are in a calm and confident state of mind. Pick a time when the others involved are calm and not preoccupied with something else. If you are properly prepared, you will have little fear or anxiety going forward. However, be careful to avoid finding reasons and excuses not to follow through with your determined decision. The sooner the better here. When dealing with another, make time for hearing their side of things before you communicate your planned action. *Be the relationship listener* and give them a figurative "Indian Talking Stick" prior to your planned comments. Do your best to ensure they feel heard. Barring legitimate extenuating circumstances, do follow through with your planned action or comments.

STEP #3: APPLAUD YOURSELF ... "BRAVO"

After you have followed through with your Determined Decision, congratulate yourself. Say, "Bravo to me, I did what I planned to do, I did the right thing!"

It may, however, be that despite your well-thought-out plan, things did not go well. Remember this was your best plan at the time for coming up with your *Determined Decision.* At that time, it was the best preparation and level of understanding available to you. It was as good as you could do. *Do not second guess yourself here.* Focus on seeing you did the best you could given the circumstance. When you do your best, that is all you can hope to do. Second guessing only diminishes self-confidence and puts you in a continual state of anxiety with any future actions. You did the "right thing" for that time in your life. "Bravo, bravo, bravo to me".

If the outcome of your *determined decision* was undesirable, put this issue into your FUSS log for future handling during your *week in review* meeting. Take the win and the applause, as you did the best you could. You will do even better in the future.

The reward in having gone through the One, Two, Three Determined Decision process is with the level of self-confidence you will have in knowing you did your best with integrity and wisdom. There is no need to second guess yourself; to the contrary you deserve to congratulate yourself and pat yourself on the back for a job well done. You will believe that even better days lie ahead for you. Your wise contemplation and consideration and follow through are your reward. De-link the actual outcome from your prepared determined decision and you will avoid second guessing yourself or having resentments. You did the right thing, now move on. Trusting your process with the FUSS log will ensure any needed follow up action will be handled appropriately. This process allows us to continue to move forward and not become stalled or derailed.

Do the *right thing* without malice but with kindness:

With malice toward none; with charity for all.
-Abraham Lincoln.

We do the *right thing* not because someone else deserves it or earns it, but because your moral code of values of right and wrong tells you that it is the correct thing to do. Don't expect reciprocity with this. This is an unconditional decision that we do because we believe it to be correct.

Here are three examples for Determined Decisions:

1. Having a child or parent who is making self-destructive decisions. Think through a short "elevator speech" that communicates on their level with their perspective in mind, and at the right time say it with respect and calmness. Read and study the book "I Am Not Sick I Don't Need Help!" by Xavier Amador, Ph.D., which has remarkable ideas for communicating by building our relationship with another in the most difficult of circumstances, as with severe mental health challenges.

2. My boss at work is close minded to my suggestions.
Read and study several books and articles such as *The 5 Love Languages* by Gary Chapman, *The Platinum Rule* by Tony Alessandra and Michael J. O'Connor, and *Winning with People* by John Maxwell. Think through how best to build your relationship and better foster the boss's interest with listening to you in the future.

3. A friend or loved one is struggling with a particular issue.
A person we care about is talking to us frequently about a problem they are facing, such as their weight, their finances, work, or a relationship with another. Think through how best to communicate with them. Let them know we believe in them, then encourage and guide them

to find a way to make incremental improvements with baby steps. Empower them with your confidence in their ability to make things better for themselves.

I conclude this chapter with a biblical New Testament quote. My interpretation of this quote is that we can cast the seeds of good in many places. Sometimes they take root sometimes they do not. Let us continue to cast the seeds for good regardless. This exemplifies our role with doing and saying the right things. These wise actions on our part are not guarantees for a successful response or action by another, yet they give us the peace of mind and confidence in knowing that at that time in our lives, we did about the best we knew how.

When a large crowd was coming together, and those from the various cities were journeying to Him, He spoke by way of a parable: "The sower went out to sow his seed; and as he sowed, some fell beside the road, and it was trampled underfoot and the birds of the air ate it up. Other seed fell on rocky soil, and as soon as it grew up, it withered away, because it had no moisture. Other seed fell among the thorns; and the thorns grew up with it and choked it out. Other seed fell into the good soil, and grew up, and produced a crop a hundred times as great." As He said these things, He would call out, "He who has ears to hear, let him hear."

–Luke 8:4-8 (NIV)

CHAPTER 17

Evolutionary Learning, Mistakes are our Friends and Teachers

How do I respond when I experience a setback?

"Be the Apprentice"

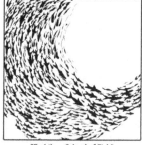

"Be Like a School of Fish"

Learning from an undesired experience is one of our best opportunities to grow and reduce future upsets.

–Michael Starr

After my time served in the Navy as a submarine officer, I next worked for the railroad. I began as a staff manager at the San Francisco headquarters for the Southern Pacific Railroad. There, I was part of a team that set standards for locomotive and freight car maintenance and manufacturing. We were responsible for determining the safest and most cost-effective way to do work on train equipment that complies with regulatory, union and company standards. This was a role I was comfortable with, having come from the Navy's nuclear power world, where equipment maintenance standards were sacred tenets.

After seven years on staff, I made a substantial shift with the railroad and was transferred to field operations. There I managed the servicing, maintenance, and manufacturing associated with locomotives for the remainder of my career. I worked in three different states and at five different facilities for the next thirty years. I began my time in the field like a fish out of water. It was stressful for me to deal with the uncertain and confrontational nature of regulatory inspectors, labor union leaders, and the day-to-day complaints and problems with personnel under my direct area of responsibility. All this in the face of daily material and tool shortages, as well as facility breakdowns involving cranes, track, pumps, lathes, etc. It did not take long for me to understand that old saying that you can't make everyone happy all the time. At times I felt that I could not make anyone happy any of the time.

I found myself often angry and frustrated. I felt I was doing my best to satisfy upper management as well as all those who worked at the facility I managed. At times, I felt like the westward bound wagon train travelers that had formed a circle while being barraged by attack from all sides. Rather than standing back to learn a better way to handle things, I just plowed forward working harder, but not smarter. My health suffered and my family eventually unraveled around me. I often worked over seventy hours each week.

My efforts to improve facility productivity did lead to dramatic progress, however. These performance improvements came at a cost of near mutiny by my staff and team. I was an effective change master with improving facility performance but at a dire cost which diminished loyalty and employee satisfaction. My commitment to rapid change and reluctance to hear out complaints and concerns led to a much-improved facility with a much-disliked leader. Later, I came to see this experience was a necessary part of my education and evolution. It taught me the importance of listening to and caring for the needs of the team before and during the implementation of improvement initiatives. If we take care of those around us, they will take care of us. I eventually matured into a much better servant leader by the time I was transferred to my third field facility. Five years after my first field experience, I was assigned to the Houston Locomotive Repair Facility as plant manager.

It was a humid and hot afternoon in Houston, Texas, as I stood in the middle of an old red brick railroad factory building. This grand old structure had been built long before the neighboring modern skyscrapers of downtown Houston, which stood majestically less than one mile away. It was a huge shop building with a ceiling over fifty feet high that spanned a football field–sized area inside. It had been used for locomotive maintenance and repairs for decades, with its large arched doorways on two of its opposing walls that allowed locomotive movement into and out of that shop. I was a relatively new plant manager at this facility, having been transferred there several months beforehand from Los Angeles. I was conducting my daily tour of the facility when the machinist union representative Mario approached me. At this time in my career, I was ready to listen and be a servant leader. It took five years in the field for me to get to this point. It took forty-two years of living my life for me to get there.

WISE CONFRONTATION CAN STRENGTHEN A RELATIONSHIP

We were in a location where we were able to speak privately without being overheard by others. Mario asked me, "Do you think you are doing a good job here?"

His tone of voice dared me to respond. My response was calm and humble, "I think I am."

He countered with the following comment, "Well I think you are f@*#**g up things around here with all the changes you are making!"

I now had enough experience to realize that his anger toward me was an opportunity for building a relationship and to learn how to be a better manager and leader, as well. In that moment, I was secretly pleased this was happening. In that moment, I was confident this experience would lead to a mutually beneficial relationship in the future. What would have once been seen as an act of defiance was now seen as a cry for help, an opportunity for contribution, and making things better for the team.

I next asked Mario, "Why do you feel this way?"

He responded with three changes he disapproved of that he believed were occurring or were soon to occur at the Houston Locomotive Facility. He elaborated in an animated and antagonistic manner on these three concerns, which I will call A, B, and C. After I heard him out, I repeated back a summary of what he had just communicated. I then responded, "As to A, that is a new company-wide policy that we are required to comply with, and I have no choice but to enforce this new policy. As to B, yes that is my idea and one I believe will be successful here with reducing injuries (at that time the injury rate per man hours worked at that locomotive facility was the worst on the system), as I have seen it be successful at other locations. As for C, that is not in the plans for happening anytime soon, as far as I am aware."

When people are upset, they tend to be authentic and sincere. They are outwardly mad and aligned with their internal feelings; there is no need to guess how they really feel. They may not be logical, but they certainly are honest with their emotions. In these moments, it is important not to get caught up with becoming defensive and focus on a calm civil inquiry with them as to what and why they feel as they do. Occasionally, it may be best to schedule a later time to talk to allow their emotions to subside.

In the years that followed, Mario and his fellow machinist union leaders became close allies, and we developed a strong mutual respect for each other. That confrontation was the beginning of a great relationship between the two of us and improved my interactions with the machinist union representatives. We worked together on numerous local concerns and initiatives for improving safety, employee satisfaction, and shop-wide quality and production performance. Over the next several years, our locomotive facility went from being the worst with its injury rate to the being the best in both safety and productivity. I am most grateful for that experience and the opportunity to be part of the team we created there.

STRIVE FOR WIN-WIN SOLUTIONS TO BUILD ALLIANCES AND AVOID NEMESES

In business, as in our personal lives, when we sincerely respond to complaints and concerns there is potential to build healthy and strong relationships and make substantial progress. This was the lesson and shift in perspective I had evolved to. When we achieve satisfaction for folks by finding and instituting a remedy for a concern they have, the loyalty and harmony that follow are far stronger than if the problem had not arisen in the first place. Nearly always this remedy benefits many others, as well. It is wise to keep in mind that allies are more desirable than enemies. Allies and enemies can be around us for a long time. They can either hinder or help us with future progress and success. Always strive for win-win solutions to build alliances and avoid making an adversary who can later become your nemesis.

The common use of the language of setbacks, mistakes, and confrontation often restricts, if not imprisons our ability to make meaningful progress. Experiences that produce pain, upset, or regret are allies to embrace, not foes to flee or disparage. Seeing an act of defiance as a cry for help is one example. Common views of mistakes often lead to a major area of suffering that impacts many of us. To help you further reduce suffering and increase happiness (the pursuit of *Betterism*) in your lives, this chapter expands on a type of learning I call **Evolutionary Learning.** It is central to addressing the age-old problem with repeating the same behavior and hoping for different results. It is essential to our ability to adapt to the ever-changing circumstances of life. If I were to list the top ten things our children should learn, I contend that on that list would be how to leverage mistakes, setbacks, and confrontation as springboards for progress. *Evolutionary learning* is learning from our experiences in life, as opposed to formal educational learning.

This chapter is about what to do *after* a mistake or setback. In these circumstances, I believe it is important to clarify and categorize mistakes into two categories. Those two categories are fatal mistakes and non-fatal mistakes. This chapter speaks to the subject of non-fatal mistakes. Driving a car while intoxicated and causing an accident that cripples yourself or others is a fatal mistake. Assaulting your boss at work is another fatal mistake.

Evolutionary learning is experiential training available to us as we proceed with our lives. Just as an apprentice learns from the master, we too have much opportunity and need to learn from life as it unfolds around us. It is wise to see the objective dispassionate reality of *what is* as our master teacher. Let us **Be the Apprentice** and see ourselves as a student of life's experiences with its many twists and turns, with its many detours and undesired outcomes that are contrary to our initial expectations. *Evolutionary learning* is invaluable with reducing suffering, increasing happiness, and making progress and peace for ourselves and others.

DETOURS ARE THE SHORTEST WAY FORWARD

It is wise to avoid second guessing actions that led to an undesirable outcome. Belaboring how we (or they) *"should have"* done something else is a destructive diversion and depletion of our energy. Rather, it is better to see disappointing results which did not meet our expectations as a consequence of NOOT; it was inevitable that they would occur as they did. Successful future advancement depends on an iterative process where, like Thomas Edison, we try one filament after another until we achieve the best light bulb possible. We grow by taking action and calmly observing the consequence of that action. We won't know a better way until we try something new and can then dispassionately say. "Okay, that didn't work . . . let me try something different . . . something better . . . something wiser."

If our journey in life is to seek wisdom (as opposed to being right), we embrace the imperfections and detours as the shortest way forward and as the tantalizing spices of life that become teachers and sages for us.

When the student is ready the teacher will appear.
–Buddhist Proverb

Let's be mindful with words like "mistakes" or "screw-ups." The common usage of these words implies being wrong as opposed to being right. They are binary in nature, a *wrong vs. right* dead-end trap for our thinking. Those experiences of disappointing or upsetting outcomes were part of NOOT and unavoidable. They had to have occurred, just as they did, given all that had happened which preceded this. Going forward, I suggest we use a better word (an acronym) which embeds within it a path forward for progress and optimism. Let's call these undesired experiences **Learning Experiences for Growth (LEGs).** These experiences provide new legs for moving forward in a most wise manner!

The perspective of approaching a setback as a LEG precludes being trapped on that proverbial carousel of insanity with doing the same things over and over again and hoping to get a different result. With a better view of these events, by seeing them as LEGs, we begin to move on a successful trajectory toward healing and real progress. Here we avoid the waste of time and energy with being defensive, victimized, or outraged that often derails or depletes us. We can avoid having our time and energy diverted into protecting our ego or justifying ourselves with that crusade of being right and engaging in a right fight. An adversarial interaction also undermines the safety, trust, and respect within a relationship. By seeing a setback as a LEG, we are now focused on looking to be better.

If our identity is not grounded in merit and core values, we can be fragile and easily threatened. This is often a root cause for a low level of self-efficacy. By the time we get done defending, justifying, or beating ourselves up, we often run out of energy, commitment, or interest with making things any better and being better the next time. Unlike the movie *Groundhog Day*, where the protagonist makes small incremental improvements that build upon each other with each new cycle, we just go back to doing the same stuff over and over again with no progress forward at all. This typical manner in which many of us deal with undesirable outcomes leaves us "without a leg" to stand on, and we are doomed to fail again and again.

MAKE IT A LEARNING EXPERIENCE FOR GROWTH (LEG)

A more desirable approach is to limit becoming derailed and depleted. After a setback, we can then quickly get back on track and then pursue a healthier route forward with fewer derailments in the future. By quickly recognizing and accepting that an undesirable result was inevitable, that it was NOOT, we keep the path forward clear. This removes a potentially huge obstacle that often causes us to stall or derail. It also circumvents any tendency for vindictive retaliation. This accelerates our ability to learn and sets us up to improve with lasting habits that minimize reoccurrence.

Yes, it is likely after an undesired outcome we will initially second guess ourselves, be angered with another, or become consumed in an emotional tempest. But this will pass quickly if we are committed and mindful of the process of *evolutionary learning*. The following is a model for interacting in a successful manner with setbacks, mistakes, confrontation, and undesirable experiences:

Moving Forward with LEGs ... Learning Experiences for Growth

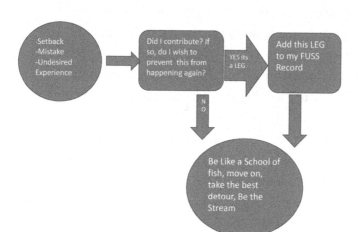

Overview of the LEG Process

When our actions result in hurt or upset for another, it is wise to err on the side of compassion and quickly show sincere remorse and apologize. However, do not admit to being wrong if you don't believe you are. Rather, it is best to say something like, "I am so sorry you feel that way," or, "I am sorry you are upset."

We can later sort that out to see the degree of our complicity (if any) and our need for making improvements and amends.

We begin this process by asking ourselves the following question: *"Did I contribute to this issue in some way and if so, do I wish to prevent or minimize it from happening again?"*

If the answer is NO, *be like a school of fish* and quickly pivot to get back on track with being a *Betterist* pursuing more good and less bad. With *Betterism,* we are committed to *being the stream,* always in an advancing motion toward the better. If the answer is YES, then it is a Learning Experience for Growth. We list the LEG in our FUSS record for later handling. We then pivot like a school of fish and continue *being the stream* with the knowledge that we will follow up at a later time to learn and improve as a result of this undesired experience.

We will handle this in the near future with three habits. Here we use the FUSS process, our scheduled week in review session, and morning routine with ISTEPs. The outcome with the FUSS process is to make things better, not perfect; to improve, not necessarily change. The intent is to reduce, not necessarily eliminate. We will generally measure our progress with observation of the duration, intensity, and frequency with this type of occurrence in the future (*durinfre*). Be careful with the term *change,* as it is binary in nature and prone to lead to disappointment. The term *change* is ambiguous and a poor measure for improvement. It is far better to notice improvements with the duration, intensity, and frequency of both the positive and negative experiences.

Be like a school of fish = when faced with a threat or upset we quickly pivot past it.

Be the stream = The state of *being the stream* is one of continually movement and motion forward with our progress. Like the stream, we quickly and easily divert around, over, and under obstacles placed in our path. Here we are committed to forward movement.

What does not qualify as a LEGs

Knowing what should or should not become a focus for later assessment and handling is crucial to utilizing our energy and time effectively. It is wise to predetermine categories of what is worthy of future follow up action. By thinking this through ahead of time before we find ourselves in a moment of concern, we can discern if the issue needs to be in our FUSS log. Predetermining categories for future handling has an additional benefit with helping us realize that some matters are not worth dwelling upon. This allows us to sort out the trivial or uncontrollable from the meaningful actions that are essential for our future happiness and progress.

Proactive classification of what counts as a LEG is an investment in your future peace of mind and ability to remain calm and clearheaded during and after a setback. When you take time to think through what does and doesn't quality as a LEG, you will actually have far fewer upsets in the future, as well. As a result of this pre-work, you will quickly discern shortly after something undesirable happens, that the event will fall in one of two categories. One category is "there is nothing to be done here, I'm moving on." The second category is "there is work to do here that will produce future benefit, I will capture it now in my FUSS log, then move on. I will come back and learn from it at a later time." What previously became an emotional storm is now calmly viewed.

You will find that the number of future upsets will decrease as you then see that some detours and undesirable outcomes are not worth taking the time and effort to avoid in the future because:

- They are outliers on the statistical bell curve of probabilities (small chance of happening again)

- They are worth passing up because they are but a small annoyance, like forgetting to take out the trash or misplacing our keys

- After a bit of reflection, we may gain clarity and perspective that *our view of the event and not the event itself was the problem* (misunderstanding, not knowing extenuating reasons for someone's emotional state, or lack of real empathy and understanding are examples here)

- We may also see that we did nothing incorrectly and it was another's issue entirely, like asking our child if they finished their homework and they in turn get annoyed with us, no follow up required.

Examples of situations which do not qualify as LEGs are:

- Shoelace breaks

- Stranger comes up to us and says they don't like our hairstyle

- While driving our car and we go over a pothole obscured by being filled with water in the rain

- Respectfully, calmly, and privately letting an employee at work know that they are not following required safety protocols and they get angry

- Uncharacteristically forgetting to pick up something from the grocery store

- Being a line of demarcation with our children and letting them know when they are behaving in an unacceptable manner and that there will be consequences for their behavior despite an adverse reaction by them

There is another category of mistakes and setbacks which will not require our follow up, and those are fatal mistakes. By their very nature, fatal mistakes are those that lead to dire outcomes. They leave little room for learning, as these actions often take us to a point of no return. Punching the boss in the nose would be a fatal mistake. Driving without a seatbelt then being seriously injured in an automobile accident would also quality as a fatal mistake. The consequences with these mistakes are unmistakable and compel obvious future action.

Keeping it on the Radar (or Sonar for our Navy sailors) the Follow-Up Setback System (FUSS)

Learning from an undesired experience is one of our best opportunities to grow and reduce future upsets. Our evolution as a species, with its many marvelous achievements, has resulted from learning largely from the process of trial and error. We learned from those actions that worked as well as those that did not work. On an individual level, we too can best improve by seeing this process of mistakes and disappointments as part of NOOT with how progress is made. We can embrace and welcome these events for the future benefit they will bring when we see them as our mentors, teachers, and coaches.

After a disappointing or upsetting experience, it may be wise to keep this event on the radar for later review. At a later time, we follow up and decide whether to make this a true *Learning Experience for Growth*. Here, we identify important areas for personal improvement. It is essential that we have a system for recording them for later follow-up review and possible action. That is the purpose of your FUSS log. Here are the steps for this follow-up process:

1. Decide what goes into the FUSS log. Be selective here as to avoid focus on the stained living room carpet while the kitchen is burning down.

2. Review your FUSS log weekly as part of your sacred habit of holding a scheduled *week in review session* to see what worked and what didn't work during the week.

3. Decide which focus you will pursue and work on (if any) for improvement in the upcoming week. Consider adding a daily ISTEP to your morning routine if it will require a period of time to make the progress you desire.

4. If it can be handled with one future action, use the *One, Two, Three of a Determined Decision* process to progress your LEG.

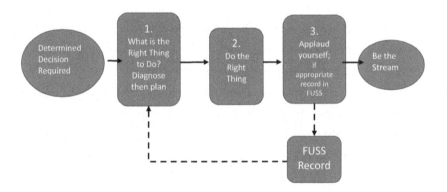

For this system to effectively work to help you find more peace and progress with less frustration and upset, you are best served to have **Three Key Sacred Habits**. Remember "Sacred" implies it is absolutely non-negotiable and foundational to your healing, truth, and progress. Those three sacred habits are:

1. Use the *Follow-Up Setback System*

2. Have a *Morning Routine* that includes plans for a daily ISTEPs action(s)

3. Hold a scheduled *Week in Review* session with yourself, where you develop strategies for following up with FUSS log concerns

1. Use the Follow-Up Setback System (see Using the "Follow-Up Setback System" for details★)

With the *Follow-Up Setback System*, practice and master the habit of recording setbacks and detours for future analysis. You can use a smart phone for dictating into a designated "note section," leave a voice mail for yourself, or carry a small pad with you to record the event in a brief manner. Usually, when we are emotional over something that has just happened, we are not in the mood for doing that. That time, however, is precisely the right time to record the occurrence for two reasons.

First: It captures the issue for later handling, and it is not lost or neglected because of subsequent activities and events that can distract us.

Second: It limits the negative impact of an emotional upset. It helps us to pivot away from being distracted. Instead of depleting our time and energy with the *should have* and *could have* thoughts, where we second guess ourselves or get angry with the situation, we focus on future beneficial action(s). We can quickly "move on," knowing it will be handled. It calms us, and as a result our focus shifts to solution and resolution and away from disappointment, frustration, or anger. The value to one's self-efficacy here is immeasurable and profound. It will generate confidence and hope in that moment of turmoil, despair, or anger. You know that in the near future it will be handled well and in a manner that will make you even better. You will use it as a stepping-stone for progress in your life that will also have a positive benefit for the people you care about.

2. Have a sacred Morning Routine (see Worksheet "Marvelous Start Morning Routine" for details★)
Within your morning routine, you will decide and plan specific actions for that day that will be building blocks for progress. These daily actions are called ISTEPs, Intentional Simple Tiny Efforts for Progress, that are your actions for traction. These are small daily activities to keep you on track with making real progress. They support your follow-up plan developed and identified in your *Week in Review* session.

3. Have a sacred Week in Review session (see Conducting a "Week in Review Session" for details★)
It is recommended that you schedule a reoccurring weekly meeting for yourself (this is to be a sacred habit for yourself much like a weekly attendance of a religious service or AA/NA meeting) at which time you will review your FUSS log record and initiate an appropriate follow-up plan for handling the problem using the *determined decision* process and/ or your ISTEPs daily activities that you select each morning as part of your morning routine.

Here you will design a strategy for determining the best course for future actions to learn from the experience. You will determine if a new habit is necessary and what daily types of activities you wish to and can sustain.

★*Note: all worksheets can be found at www.executivecoachingservices.net*

Examples of what qualifies as a LEG:

a. We decide to quit our job and take work with a much higher paying organization. One year later, we find our new position grueling and frustrating, and we are fatigued with hours spent keeping up with the job. We regret having quit our previous employment and previous organization. This is a LEG where we can develop clarity for ourselves as to what is and is not important for us through our clarity and certainty with our values. Next time we will research better to assure our values and the job requirements are aligned.

b. We respond in an emotional and angry manner to someone in our family over a decision they have made. They become very upset and respond with an escalating emotion. We see that our disapproval has been smoldering for quite a while and like the straw that breaks the camel's back, led to an emotional eruption. The LEG here is to take the time in the future to understand another and have a sincere compassion and empathy for them all along. Yet, at the same time recognizing which behavior(s) is off limits and requires a boundary because of its toxic impact on us. Then we implement a planned calm and respectful consequence toward the other by setting boundaries with consequences. This was addressed previously with the *Symbiotic 3: Empathy, Boundaries and Consequences.*

c. We communicate with a loved one by telling them they are creating problems in the relationship. Afterward, the other explodes into a tirade of accusations and upset. In the future, the better path forward is to work to understand who they are, their likes and dislikes, their fears and joys, and their insecurities, as well. Learning about what our own boundaries are as well and having dispassionate consequences that come into play are crucial. Lastly, we must be be mindful with our timing and tone as well as use of empowering wise language so to focus on the behavior and not the person.

These examples are but a tiny sample of the numerous setbacks, detours, and undesirable experiences we may face. This is life. However, we have the potential for limiting these negative experiences and their impact on us in the future. We can be optimistic with our belief that no matter what life delivers, we will find a way to get past a problem and become better for it. It is possible to limit the duration, intensity, and frequency of their future impact on us. Far better to be angry for five minutes than five hours or once a week versus twice a day. We can ultimately have a view that sees detours to our expected progress as adventures and opportunities. Instead of being upset over a need for a detour, we focus our energy on selecting the best detour and using the experience to be better in the future. We can embrace setbacks and become grateful for them, as well. This perspective is where our peace of mind resides. The path to heaven (on Earth) is often through the gates of hell. Keep on walking forward my friends, use wise empowering language, and learn from your experiences to be ever better each and every day. When we recognize these as opportunities and have the confidence in ourselves to follow through with an improvement plan, our peace and progress flourish.

CHAPTER 18

Proactive Learning, the Poison of Stupid

What do I wish to learn next?

"Be the Brave Velcro Turtle"

Without empathy, we limit our understanding of what is occurring around us and subsequently reduce the effectiveness of our responses and future actions to improve.

–Michael Starr

John had a congenial way about him. Being six-foot, one-inch tall, physically fit, and handsome he had a commanding presence. His stature and appearance gave him confidence and a degree of fearlessness that made it easy for him to joke with his friends and baseball teammates. He was bold and at times brash. His dedication to baseball practice and openness to being coached ensured he had a promising future as a shortstop baseball player. His self-motivation for improving his sports talent was high, and he was intense when it came to honing his baseball skills. Yet despite his often happy go lucky nature, he could be easily offended. He was a hot-headed baseball player much like another infielder, the great combative Yankees player and coach, Billy Martin.

Early on in his life, John was enthusiastic with a promising view of the future. John married young and soon had two sons. His optimism and enthusiasm came to an early end as a result of an initial injury in baseball and another subsequent injury at work. A once hopeful future was replaced with despair. His feeling of self-worth came to an all-time low. His temper flared ever more, and his past dysfunctional childhood upbringing surfaced with increasing levels of anger. He came to a point in his life where he could find no reason to go on.

I have mentored hundreds of folks during my forty-plus years in my professional capacity as a Naval Officer and as a manager in business. Likewise, with my personal coaching business, I have guided many through a number of programs for self-improvement. John (not his real name) is one person who particularly stands out as a success story. He is an excellent example of how progress can occur for people when two key components are present: self-motivation and wise strategy. Just as a rocket needs both a consistent propellant and a guided trajectory to be successful with its mission, so it is for us to be able to hit the targets and goals we desire. Self-motivation is the propellant. A wisely guided strategy is the trajectory.

When we started our coaching relationship, John's life was in turmoil. He had been despondent for several years and involved in an abusive relationship. John had little confidence in his ability to make any improvement, let alone have a feeling of success. He had been unemployed most of the previous five years and on the verge of losing his family. Yet, despite a long history of physical pain, missteps, and stagnation, he was highly self-motivated to do something different, something better, when we met. For him, now was the time to do something different. I was fortunate to meet him at just the right time for us to have great chemistry for progress. Yes, indeed, when the student is ready the teacher does appear. So it was for us both, as John became my teacher, as well.

Ongoing self-motivation is one of the two key components for progress. The other is having a path forward that is both wise and sustainable. John brought the self-motivation. My coaching philosophy assisted with a guided trajectory. Like a guided missile moving toward a target, the propellant and guidance system where in place and working. For John, today there are multiple destinations and journeys ahead that are certain to be filled with success and satisfaction.

PERSONAL PROGRESS BUILDS ON
FOUNDATIONAL KNOWLEDGE

John had a limited level of formal education. He did not have a high school diploma. He often spoke with poor grammar that detracted from his communication with others. However, he had great common sense and the ability to grasp the new knowledge and perspectives I presented. Once exposed to new ideas, he could easily sort the wheat from the chaff and see the core principle. He was a quick study. In our coaching relationship, my focus with him was with his *foundational background* and *learning distractions.* These two perspectives formed the launch pad for future progress. John's path of *Betterism* with seeking more good and less bad was off to an encouraging start.

With my coaching clients, I share the following: "At the age of __ (the age I am at the time) I have likely had more setbacks, made more mistakes, and had more screw ups then you can imagine."

It is important that people know they are not alone with their life challenges, past and present. I share with them that I have experienced many setbacks, and as a result have learned to be a far better person, yet I am still a work in progress seeking to be even better. I also explain that

I am grateful to have a strong interest in learning from my undesired experiences. I am most fortunate to have arrived at a perspective which recognizes my mistakes and setbacks as friends and teachers. Perhaps due to having parents who nurtured and loved me unconditionally, I am not easily offended and eagerly seek out critical feedback from others to improve myself. This inclination toward *evolutionary learning* (presented in the previous chapter), has given me some degree of wisdom and success. John wanted this for himself. He did not know how but was primed to learn. The student was ready.

John was coachable; he was very coachable. He had the self-motivation to be better. He also trusted me and felt confident I was looking out for his long-term best interests. My coaching with him was pro bono. He recognized that my efforts were altruistic and had no financial motive. I was selfish, though, with this experience and commitment to John. To be more precise, I was *wise-selfish*. My self-motivation was with the satisfaction in seeing him make progress and believing his progress would have a positive ripple effect on his children and people around him in the years ahead. W*ise-selfishness* always seeks a win-win outcome.

JOHN BEGAN WITH DAILY ISTEPS

We started with one small achievement, daily walks, as success does indeed breed more success. He began a daily routine of walking outdoors and recording and reporting the number of minutes walked each day. As with the Chinese proverb that every journey of a thousand miles begins with the first step, he had begun his journey. This daily habit of outdoor walking and recording time walked was the beginning of his positive forward trajectory.

I did my best to reinforce my belief in him and his ability to make significant progress for himself. With help from relatives and with his renewed drive to succeed, John was soon back working full time. He had set up a new living arrangement for himself that assisted with his peace of mind and disengagement from the abusive treatment he had long experienced. He was saying things like, "Look at me, I'm really making progress!"

John began reading self-improvement books and listening to motivational audios featuring speakers like John Maxwell. He was thirsty for learning to be better for himself and his children. The mutual reward for him and for myself with his progress goes beyond words. What helped me to help John, to guide him with his *proactive learning,* was the use of wise language that led to wise thinking. In particular, the wise language for *proactive learning* has two specific terms: **foundational background** and **learning distraction(s).**

The previous chapter discussed **evolutionary learning,** which is reactive as it addressed *learning after the fact* from our mistakes and undesired experiences. This chapter focuses on another type of learning I call **proactive learning**. This is a preparatory learning which is accomplished ahead of achieving a desired outcome, such as becoming an accomplished musician or a successful health care provider. This is the way we gain new knowledge and wisdom by intention. This is learning that prepares us to be better in the future.

Some examples of *pro-active learning* are:

- Attendance of a class, seminar, or workshop
- Enrollment in a formal education program, such as high school or college
- Reading a self-improvement book
- Studying the Bible, Koran, or Tanakh
- Interactions with a coach
- Being in an apprenticeship program
- On the job training
- Watching an online video, such as one found on YouTube, to learn how to do something

- Observing or listening with the intention of learning something new
- Honing our skills in an area important to us
- Following up on our natural curiosity

PROACTIVE LEARNING FIRST DETERMINES WHAT'S IMPORTANT

Proactive learning often does not occur as well as it can. Our ability to learn new things within the context of being better in the future often stalls, is diverted, moves painfully slowly, or progresses with erratic spurts. At times, what starts as a laser beam of focus quickly diffuses into a feckless glow. New ideas don't stick, especially when it comes to applying them in real life. There is a disconnect between what we memorize and what we actualize.

Improvement begins with a clarity with what is important and what is not so important for us. The *Ten Convictions* you developed (hopefully you have) are foundational to this wisdom. Your *Ten Convictions* are who you are; they are at the core of your identity. Clarity comes with this understanding of your creed of what is right and what is wrong. Priorities for making decisions about what to do and when to do them improve substantially when you have a core set of wisely-written convictions. I encourage you to choose wisely what you seek to learn. Be selective with what you pursue to be better in the future. When we desire everything, we often end up with nothing.

THE POISION OF "STUPID"

One large obstacle with being effective with proactive learning is use of dangerous words that harm, i.e., tyrannical words. Often, we hear comments such as he/she is "a moron" or "dumb." We, ourselves, may be concerned about that and thinking, "I don't want to look like an idiot."

Let us recognize that these words of dumb, idiot, stupid, moron, etc., are a tempting boost to our identity when we apply them to someone else. They are toxic when we apply them to ourselves. In either case, they are dysfunctional and just flat out wrong. They are a poison to both the accused and accuser. As we look at well-known quotes by the famous and accomplished, we see they often use this demeaning language, as well. Even these geniuses and well-respected folks have a fundamental misunderstanding of human nature. Perhaps they, too, are guilty of falling prey to the temptation of wanting to feel superior. Perhaps this attitude may have been a contributing factor and motivator for their achievements? From Einstein to Martin Luther King Jr. to Napoleon Bonaparte to Stephen Hawking, they use "stupid" in a disparaging manner that misses the core understanding of humanity with empathy and compassion.

- Only two things are infinite, the universe and human stupidity, I'm not sure about the former. –Albert Einstein

- In politics stupidity is not a handicap. –Napoleon Bonaparte

- Stupidity is a talent for misconception. –Edgar Allen Poe

- We are in danger of destroying ourselves by greed and stupidity. -Stephen Hawking

- There is no sin except stupidity. –Oscar Wilde

- Stupidity has a knack of getting its way. –Albert Camus

- Nothing in all the world is more dangerous than sincere ignorance and conscientious stupidity. –Martin Luther King, Jr.

- A stupid man's report of what a clever man says can never be accurate, because he unconsciously translates what he hears into something he can understand. –Bertrand Russell

In the instance that we say or think "you are a moron," it makes us feel and think, "I am not a moron but you are, therefore I am superior to you."

This view is a contributor to *contra-identities* referenced in previous chapters, where our importance is based on finding fault with others. There is a great temptation to go there, as it is a quick affirmation for ourselves. Not only is it wrong to use this, as it is demeaning, it actual says nothing meaningful to improve matters. It embeds a relationship dead end with its use. This language dooms our view of another as unredeemable and an easy write off. This judgment leads to a view of certainty that another is a hopeless case. We can develop a belief such as, "What did I expect? He's a fool! I am wasting my time talking to him."

Woven into this language is a self-fulfilling prophecy that discourages another and sends a message either directly through words or indirectly through body language of no confidence in them. Some people respond to that abusive language, and as a result do work harder to overcome the image, but most of us flourish when others believe in us and show empathy for us.

When we think and speak with words such as *stupid* directed at another, it can be a way for us to cope with unmet expectations, as well. Our disappointment or frustration can lead us into a temptation to get some instant gratification with revenge. Thinking or calling them a derogatory term may release our contained upset and temporarily appease our dark side with a thought like "that idiot should have known better." Unfortunately, this behavior and perspective is counterproductive. It diverts us away from being effective and influential as well as shattering our peace of mind. It promotes unhealthy relationships as it kills empathy in the crib before it can grow. *Without empathy, we limit our understanding of what is occurring around us and subsequently reduce the effectiveness of our responses and future actions to improve.*

FOUNDATIONAL BACKGROUND AND LEARNING DISTRACTIONS LIMIT PROGRESS

When we strip away this immature explanation with why another does things that don't meet with our approval, we can then begin to achieve progress and harmony. Going beyond myopic superiority, we are wise to see that the person is at an undesirable level with their current ability to learn new things. This undesirable level with their ability to learn has a reason for being that way. The key terms which provide empowering clarity here are:

1. *Foundational background*—preexisting knowledge and experience

2. *Learning distraction(s)*—emotional predispositions and/or pre-occupation distraction

Foundational background and *learning distractions* are major reasons why people (including ourselves) learn slowly or not at all. It is often why they repeat the same mistakes over and over again. However, when we can discern these two wise language terms, we are on track for progress and success. With this view, we can now ask empowering questions that help properly diagnose root causes, and as a result point us toward effective actions for achieving desired results. Instead of thinking "they are stupid" or "I am stupid," we can now ask empowering questions that lead to effective diagnosis and remediation. The empowering questions begin with, "What foundational background or learning distractions are limiting progress here?"

Imagine how differently the communication between individuals and within an individual themselves would be if they were to think:

"My/your lack of *foundational background* with this subject limits my/your ability to learn about it. It is time to make a plan to acquire more background understanding."

Or, "My/your *learning distractions* are preventing me/you from being able to focus on hearing or seeing knowledge that could benefit you. Time to pursue identifying what distractions are getting in the way."

This enlightened perspective shifts our view to one that leads us toward a more prudent direction that focuses on achieving results and away from fear or harmful self-righteousness. We now have embedded and woven into our language a predisposition to ask empowering questions that can make things better, in contrast to a binary label that pigeonholes us into a dead end, stifles progress, and undermines healthy relationships.

Foundational Background

When I speak of *foundational background,* I speak of preexisting training, understanding, education, and experience. Attempting to learn trigonometry before learning algebra would be very difficult. Having success with conflict resolution would also be difficult if we do not understand how to listen effectively. With an absence of *foundational background*, we just don't know certain things; we are ignorant of them. Both knowledge and experience are key components with foundational background. Experience helps us to relate to what we see and put things into perspective. It supports our certainty and convictions, as well. Without a certain level of life experience, it is difficult to truly be empathetic toward others or confident that brighter days lie ahead.

VELCRO NEEDS TWO OPPOSING SURFACES TO STICK AND HOLD

Our existing knowledge and experience help us understand and remember. We are able to put things into a context that interrelates to things we currently know and believe. It allows us to make sense of things and solidly build upon them as we would with framing a home on a solid concrete foundation. Without *foundational background*, new information just goes in one ear (or eye) and out the other. We are wise to see new effective learning as **Velcro Learning**. Velcro needs an opposing strip to work properly. Likewise, for new experience or informational knowledge to be retained, it must be within some pre-existing context for it to stick with us and be retained.

We all have limitations with our experiential or educational backgrounds. Learning in a vacuum is difficult. If we were to attempt to understand an advanced complicated subject without understanding the basics, we would find that there is nothing for the new information or experience to stick to. Instead of an opposing Velcro strip that allows us to connect and attach, we have Teflon surfaces that slide past one another. Some examples where *foundational background* is important are:

- Home maintenance and repairs require understanding of plumbing, electricity, carpentry, etc. Learning to make home improvements and repairs requires background understanding of tool use, repair materials, and techniques.

- Meaningful self-improvement requires understanding of how to decide what is important in your life, how to create habits that are sustainable, and how to keep your self-motivation going.

- Learning a new technique in software programing requires an understanding of the basics of that software design.

- Relationship improvement requires relationship listening skills.

- Getting past hate and resentment requires knowing how to set boundaries and have empathy for others, as with the NOOT concept introduced earlier in this book, as well as with the *Symbiotic 3* with empathy, boundaries, and consequences.

- Being an effective teacher requires subject matter expertise and a solid understanding of human nature and wise use of communication skills.

Learning Distractions fall into two subcategories:

1. The first is with the *emotional predispositions* we have with incli-nations toward feeling threatened, wanting to be liked, or need for superiority.

2. The second has to do with being *preoccupied* with concerns and worries.

Both will limit, if not prevent, our ability to absorb new information and ideas for improvement.

1. Emotional predispositions

Turtles are quick to retreat within their shells at the slightest perceived threat. While within their shell, their ability to see or hear what is going on around them is greatly restricted if not stopped. When we become defensive with our communications with another, we are retreating into our shell and shutting down our ability to learn. Likewise, when we are overly eager to please, we may exclusively focus on being nice and say things that make the other person feel good, and as a result lose an opportunity to learn and notice worthwhile information. Excessive desire to please is a form of retreat from observing. Perhaps the most disturbing trend these days is the quickness with which some people become offended and are eager to stand on a moral stool of superiority. This once again is another form of retreat away from being open, vul-nerable, and available to learn. These are turtle retreating behaviors that put people within a shell that is impervious to noticing opportunities and lessons for improvement.

When a turtle remains within their shell, they are not in a posi-tion to observe or process what is going on around them. When we emotionally retreat, our heads are visible, but our minds are largely unavailable and not present; our minds are in a turtle shell.

These emotionally distracted ways of being cause potentially valu-able information to be diverted and restricted from being heard, seen, or considered. You can't absorb new information if you are inside your mental shell. We may have the *foundational background* but are not able to capitalize on it. We are isolated from opportunities for learning, and as a result none occur.

Some examples of emotional predispositions that limit our ability to absorb and process new information are:

- Excessive worry with looking stupid of foolish, which may indicate we believe that we are not good enough.

- Having a *contra identity* that is built on making ourselves important by making others wrong, unimportant, or less than we are.

- Fear of things we don't understand or are contrary to our current views, and as a result make us feel threatened and become defensive or self-righteous. This fear can stifle our natural curiosity and preclude valuable learning from taking place.

- Preoccupation with a need to be liked and approved.

- Being easily offended—hurting people are easily hurt. Here, unmet expectations from the past can surface as anger in the present.

With *learning distractions* that are emotionally triggered, we react with defensiveness, right fights, blame games, or shutting down any interest for further communications. Here our emotions spring up as an unconscious response. There is a déjà vu feeling that arises from some past trauma, disappointments, or exposure to disempowering language. Emotional triggers derail our ability to calmly listen and later follow up and make needed improvements to reduce the recurrence of upsets. A need to compete and beat another falls within this category. We can get caught up with defending why we are "right" and why they are wrong. This is a classic category called "right fights." These emotional responses are often major contributors with poisoning relationships, as well.

As we become more self-aware of our emotional triggers, as with our need for approval or need to be right, we improve our ability to learn. We are more likely to stay outside our protective shells to hear and see what is going on around us. This allows us to better absorb valuable information. With this understanding of self, we can recognize the harm those retreats do. As we face these emotional inclinations, we can notice them early before they take over our behavior. With self-awareness of our emotional inclinations, we are more likely to face these imperfections and allow ourselves to be vulnerable and open. The result is that we get smarter and wiser. Our relationships improve rather than devolve. We do not retreat prematurely, and we become better at processing valuable information that promotes personal and interpersonal improvements.

As we align our actions with our beliefs, as with our *ten convictions*, we are less vulnerable and more willing to do the right thing, and as a result more willing to learn.

2. Being Preoccupied

It is difficult to concentrate when you are preoccupied with a major concern or worry. When we are preoccupied with worry or focused on an agenda, we are mentally closed off. Whether we are listening, reading, or observing, our thoughts are distracted beyond where we are at the time, and as a result, we limit our ability to learn and see what is going on in the now. Many of us can become embroiled with life's challenges; sometimes we are so familiar with this state of constant anxiety or worry that we may have a tendency to unconsciously perpetuate it. Recognizing that this is going on is important. Learning to focus on things within our control and having a plan to address concerns can help compartmentalize these fears and insecurities. We can achieve a state of mind where we believe that current challenges are in the process of being handled the best they can be. We can become confident that they will definitely be handled in the future as a result of our habits and guided trajectory for mitigation or resolution. In the subsequent chapter regarding "Results Matter," a method for getting important things done is presented to further your ability to succeed and believe in your ability to achieve. You will find as you build wise habits and empowering ways of seeing the world around you, your self-efficacy will improve and the tendency to immerse yourself in constant worry and anxiety will diminish.

Some examples of learning distractions that limit our ability to absorb and process new information are:

- Preoccupation with projects or commitments, especially when we overcommit.

- Preoccupation with a deadline.

- Personal turmoil, worry, or upset with a mistake, setback, or a family crisis such as with debt, unhealthy relationships, or work uncertainties.

- Preoccupation with ourselves. In contrast, as we increase focus and interest on learning from others and learning from our life experiences, we decrease focus on our own personal worry and fear. Likewise, as we seek to help others by best understanding and responding to them so as to empower them to succeed, we also reduce our own preoccupation with self.

Yes, genetics play a part with our *proactive learning* ability, but not a dominant one for most of us. Few of us are born prodigies or savants and destined to be the next Einstein, Marie Curie, or Katherine Johnson. For most of us mere mortals, the limitations and restrictions to our progress and potential fall more into the arena of "nurture" than the domain of "nature" with its DNA roots of our humanity. When we recognize our tendency to retreat away from certain conversations or information, we recognize our turtle nature and the importance of staying outside our shells. When we are mindful with our listening and observation, we are far more willing to ask those "stupid" questions that previously we may have been embarrassed or afraid to ask. As a result, we will absorb more important information and get things right the first time. This will add to our foundational background and our ability to better process information and feedback in the future. If we can combine our Velcro learning with our awareness of *learning distractions,* we can **Be the brave Velcro turtle** which builds foundational background and avoids learning distractions.

Institutional Education—Be Cautious

Institutional education is one of the most common means for building foundational background knowledge in our culture. Schools and colleges are at the core of this background knowledge. In them, we hopefully learn principles and foundational information which become steppingstones for achieving bigger and better things in the future.

Our life learning is best served when we combine and optimize both *proactive learning* and *evolutionary learning.* Unfortunately, there appears to be an unhealthy trend away from the principles and practice of *evolutionary learning.* Too often, we fail to learn from our personal experiences to determine what is effective and what is not, where we learn from what we ourselves see, hear, and experience. There is an increased level of tyranny being introduced in our common language, especially in educational institutions, that works against clarity and objectivity. Educational institutions, political leadership, social media, and media in general are complicit with a new *Brave New World* view that it is their place to tell you "what" to think as opposed to "how" to think. Civil debate is often discouraged and opposing views demonized. Bastions of education are trending toward adopting and encouraging a position of: "we will tell you what you are really seeing and hearing."

This is a dangerous development that is moving our culture and citizens toward confusion, anger, and divisiveness and away from critical thinking and civil debate. It is a near blatant assertion of "don't believe your lying eyes," which is being promoted to achieve someone else's agenda.

Many believe that today's formal educational learning has been largely over emphasized and overrated. In many instances, educational institutions are actively contributing to confusion and conflict. The cultures within these institutions have persecuted those who disagree with a prevailing politically correct view or the existing culture of identity politics on campus. They are promoting absurd beliefs as with the current gender identity debacle which conflates gender with sexual preference. Perhaps a wise attitude and approach with institutional learning is to first understand what is being said, then next challenge it to see if it rings true for you. Be mindful to discern objective educational information from indoctrination aimed at some political agenda.

How to Improve Your Foundational Background

- Have a natural curiosity and follow up quickly to better understand through personal research.

- Identify important areas for your self-improvement then seek out mentors, readings, videos, classes, etc. to make progress there. Make a plan that uses ISTEPs within your sacred Morning Routine. (See Worksheet "Marvelous Start Morning Routine")

How to Reduce Learning Distractions

- **Self-awareness**—Work on objectively identifying your fears and needs and face them courageously. Therapists and life coaches can be helpful here. Pursue identifying the harm that emotional triggers do to you and the people around you.

- **Empathy**—The more you can understand why another is as they are, the more likely you will communicate effectively with them and perceive them in a healthy way. This is a win-win approach that benefits all.

- **Compartmentalize**—Work on one problem at a time with a clear understanding of what the problem is and what you can do about it. Have a plan and work that plan. Focused action is an excellent elixir for worry.

- **Listen**—Mature your listening skills in line with the relationship listening advice in the previous chapter. Increase your focus with caring for another and placing your concerns on the back burner when communicating with them.

- **Develop Clarity**—Learn to determine what is and what isn't, and see where you have some influence and work on that. In places you have no control, move on and surrender to reality.

- **Limit your commitments**—avoid the tendency to agree to do more than can be comfortably accomplished. Better to under promise and over deliver than not be our word, create unmet expectations, or be in a frenzy with our "doings".

- **Encourage**—Seek to be better at lifting others up and guiding them and spend less time being preoccupied with self.

When we grow and improve, we can live our lives with vitality and purpose. *Betterism* is a philosophy of continual pursuit with having more joy, satisfaction, and harmony with less fear, upset, and conflict. As you hone your ability to learn both from your experiences and with your desired interests, your peace of mind, progress, and healing will go well for you.

CHAPTER 19

Results Matter: Diagnose Properly Before Prescribing

Is this a symptom or an underlying root cause?

"Be the Diagnosing Doctor"

Albert Einstein was once asked: "If you have one hour to save the world, how would you spend that hour?" He replied, "I would spend fifty-five minutes defining the problem and then five minutes solving it."[22]

In the previous two chapters, the subjects of *reactive learning (evolutionary learning)* and *proactive learning* were discussed. In one case, we are looking to make things better after the fact, as with a setback, mistake, or undesired experience. In the other case, we pursue knowledge and skills we wish to acquire that are aspirational in nature prior to a desired accomplishment. In this chapter, we take a deeper and more detailed look at what it takes to best guide these learning efforts toward real results.

The philosophy of *Betterism* melds journey with destination into a symbiotic relationship. The destination creates the vision that drives your daily actions for progress. With your pursuit toward a particular destination for improvement, you may make a large investment with the use of your time, effort, and money. These pursuits may take weeks, months, or even years of action. When it comes to making things better for ourselves, it is important to have a proper definition of the concern we wish to deal with. Without a proper assessment of the problem, the underlying causes can easily be misdiagnosed. We may waste time, energy, and money and possibly even make things worse for ourselves and others. It is very important that we properly select and define a concern or interest to achieve a clear diagnosis and begin a meaningful journey forward. Many spend their careers working to achieve something they think important, only to lose their health and important relationships in the process.

Achieving meaningful results begins with a concise, wisely written problem statement. In order to separate symptoms from causes, the problem statement must be objective and untainted without any bias as to the cause. Symptoms are usually what brought about our interest for improvement in the first place. Causes are the underlying reason the symptoms appeared. We may have a recurring experience with arguments in a relationship. Those arguments are symptoms of deeper issues. In this case, the path for real progress is not necessarily to limit conversation so that there is nothing to argue about, but rather to seek to understand more fundamental causes such as poor listening skills or personal dissatisfaction with our own lives being projected onto another.

This chapter will focus on the first half of successful problem solving, that being proper definition and diagnosis of the concern, as opposed to the subsequent countermeasure action strategy for achieving the desired improvement. The following chapter on Leadership will address taking subsequent action for getting better.

The following experiences are intended to give context to the overall process toward achieving results with a team, family, or work group.

My Early Years—The Golden Rule Hurt Me

I have always embraced and solicited direct feedback about what I may have done wrong. I am not easily offended by candid criticism, as I see how important it can be to become a better person. I often wondered why others would not want to hear "the truth" so that they would be better able to determine where to improve. In the past I was more than willing, if not eager, to share my truthful and candid observations of others with them. When growing up, as a teenager my buddies were a tough lot and we would shovel the feedback back and forth, poking fun at one another with our mistakes . . . we thrived on that. In retrospect, we enabled each other with a level of insensitivity and brute directness that would later come to hurt others.

TREAT OTHERS THE WAY THEY WISH TO BE TREATED

For me, the use of the principle of the Golden Rule has been a mistake. "Treating others the way I wish to be treated" has generally not served me well with my relationship interactions and team leadership. I learned later in life that *treating others as they wished to be treated* is a far more valuable principle. This principle, called "The Platinum Rule," is presented in a book by the same name by Tony Alessandra and Michael J. O'Connor.

My habit of seeking and giving honest criticism has been both a blessing and a curse for me for decades. Someone forgot to send me the memo to be sensitive as to how and when to approach others about their mistakes. On a personal level, with achieving results, that view advanced me through crises and chaos. It sustained me with staying the course with actions I believed to be right, especially when my actions were unpopular with others. On the other hand, when I later came to manage and lead others, it did not work out so well. I had a perspective of "a much better outcome will be coming folks, just hang in there till a time later."

I found it difficult to sustain loyalty and teamwork with that approach. It is not enough to be right. Mutiny is never a desirable occurrence during a transition toward improvement. I have experienced more than my fair share of unhappiness with my leadership and managerial style.

I was (and suspect I still am) an exceptional problem solver when working alone; working with a team was initially not nearly so successful. Later in life I "got it" and was able to combine the clarity and wisdom of a solid diagnosis and visionary destination with an action plan that included others. More heads thinking is better than just one. I eventually came to realize that respect, empowerment, and engagement with the team was crucial for long term sustainable improvement and teamwork. I found out the hard way that the shortest distance between two points was unequivocally not a straight line when dealing with people.

What works well for us as an individual performer at times does not always translate to success when dealing with others. When it comes to the plan and execution of actions for improvement, consideration of team members' participation, input, and motivation is vital. Some of the greatest athletes came to be some of the most mediocre coaches when they advanced to the next levels with their careers. Two examples are with hockey's "the Great One," Wayne Gretzky, and my namesake, Green Bay Packers' quarterback Bart Starr. The very characteristics that made them exceptional individual performers worked against them when leading others.

My Later Years—Production Team Successes

In the latter years of my business career, I was fortunate to have had the opportunity to work in a manufacturing environment where locomotive components and the locomotives themselves were rebuilt. At one point in time, I was responsible for well over 100 personnel with a budget of $100+ million that supported this business. I oversaw managing the production lines where locomotives and locomotive components were disassembled and then rebuilt. Our facility was in competition with other builders and suppliers, so improvement was not an option but a necessity to remain competitive and keep that business "in house," and subsequently keep our employees employed.

A locomotive is a huge piece of machinery that is used to pull trains well over a mile long. Given the commodities carried on trains and the nearness to communities with their travels, it is essential that they be safe and reliable. A stalled train caused by a locomotive breakdown could back up multiple trains and thousands of freight cars on the main line. A derailment or collision could have severe, if not life-threatening impacts for both the crew as well as the surrounding communities. A train may carry hazardous chemicals and potentially dangerous explosive fuels such as liquified natural gas.

In our locomotive rebuilding business, it was critical that we safely produced a high-quality product at a competitive price. This was done through reducing waste, such as with rework, by doing things right the first time. Written best practice standards for our work were essential to improve with reducing the rework (mistakes), performance shortcomings of the product, as well as with improved efficiencies in safe quality production. As with *evolutionary* and *proactive learning*, our opportunities for improving our competitiveness were both reactive and proactive. Learning from mistakes and problems identified by our employees and customers was invaluable. Likewise, studying the successes of other industries and companies, such as the automotive business and the Toyota company, helped us find better ways to do business. It was essential that we made continuous improvement a vital principle.

In the railroad business, safety, reliability, and productivity are inseparable and an absolute necessity. Given the magnitude of commodities hauled by railroad transport, it is indeed a safe and reliable means of moving goods around the country. As a supplier of rebuilt locomotives for our railroad, as well as for replacement locomotive components used at various repair facilities, it was necessary to have high standards for our safety, quality, and productivity.

As a result of my company training, as well as my own self-study, I was able to successfully lead well over a dozen improvement teams to assist with reducing injuries, reducing waste, improving quality, and making advances with productivity in this business. We were highly successful on all counts. Our employees' involvement with both identifying opportunity areas for improvement as well as solutions to those problems was crucial. We were able to continue momentum forward as we empowered and engaged our team members to be part of the solutions. As a result of these improvements, our employee satisfaction and engagement greatly improved. This chapter reflects a number of the concepts and methods used to achieve the results and successes that made this business succeed at an unprecedented level. As is often the case, success in business can often be translated into success in our personal lives, as well.

Prioritize then Define Objective Problem Statements

When it comes to you as an individual, whether a leader or not, it is very important that you avoid tainting your problem assessment with premature unsubstantiated conclusions. Be objective and open to seeing "what is," independent of preconceived biases or desires. As with the principle of innocence where "people are innocent until proven guilty," the definition of the problem and its diagnosis should be considered "unknown until reasonably examined." Initially, be open to all possibilities, however unlikely they may seem. The error of focusing on the wrong problem and the wrong underlying root causes has huge implications, whether it be a marriage, a production line, or a medical initiative.

One example for best identifying what problem to work on is with the pro-life and pro-choice quagmire we find ourselves embroiled with today. The wiser approach would be to focus on significantly reducing unwanted pregnancies (the vast majority of unwanted pregnancies are the result of irresponsible sex between the engaging partners). Another example would be the well-meaning but disastrous results of Lyndon Johnson's "Great Society" that led to long term increases with illegitimacy with an increasingly large percentage of fatherless families. The focus on government dependence rather than empowered self-independence is rarely a successful long-term solution for improvement.

As pointed out by Thomas Merton, the American monk, we may spend our whole life climbing the ladder of success, only to find when we get to the top that our ladder is leaning against the wrong wall. This is a tragic commentary on one's life. Often, many people find themselves in that position as they advance into their fifties and sixties. They come to believe that they missed out on important relationships and investments in a healthy future for themselves. They see that perhaps the fragrance and beauty of the flowers along the way were missed. Sometimes this mature enlightenment with what is truly important comes too late, with lost opportunities and failed relationships. People die before we make peace with them. Relationships can move from love to acrimony. Our health can prematurely degrade from vigorous vitality to pain and suffering with restricted mobility. We can wake up one day feeling a profound emptiness inside ourselves and a sense of aimlessness.

As you may have gathered with the reading of this book, the key to a wise life is not necessary about which wall you lean your ladder for success on. Though it is important to prioritize our destination goals, it is perhaps even more critical how we live our day-to-day lives as we climb that ladder and move forward in life. It is essential we have both a long-term perspective with our life destinations as well as the journeys in pursuit of them. Define your current problem/concern objectively, and then frame them within a larger perspective of how important they are. Some battles are not worth fighting, especially if engaging with them neglects far more important initiatives. Why work on repairing a broken window when the kitchen is on fire?

It is worth examining how we determine what the root cause of a problem is, as opposed to a symptomatic concern. The doctor looks beyond the fever temperature to determine the underlying cause of illness. They do not jump to the conclusion that a cold bath is all that is needed and neglect a root cause such as a bacterial infection. After gaining clarity about what the problem is, next is determining how much of a priority it is. Hiring a coach to improve our tennis game while our spouse or child is becoming increasing distant with us may be a mistake. Perhaps hiring a family therapist or counselor would be a better focus. Working long hours on career advancement and work improvements may be a mistake as well if we neglect our health and important relationships along the way. It is also important to consider that our action plans are not being subconsciously conceived with a desire to "run away" from real problems, ignoring the elephant(s) in the room. Careers and hobbies are fraught with numerous examples of this running away and being "busy;" fiddling while Rome burns.

As a result of my personal experiences with coaching others, leading business teams, and overcoming family challenges, I have come to see that later in life, our concerns mature and come full circle. What was once important is now seen as "small stuff" and we no longer "sweat the small stuff." Eventually, many come back to the basics of desiring healthy relationships, good physical health, and peace of mind with mental and financial health for themselves and others they care about. Often, the impetus for this clarity and realization is loss . . . loss of a relationship, poor personal health, or a sense of just being lost with their lives. Being competitive and better than another tends to lose its appeal over time. However, in many, many cases it is not too late to get our lives onto a joyous and fulfilling track. Better late than never.

Many so called "problems" are best addressed simply by improving our perception of them; changing our vantage point. Perhaps our problem isn't that our closet is too small but that we just have too much unimportant stuff to store away. Perhaps the problem isn't that I need to earn more money but that I need to be wise and thrifty with my spending. Perhaps the problem isn't that I need to spend more hours working and helping others, rather I need to learn to better discern when to say "no" and set boundaries with my commitments. Perhaps helping a friend or family member financially with their problems stemming from addiction or irresponsible life habits is the wrong course to be taking as opposed to seeking wise family therapy for ourselves.

Strategy for achieving meaningful results:

1. Determine worthiness. Is it worth investing future time, effort, and money to make improvement with a desired outcome when it is put in perspective with other desired results?

2. Write a clear, unbiased objective problem definition.

3. List symptoms and gather data that quantifies and qualifies the problem using the measures of *durinfre*: duration, intensity, frequency.

4. List possible causes and select the top root causes, with a set of a critically few countermeasure actions.

Defining & Diagnosing the Problem

1. Determine worthiness. Is it worth investing future time, effort, and money to make improvement here?

As you are about to embark on a substantial effort to improve an area that is important, be careful to prioritize it with other initiatives that are also important for you. There is only so much we can realistically hope to accomplish during any particular time in our lives. Choose wisely, pick focuses that address truly important issues for you and the team you may be involved with. Remember the economic principle of opportunity costs: the time and resources spent on "X" cannot also be used for "Y."

2. Write a clear unbiased objective problem statement.

When defining the problem/concern, seek to get it in a one sentence statement form. Do not embed a solution within the problem definition.

Incorrect examples of a problem statement:

- "We are having too many injuries at work because our supervisors are placing productivity ahead of safety."

- "I am having financial problems because I am not making enough money."

- "My spouse and I argue too much because he/she is extremely defensive with feedback."

- "I am overweight because I am eating too much."

- "I am not getting promoted at work because my supervisors and management are racists."

- "I don't have enough room in my garage to store all my things because it is too small."

- "Joe is not getting his work done because he is undependable."

You can see that embedded within these problem statements are predetermined solution areas for focus . . . this is a mistake. More often than not, these preconceived biases lead us down an ineffective path and away from making substantial real progress. I encourage you to notice and avoid this.

Correct examples of problem statements:

- "We are having injuries at work which cause pain and suffering and impact the team's effectiveness."
- "I have debt and expenses which I am not currently capable of paying."
- "My spouse and I argue frequently, and this causes both of us great upset."
- "I am overweight, and this is reducing my energy levels and hurting my self-image."
- "I am not advancing at work with position and compensation on pace with my expectations."
- "There is not enough room in my garage to store all my current possessions."
- "Joe is not completing assignments on schedule."

With these improved problem statements, we keep the door open to many possible causes, especially with those we are not currently considering. We are now much more likely to address root problems versus symptoms. We may also come to see that the real issue is not our original concern at all, as with storing things in our garage. Here, we may determine that the problem is not storage space but owning too many possessions. We then decide it best to have a garage sale or to drop off donations at the Salvation Army donation center instead of constructing a building extension or renting storage space elsewhere.

3. List symptoms and gather data that quantifies and qualifies the problem.
List symptoms and gather data that quantifies and qualifies the problem using the measures of *durinfre*: duration, intensity, frequency.

If the problem statement is: "We are not achieving adequate production levels," the symptoms may be:

- Customer complaints with not receiving orders on time, with an average of twenty per week.

- Low or no profits, with a current level of only 2 percent profit.

- Excessive backlog of twenty units of "in process" work with some parts of the business waiting for completion of work ahead of them before they can be worked on.

- Late in paying subcontractors and vendors suppling us parts, with the average payment being over three weeks late.

If the problem statement is: "I am having frequent arguments with another person (spouse, child, co-worker, etc.)," the symptoms may be:

- Daily arguments that leave me upset for long periods of time afterward.

- Not following through on my commitments because I am preoccupied with my upset over the argument.

- Not sleeping well, getting only four to five hours per night.

- Feelings of intense anger or despair.

- Loss of appetite or excessive eating, slammed doors, thrown dishes.

- Threats of divorce or quitting.

4. List possible causes, then select the top root causes.

Brainstorm causes to the symptoms, then select the top best critical few that you will pursue.

Root causes to production concern:

- Proper tools not readily available to employees when they need them.

- In process, standards and specifications are inadequate and as a result rework is often needed at the final step of the production line.

- Flow of work is not consistent; some areas get ahead quickly while some routinely fall behind schedule.

- Not having enough people or not having the right people in the right place.

- Employees are not getting adequately trained.

- Communication breakdowns between shifts.

Root causes to concern with arguments:

- Clear expectations, boundaries, and consequences not communicated effectively or enforced consistently.

- Personal unhappiness spill over.

- Deep seated resentment.

- Inadequate relationship listening skills.

- Engaging in confrontational communications with angry tone of voice or repeating the same things over and over.

- Lack of empathy for another.

- Focus on trying to change another as opposed to how we will better respond to them.

When prioritizing root causes for action, consider their impact on the problem as well as the feasibility with having them be addressed through possible countermeasure. Skip over root causes that cannot be addressed at this time, such as facility, money, or hiring limitations. If you find that root cause remedial actions are not possible currently, move on to another problem to solve or improve upon.

Keeping your eye on the ball = results and healthy relationships

My number one priority with selecting a doctor is their competence. Can he/she properly determine if a concern is significant or just a minor nuisance? Can they properly diagnose symptoms to determine the root cause(s) of a problem? In most cases, the treatment is easily determined *after* a proper diagnosis is made. Yes, the old adage of "a stitch in time saves nine" is right on target. A dear friend of mine went years with the wrong diagnosis of their Lyme disease. This led to an excruciating physical degradation, with much pain and suffering and an untimely death.

The doctor's bedside manner is of minor consideration for me. Frankly, if someone gave me a bag of gold, I would be little concerned with whether it was in a paper bag or a Gucci bag. Unfortunately, many folks these days are often more focused on the bag than its contents. The distinction between substance and form have become increasingly blurred these days. The genius with addressing problems with action plans that can achieve sustainable improvements is with the diagnosis. Any doctor can write a prescription, yet determining whether a pharmaceutical is necessary and if so, what the best one is, separates the good from the excellent. Whether it be a medical doctor, automotive mechanic, military strategist, or family therapist, their knowledge, experience, and ability to make a wise diagnosis can be the difference between suffering and joy, life and death, success and failure, or conflict and harmony.

Once an appropriate diagnosis is made, often the actions easily follow. It is wise to seek out experts where you can. With relationships, that may be a counselor or therapist. With money, that may be a financial planner. As with medical advice, it is best to seek out diagnosis early and be safe rather than sorry. With personal or team productivity, you may wish to seek out a proven coach, consultant, or mentor.

This chapter has addressed problem solving to get us to a point where we recognize root causes for action. The countermeasures and actions which follow and produce sustainable and meaningful results will be expanded upon in the next chapter. Two key points will be made there. The first focus is the Pareto Principle, where often 80 percent of desired results come from 20 percent of our efforts. The second is with the importance of relationships with achieving results.

CHAPTER 20

Leadership 101, Servant Leadership

In what roles am I a leader?

"Be the Servant Leader"

*The servant leader continually seeks to find ways
to make their team members' lives easier . . .
the servant leader pursues commitment over
compliance with their team members.*

–Michael Starr

Are you a leader? Nearly all of us are, with perhaps the exception of hermits. Whether we are a parent, educator, small business owner, plumber, homemaker, nurse, corporate manager, or the captain of a submarine, we all have roles where others look to us for guidance or example.

By its very definition, leadership implies being in front, being ahead, and to some degree being a trail blazer. It also implies having followers who follow. Hopefully, they follow with respect and loyalty, not with a desire for mutiny. Having lived through the Vietnam War while in college, there was a joke back then that was based in truth. *"What do you call a leader who gets too far ahead of the troops? A target."*

It was reported that this did happen at times with inexperienced people put in combat leadership positions who knew little about how to lead others and were shot in the back during battle by one of their "followers."

As leaders, we have a responsibility to look out for others as well as ourselves. In this role, it is wise to seek and find win–win outcomes whenever possible; to have outcomes that benefit the follower and the leader. The leader helps establish and reinforce the boundaries of right and wrong for the team. The leader is critical with creating and maintaining a healthy and effective team where individuals are respected, competent, committed, and feel valued.

WHEN WE HELP TEAM MEMBERS TO SUCCEED, WE ALL SUCCEED

The servant leader seeks to improve things for those they lead, as well as for the team as a whole. The servant leader effectively communicates his concern for the team, as with Theodore Roosevelt's famous quote, "People don't care how much you know until they know how much you care."

Remember that it is not enough to care for your team in your mind. You must convince them with both your actions and your words. Servant leaders understand that by helping their team members to succeed, they all succeed. To achieve this, commitment must trump compliance with an effort by the leader to sell and not just tell.

The subject of leadership takes up volumes of books and a multitude of philosophies. The scope of this chapter is not meant to address all aspects of leadership, but rather a critical few that can make a difference for you. This chapter is focused on the specific leverage wise empowering language can have, as well as the fundamental steps needed for solving problems in your role as a leader. There are suggestions here for improving your clarity of vision with *what is* as well as determining effective actions worth pursuing. This chapter will provide you knowledge and perspective that will assist you with becoming both a better change master as well as a respected leader who can achieve results that matter.

Today, there is a compelling and critical need for healthy leadership in our country, communities, and families. The leaders needed today must be competent, respect others, and seek to leverage common ground. They must pursue harmony, teamwork, and healing over conflict, division, and confusion. These leaders must have the motivation, experience, and understanding of how to achieve desirable win-win outcomes. Today in 2023, unfortunately, few meet this bar on a national or international level.

HOW TO DETERMINE AND IMPLEMENT COUNTERMEASURES FOR PROGRESS

In the previous chapters, we reviewed how to select a problem for action and how best to diagnosis its top root causes. In this chapter, we will discuss how to determine and implement countermeasure actions to produce the progress and results we desire. Two key elements for accomplishing impactful countermeasures are:

1. *Decide which efforts and actions we will pursue to address root causes; identify the critical few.*

2. *Work with others to help them to help us all succeed. Strive for commitment above compliance.*

1. Decide what efforts and actions we will pursue to address root causes.

The Pareto Principle, also known as the 80/20 rule, states that 80 percent of our desired results come from 20 percent of our efforts. Though this is not rigorously exact for all cases, it emphasizes the importance of identifying a few critical actions that provide the biggest return for our investment with time, effort, and money. This principle helps us succeed by guiding us away from a focus on perfection and unsustainable complexity toward sustainable simplicity and results that matter. It is as much about what we decide "not to do" as what we decide "to do."

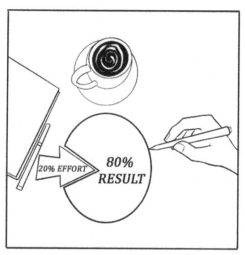

Pareto Principle

An action taken to address a root cause of a problem can be called a countermeasure, as it is a "measure" or action that is meant to "counter" a problem and move us toward a solution or mitigation. Countermeasures are selected to minimize the bad and maximize the good with the *durinfre* of outcomes. With your efforts to improve and make progress, take time to include others who have a stake in the matter to help decide the best course(s) of action. By doing so you, will find better ideas for action that are sustainable and met with commitment (as opposed to compliance only). Often, identifying the root cause(s) will in and of itself lead to seeing the needed action(s). Initially estimate, then later measure the impact these actions have toward reducing the severity of the problem and increasing the extent of the improvement.

Some example problems, root causes, and countermeasures:

Problem statement: Frequent arguments with significant other

One root cause: Our values with financial spending differ

A countermeasure: Write out an agreement for spending decisions and clarify who is responsible for what, then review together on a weekly basis. Perhaps open separate checking accounts. Consider a family counselor or financial advisor to help you both navigate through this process.

Problem statement: Our company has many customer complaints, and we are losing valued customers.

One root cause: Material availability is a problem and contributing to the late delivery of products that do not meet with the customer's expectations.

Two countermeasures:

- Identify supply chain weak links and seek out alternative vendors.
- Ensure customers are given realistic expectations as to delivery time. Better to under promise and over deliver than to over promise and under deliver. Let customers know in advance when and why a previous commitment will not be met. Measure what was promised versus what occurred to keep focus on efforts to close this gap to zero.

Often, the process with wisely selected countermeasures is an iterative one. One where we try one thing, give it time to work, then evaluate it its effectiveness. We next refine this countermeasure and try yet another. This process is summarized in the classic quality improvement cycle of PDCA: Plan, Do, Check, Adjust. It is important to give the countermeasure a reasonable chance with time and commitment before changing it.

2. Work with others to help them to help us all succeed. Strive for commitment above compliance.

The two most important partners in any business or organization are their employees and their customers. It is wise to invest in both groups by fostering healthy relationships. Healthy relationships lead to healthy teams. As we embark upon some new initiative, it is very helpful to have healthy relationships in place. This fosters trust, fluid candid communications, and confidence. If it is not in place now, work to build it along the way. These relationships must be grounded in trust, integrity, competence, and respect. They foster loyalty, engagement, and motivation. Always strive for 100 percent when it comes to being your word and doing what you say you will do.

BE COURAGEOUS AND CAPABILE OF RECOGNIZING THOSE NOT SUITED FOR THEIR ROLES

As a servant leader, we care about team members as individuals with their own sets of personal life challenges. We see that each has talents, shortcomings, fears, desires, and insecurities. The servant leader must have sincere empathy for those they lead. This empathy can only exist if they strive to know and best understand each team member within and beyond the organizational environment. When we identify the strengths and shortcomings of our team members, we can ensure they fit the roles they are expected to have with the team. A wise leader must be courageous and capable of recognizing those not suited for their roles and take action to either reassign them other responsibilities or frankly just cut them from the team. In the long run, this is best for everyone and avoids inevitable frustration, conflict, and failure with having someone in a role they are not suited for. Having someone in a position that is not a good fit for them is detrimental to that individual, other team members, and the organization (team).

Perhaps one of the most important decisions of any organization is who they select to be part of their team. After wise interviewing, vetting, and hiring has occurred, it is then the organization's responsibility to ensure that the team member succeeds. The servant leader's top priority is to ensure their team members have all reasonable tools, resources, and encouragement possible for them to succeed. They ensure training, understanding of the mission and vision, technical tools, and time are available for their folks to achieve that which is expected. It is important that any environment, be it at work, home, or in the community, be reasonably safe both physically as well as making sure that each team member feels free to express concerns and ideas for improvement. Coupled with a freedom to express a concern we should also encourage them to propose possible alternative solutions. with their concern.

I found through years of leading production improvement teams that one of the most valuable questions I could ask to solicit improvement ideas, sell my servant role, and build commitment was to ask, "How can we make your job easier?"

I met with a number of improvement teams each week. I felt these sessions were critical for our ongoing success. These teams represented the different shifts and work groups in my areas of responsibility. Each work group had its own supervisor. The weekly sessions consisted of the supervisor and several volunteer members from the group who attended a thirty-minute session that started and ended on time. The agenda always began with review of the "Obstacle Log." This log was a record that was posted in their work area weekly with updates of new concerns and comments concerning progress as well as any resolution of previously logged "obstacles." Next on the agenda, I always asked "how can we make your job easier?" We documented all reasonable concerns and added them to the log. This "obstacle log" also showed who was assigned to lead the efforts with resolving a particular concern. This was a remarkable tool for improving employee engagement as well as safety (reducing injuries), productivity (reducing waste), and quality/ reliability with our work of repairing and rebuilding locomotives and their components. In one of the work areas (over a period of two years), approximately 330 items were on the log with nearly 300 resolved.

When we ask team members how we can make their jobs easier, we encourage their engagement and will be sincerely told what they need to become safer, happier, more productive, and more committed. Great ideas are born in an environment where servant leadership solicits requests to know their team's needs and desires. Likewise, misunderstandings were easily identified so we could correct them, especially when it came to the shift-to-shift hands offs of in process work information.

LOYALTY, ENGAGEMENT AND TALENTS WILL MAKE OR BREAK AN ORGANIZATION

People are not just important, they are essential to life and our enjoyment with sharing, contributing, and our ability to improve things. As masterful as Jesus Christ was with his message, it was ultimately the apostles who carried the Christian doctrine forward and planted the seeds for its flourishing around the world as one of the largest practiced religions. In the long run, the loyalty, engagement, and the talents of team members will make or break an organization. Their commitment to success is paramount, as they are the people who do the work and produce the results.

Assuming that we as leaders are competent and proficient in our field (which perhaps is a big assumption for some), our effectiveness lies with our ability to get things done through and with people. The below are a few critical values that will serve you well with being an effective and respected servant leader. I call them "I C7."

1. Integrity

2. Caring

3. Competency

4. Consistency

5. Clarity

6. Commitment

7. Calm

8. Consequences

1. INTEGRITY

Integrity includes trust, honesty, being our word, and being true to ourselves:

- **Trust:** Followers must believe in the competence, commitment, and motives of the leader. They believe the leader knows what he/she is doing and is striving to do the best for the organization as well as the team members. They believe the leader is commited to the team initiatives and responsibilities.

- **Honesty:** Never lie to the team. At times it may be prudent or required to withhold information, as it may be confidential or just premature to present it, but never lie and say things you know not to be true at the time.

- **Be your word:** If you say you are going to do something, it is critical you follow through and do it. Should some extenuating circumstance arise that prevents this, then get back to those involved ASAP to explain the need to change the commitment. It is also important to avoid the temptation to commit to too many things; be selective and mindful to limit your commitments. Better to under promise and over deliver than to over promise and under deliver.

- **Be true to yourself:** Review and recommit frequently to your *ten convictions.* Ensure you align your personal actions with your core beliefs and creed, with what you believe to be right and wrong. Right is right and wrong is wrong when it comes to your *ten convictions* creed.

2. CARING

Let people know you do have an interest in them. Ask questions about their activities outside of work in addition to showing your professional desire to help them succeed. Be sincere and truly interested in them. As a result, you will learn things that help you be both a better person as well as a better leader. Be their student. Seek to understand them the best you can to develop both your respect and empathy for them. Empathy will set the stage for sincere respect for another.

When you see NOOT with why people cannot help being who they have become, you can make objective decisions. NOOT provides a dispassionate clarity in seeing the strengths as well as limitations of team members. The Platinum Rule of treating and speaking to people in the way they wish to be treated is essential.

Your communication with them is best framed with an empowering tone and messages of, "You can do it," and, "I believe in you." Avoid binary language and dead-end language such as stupid, unfriendly, or some other negative identity. Place more emphasis on the desired outcome and provide them as much latitude as possible for how they go about getting to that outcome.

Caring is especially important when there is a need to give feedback for improvement. Take your time in advance to think through how and when to best communicate whatever issue you might be addressing; focus on the desired results and actions as opposed to their being inadequate. "When we miss our deadline, it affects our customer's needs and future business we receive from them." Strive to be kind as much as possible.

3. COMPETENCY

To be skilled and effective, there is a need to have lived life with a certain about of experience, honing of talents, and understanding of reality. There is a need to have had a number of bumps and bruises with actually playing on the field of life as opposed to being professional spectators who do little more than find fault with others. Ensure you strive to learn from your mistakes and the mistakes of others. Aggressively pursue building your knowledge base with both people skills, such as relationship listening, and technical skills required within your organization.

4. CONSISTENCY

It is important that those you lead see you as predictable. Be consistent with how you treat all team members with praise or feedback for improvement. It is a challenge to start up a new initiative or begin a new action. Think things through and include others before prematurely going forward with any significant plans. This will inspire the confidence of the team in both the leader and the organization. It is important to minimize rework and redundancy. An effective leader strives to get it right the first time and minimizes the need to reverse course or second guess a strategy shortly after putting it in place.

5. CLARITY

Ensure the team understands the mission and vision. Ensure they understand the WHY behind new initiatives and existing projects, programs, and policies. Ensure they feel safe to express concerns or reservations. Take ownership with getting this accomplished. Saying

"I told them three weeks ago to do that" does not excuse you from being responsible for the selling and their understanding of what is expected. Incorporate as much of their feedback as reasonably possible. That said, there needs to be a clear agreement of what and when things are expected to be done with an initiative or assignment. Take time to sell them on this and ensure they fully understand the what and the why. Don't rush this. Spending extra time in the beginning with the what and why discussions with team members will be a worthwhile investment that leads to building their commitment beyond just their compliance.

Know how to delegate with follow up, have a system to follow up on the assigned actions well ahead of a deadline for completion. In time the amount of follow up with some becomes minimal, while with others it is ongoing. This is just one of those *it is what it is* realities. Ensure they understand that if an action cannot be completed as was agreed upon, they are to get back with you ASAP to discuss a plan B.

6. COMMITMENT

Include others in developing plans to select and execute initiatives for improvement. Take time to listen to their concerns and address them as well as you can. Place emphasis on the WHY for the new initiative or existing project or program.

7. CALM

A leader is most effective when drama, fear, anger, or upset are replaced with calm confidence. Do not engage in gossip. Avoid admonishing any team member in public but do praise them in public. Focus on the impact of undesired results and the need to improve the process. During times of challenge and turmoil, the true metal of a leader is revealed. Strive to be a calm presence for others. In conjunction with being calm, also be kind, as opposed to being stoic and non-emotional.

8. CONSEQUENCES

There is a reluctance these days to clearly define boundaries for expected and appropriate behavior and performance. Even more reticence exists with being consistent with implementing consequences to misbehaviors.

Clear boundaries with clear consequences actually lead to happier and more effective teams. Not to do so leads to a dysfunctional organization where standards appear arbitrary and as such can become mired in accusations relating to favoritism, race, religion, ethnicity, gender, age, etc. As with our families and children, people seek consistency, certainty, and clarity with what is right and wrong. It is important to communicate clearly the consequences with misbehaviors and implement them fairly and consistently each and every time. Be a clear line of demarcation with acceptable and unacceptable behavior and performance.

As with the *EBC Symbiotic 3*, it is important that you have true empathy for them and care about them, that they clearly understand the boundaries with performance and behavior, and lastly that there is an unmistakable understanding of the consequences when those boundaries are crossed. This also allows us to implement dispassionate consequences when behavior goes out of bounds and crosses boundaries with what is acceptable and what is not.

Be well versed and skilled in the use of the concept of the *EBC Symbiotic 3* with your empathy, boundaries, and consequences.

My vision is that you become a better team leader in your family, community, and career. My desire is that you will achieve results expeditiously that can be sustained and include the engagement of others.

Ultimately, the best leaders create other leaders. My hope is that you, too, create other successful leaders as you improve your own leadership skills. Please take the knowledge you gain from this book and use it to help others. Go forward teaching and encouraging others to recognize that the potential for more harmony and common ground exists by improving their use of wise empowering language.

If you are wise enough to ask the right questions; if you are ethical, competent, and have a true empathy and caring for the success and self-images of your team members, you will be well on your way to becoming a successful servant leader.

I published the below article a number of years ago and am reprinting it here. It speaks to the value of asking the best questions you can as an individual or leader. Effective leadership of others must be grounded in effective leadership of ourselves.

New Beginnings
The Answers Lie with the Questions

MICHAEL STARR

LISTENING FROM THE HEART

Mancos Times
April 4, 2012

In my listening to others—myself as well—I often hear how a critical event or a poignant relationship went south, how something that meant perhaps the world to us failed, and with it great hopes and dreams went unrealized. I hear how life becomes meaningless and full of despair at these times. Moving forward and "getting on" with our lives afterwards can seem oh so difficult and even feel futile, as if we were just stepping through our days like the "walking dead." Certainly, time must pass as we move through and past this pain and disappointment. There are indeed stages of grief and loss, with denial, anger, bargaining, depression, acceptance (Elizabeth Kubler Ross) that we must journey through.

A period must pass before we begin our healing to begin our new beginning.

Tragically, however, for some of us, we often find ourselves immobilized and mentally going in circles with this for a long, long, long time. It is as if we are in a coffin cocoon, trapped and doomed with no way out, dead and buried alive in our regrets, our anger, our frustrations.

What if the best cure for this lengthy malaise was a simple prescription of "CHANGE MY QUESTIONS?" Instead of the disempowering question we have been asking ourselves, we make an intentional effort to change them into EMPOWERING QUESTIONS.

We ask those dis-empowering questions like: WHY did they? Why didn't I? I can't believe they . . . As we demonize others, demonize ourselves, make ourselves victims of the past, we only dig ourselves deeper into a sense of despondency and helplessness. When we find ourselves in a hole, perhaps the first order of business is to stop digging.

So, try it. Let us change the questions we ask ourselves. Change them to empowering ones such as:

- What will I learn from this to make me a better lover, partner, worker, parent, friend?

- How will I take this experience and use it to find ever more joy, inner peace, more FUN?

- What will I do differently to keep this from happening again with another person or in a similar circumstance?

I have come to believe that our path ahead and important life answers lie with the questions we ask ourselves.

I believe these questions do direct our thoughts and efforts. They lead us to what it is we either notice or ignore, actually creating a path, a future course to navigate ahead for us. As such, we must be mindful to ensure we are asking ourselves questions that are lifting us up and nurturing us toward success and hope. Questions that direct us toward constructive improvement.

These self-talk questions manifest a path that either takes us to greater heights of serenity and joy or one that has us descend into a hole of hopelessness, gloom, and doom or perhaps one that just has us futilely go round and round, living out the definition of insanity daily (doing the same thing over and over, getting the same results), eventually becoming exhausted, angry, frustrated, or resigned with people and with ourselves, eventually being conditioned to believe that mediocrity and resigned survival interrupted with going to dinner, shopping, or going fishing is as good as it will get. I say change the questions, change your life!

Perhaps, my friends, the answers we seek indeed do lie with the questions we ask?

CHAPTER 21

Saving the BEST for Last ... Breathing Energy, Savoring Thought

What are some things I can appreciate and savor today?

"Be the Savoring Breath"

Positive thoughts will nudge out and displace negative thoughts and feelings.

–Mike Starr

In this concluding chapter I present what I believe to be a profoundly valuable practice that will promote your healthy progress as a *Betterist*. This is the practice of *BEST*, which stands for Breathing Energy with Savoring Thought. This is a breathing technique coupled to an empowering thought. I believe it literally is one of the "best" daily practices you can do to maintain and improve your health and overall well-being.

Before I elaborate on the whys and hows with the state of being called *"Be the Savoring Breath,"* I will digress a bit to reflect on destinations and journeys for seeking more good and less bad in our lives.

My ultimate desire for you is that your improvements with health, sense of meaning, harmony, peace of mind, and happiness will occur automatically and naturally for you. May you know that where you are is where you are supposed to be. May you believe that what you are doing is exactly what you should be doing. I hope you have an optimistic view of a future where tomorrow will be better than today. May the life you lead be one where your actions are in alignment and harmony with your core beliefs. May you be in constant pursuit of win-win outcomes and a desire to serve others.

Of course, we never do reach perfection and attain a state of nirvana. There will always be opportunities to make things better for ourselves and for others, as well, with healthy destinations and journeys toward them. Stay hungry with your desire to be better. These endless opportunities are a good thing, as the process of moving forward is the true adventure and spice of life. The advancement with the pursuit of the better gives us meaning and challenge.

Hopefully, as a result of reading and studying this book, you have considered and incorporated a number of the wise empowering language suggestions into your views of self and the world around you. Likewise, as you hone your ability to discern "useless" and "tyrannical/ dangerous" language, your *Journey into Peace* improves your perceptions of *what is,* and as a result improves your responses. It is not a Pollyanna approach, but rather one focused on seeking and finding LEAR. It is a vantage point from which we fully understand NOOT; that things had to occur as they did, that people had to become as they have. As a result, we will make wise and dispassionate choices that best improve our probability for success with self and others.

WE CAN RETRAIN OUR SUBCONSCIOUS BRAIN

A simplified description of brain functions is that they occur on two levels. These two areas in which our brains operate are with conscious decisions and with automatic, unconscious actions. The *autonomic nervous system* controls things that happen automatically, as with breathing and digestion, without us having to make conscious decisions. When we immediately react to an event in an emotional manner, such as with fear and anger, this is actually our brain automatically kicking in our *fight or flight* response. This automatic response of the brain triggers the release of hormones, which in turn make substantial changes with our body functions.

The autonomic system of the brain has two major components the "fight or flight" system and the "rest and digest" system. These are called the sympathetic nervous system (SNS) and the parasympathetic nervous system (PNS). These two systems activate hormones that affect our body functions such as heart rate, blood flow, blood pressure, digestive processes, and muscle tension or relaxation.

As is the nature of all species, their evolution inevitably led to a programing for self-preservation within their DNA; this is the purpose of the SNS. The brain has evolved to achieve two critical goals: self-preservation and self-propagation. An important part of that wiring for self-survival is a genetic fight or flight response within us. During moments of fear, the SNS kicks in and blood flow is redirected toward arm and leg muscles while blood pressure and heart rate increase. These changes to our body functions are triggered into action by the release of hormones such as adrenalin and cortisol. This served the human species well in millennia past when the need for immediate attention to a threat was necessary to survive. For many of us today, especially in the more advanced societies like the United States, this type of survival need is minimal. Yet, we often are on guard for external threats and worries that never materialize. When we spend our time worrying, without having a plan of action to address it, this further aggravates our anxiety and fear. This works against our health and peace of mind and is unnecessary.

With the practice and use of wise empowering language, we can retrain our subconscious brains to see and react to the world differently. We can reduce our fears and the threats we feel by:

- Pursuing healthy destinations and journeys toward them
- Learning to accept things that are out of our control (not necessarily agreeing)
- Improving relationships
- Building our empathy for others
- Setting boundaries with consequences
- Becoming eager to learn from mistakes and setbacks and embracing them as opportunities to improve our relationships and our future results

This enlightened view grows our personal level of empowerment, self-efficacy, and peace of mind while at the same time builds our empathy and compassion for others. This in turn impacts the SNS and PNS automatic reactions with the fight or flight verses rest and digest unconscious responses. Our habits and perspectives in the conscious world can in turn impact our unconscious reactions. Wise habits and views lead to a healthier and calmer state of clarity with a much-reduced tendency toward fear, anger, or despair. We now have interactions and responses that move us away from the *fight or flight* (SNS) mode and more into the *rest and digest* (PNS) mode. This promotes healing body activities with blood flow, blood pressure, heart rate, and better digestion. It nurtures a stronger immune system that allows our bodies and our thinking to operate at an optimal level.

As with all new tools that make our lives better and easier, the challenge is to maintain and sustain them for the years ahead. The excitement and novelty of a new successful discovery for improvement soon wanes, and it is incumbent upon us to find ways to keep our self-motivation and focus on track with their use. I conclude this book's journey with one last acronym and one last state of being for your consideration. The acronym is BEST. The state of being is *"Be the Savoring Breath."* I believe this is a valuable and easy to do daily practice for maintaining vitality, clarity, and enthusiasm.

BEST is a practice I encourage you to do several times each and every day. It will only take a few minutes to do. It stands for **breathing energy with savoring thought.** This is an intriguing and powerful tool that has great potential for healing, relaxation, and empowerment. One of the beauties of the BEST practice is that you can do it practically anywhere and at any time. BEST is a specific deep breathing technique done in conjunction with envisioning a positive, empowering, savoring thought.

DISPLACE NEGATIVE WITH POSITIVE

Two objects cannot occupy the same place at the same time. The cue ball and the eight ball cannot occupy the same space at the same time while on the billiard table. A positive savoring thought and a negative upsetting thought likewise cannot occupy the same space and time within our mind. These two views are mutually exclusive. The existence of one precludes the existence of another at that same time. As we introduce and practice moments BEST throughout our day, we are clearing a place for empowerment to take root and prosper. Here we also exclude and prevent the germs of negativity from taking hold. This is a *Betterism* practice that grows the good and diminishes the bad. This is definitely a *"Be Like Betty"* state of being, where we actively pursue being better. No matter the time or location, you have the potential ability to step back and practice BEST as a means for renewal, reminder, relaxation, and healing.

Being frequently anxious or fearful is unhealthy both physically and mentally. This chronic tension leads to decisions and choices that can limit or undermine our long-term peace, progress, and healing. Many of us spend much of our day worrying, anxious, fearful, or preoccupied with a concern or upset. As an antidote to this tendency, I propose a state of being I call *"Be the Savoring Breath."* It is suggested that several times a day we take a break and practice this exercise throughout the day. If we find ourselves becoming upset, that would be a good time to practice this exercise, as well.

Imagine that in our normal day, with its dozens of worries and concerns, we now inject and practice several BEST exercises throughout the day. These positive thoughts will nudge out and displace negative thoughts and feelings. The more we can do this, the more wonderous moments, hope, and peace of mind we will find for ourselves.

With practicing the BEST exercise, we can do it both reactively and proactively. If we are starting to feel stressed or upset, that would be a good time to initiate this practice. I would also suggest as a proactive practice to make it part of your *Marvelous Start Morning Routine* (see Worksheet "Marvelous Start Morning Routine" on executivecoach-ingservices.net). Starting your day in a positive and empowering way is a good thing. This is also especially valuable and beneficial to do just before going to sleep. To practice it just before going to sleep puts us in a healthy state of mind that can carry into and through our sleep and dreams, and later into our waking moments.

A DEEP BREATHING HABIT IMPROVES HEALTH

The merits of specific types of deep breathing are promoted in a variety of disciplines such as with medicine, yoga, meditation, and exercise.

There are several breathing techniques I have researched and found to be most valuable and credible. For the purpose of an example, I will focus on one technique in particular. That one is Dr. Andrew Weil's 4-7-8 technique in conjunction with a savoring thought to demonstrate how the BEST practice can be used.

A bit of background about Dr. Weil:

"Andrew Weil, MD has devoted the past thirty years developing, teaching, and educating others on the principles of integrative medicine. Weil is an internationally recognized expert on integrative medicine, medicinal herbs, and mind body interactions."[23]

He is a Harvard-trained doctor who is dedicated to changing the training of healthcare professionals and educating the public about health, healing, and nutrition. He believes in the integration of biomedicine, the complexity of human beings, and the healing power of nature.

He is a best-selling author of number of books including *Spontaneous Healing*, *8 Weeks to Optimum Health*, and *Eating Well for Optimum Health*.

There are a number of YouTube videos as well as information on his website drweil.com which expand on the 4-7-8 technique.

According to Dr. Weil, the potential benefits of his technique when practiced over a period of several weeks and months are:

- Relaxation
- Better digestion
- Lowered blood pressure
- Lowered heart rate
- Improved circulation
- Reduced anxiety

Example of using the BEST practice (Breathing Energy with Savoring Thought)

Just prior to beginning the 4-7-8 beathing technique (or another deep breathing technique you choose), envision an image relating to one of the following categories:

- Gratitude for people, pets, and things you have in our life now
- Memories of a wonderful past experience
- Anticipated fun or rewarding experience in the future
- Anticipated achievement or state of being, as with a wish fulfilled

- An *in the now* appreciation of what is currently going on around you

- An empowering mantra may also be a choice for a savoring thought, such as "I will find a way" or "I live to serve" or "we are all children of God"

One image I often call up is of an experience with my wife and our two rescue dogs Rippy and Lola. We were crossing a beautiful, 150-foot-wide gurgling stream during an eight-mile hike near Calico Rock, Arkansas. The water was frigid yet invigorating. It was a sunny day with clear blue skies. The air temperature was a bit cool, but pleasant and optimal for hiking. I carried the dogs separately across the stream, as the water was just below our knees in depth and flowing strongly. The beauty and the tranquility of nature enveloped both sides of the stream with a pristine forest embracing all of it. This is a very pleasant, fun, and adventurous image for me. It makes me smile whenever I think of this time.

Three-Step BEST Exercise:

Step 1. Visualize your savoring thought image. Savor it for a few moments. Immerse yourself within it with appreciation, gratitude, smiling, and details that enrich and enhance your view. Take perhaps a minute or so to do this. While doing this, breathe in slowly through your nose and out through your mouth.

Step 2. Conduct the four breath cycles with the 4-7-8 technique, which inhales through nose on a four-count, holds breath for a seven count, then exhales through mouth on an eight-count (or the deep breathing technique you choose)

Step 3. Revisit the image and savor it again for a few moments. Again, while doing this, breathe in slowly through your nose and out through your mouth.

Do this both proactively and reactively throughout the day. Make this a MUST DO daily practice. This will enhance and promote your long-term health and peace of mind if you continue to do this each and every day.

> *Your "Journey into Peace" is a path that will guide you into a new world. Here you will take up residence in a wonderful empowering home. A home where your peace, progress, and healing grow. In a way it is a garden of Eden for you here on Earth. Wise empowering language is the vehicle that will transport you there.*
>
> –Mike

Glossary

Anchor Habit—An existing habit we are doing religiously each day 99 percent of the time. When starting a new habit, we couple an action that promotes the new habit to this anchor habit.

Betterism—A philosophy of living which continually takes action for incremental progress. Like a stream, it is defined and exists only through ongoing forward movement. A *Betterist* lifestyle focuses on achieving more good and less bad in their lives. A *Betterist* pursues more peace of mind, health, harmony, fun, meaning, prosperity, etc. They also seek to have less suffering, anger, animosity, fear, frustration, despair, etc. This belief sees that wise goals consist of two parts: destination and the journey toward that destination. Our progress within the journey continues to seek win-win outcomes for self and others. Here, "goals" focus on two outcomes: having a meaningful, balanced, and healthy journey and reaching a desired destination. The vision of the destination provides the context which gives the journey meaning and purpose. The satisfaction and sense of meaning and purpose associated with the journey of progress is just as important, if not more important, than reaching the destination. The journey is our day-to-day living . . . it is our life. Here, destination and journey are symbiotic. This philosophy of living leads to a life full of hope, harmony, enthusiasm, vitality, optimism, and self-efficacy.

Betterist—One who practices *Betterism*.

Binary Views—An "all this" or "all that" view with no gray area in between. In computer language, all information is coded with either a one or a zero, there is no other choice. An example of a legitimate binary situation would be one where you are either pregnant or you are not. Often, people use illegitimate binary characterizations of others which demonizes them and strips them of their humanity. These illegitimate binary views are often devoid of any meaningful empathy or compassion. This perspective misses seeing the larger reality and context of the mosaic of our imperfect humanity with our many roles, predispositions, biases, contributions, gifts, and talents, as well as shortcomings.

Compassion—The kindness we feel for another as a result having developed an understanding and empathy for them (including ourselves). It leads to a healthy connection with another. Compassion is the result of our efforts and desires to understand another and why they are as they are; it is a consequence of our empathy for them. Our empathy toward them is an enlightened understanding of why they became as they became and that it was inevitable that they became who they are.

Contra Identity—Personal identity based on seeing oneself as valued and superior based on finding fault or shortcomings in others. This is the opposite of an identity based on personal merit, skills, accomplishment, or ethical principles. Binary views are predominant with this type of self identiy. This self view is a gateway to dehumanizing others, leading to conflict and toxic behavior.

Crampons—A tool for dealing with mistakes and setbacks after the fact. There are two phases with the use of crampons:
First Phase = damage control
Second Phase = step back handling with the FUSS process

Damage Control Phase—Shortly after experiencing a setback, we take damage control action as necessary to mitigate harm. Although this is a reactive response, we can be proactive with preparing for it, like having a spare tire in your automobile trunk, knowing CPR, or a dollar fund set aside for emergencies.

Dangerous/Tyrannical Words—Words that lead to beliefs that make matters worse in elationships, views of others, and our ability to improve things. Some of these words have been intentionally designed and promoted to achieve agenda that seeks to create fear, distract/divert, divide, discredit with slander, or promote conflict. This language can work against having empathy for others and having civil debate by dehumanizing others. It also pigeonholes views of another into a disempowering dead end.

Delightful Detours—The view that mistakes and setbacks contrary to our expectations lead to unavoidable detours from our original plan. These detours are seen as the shortest way forward and are our potential teachers and friends. These detours are springboards for our future progress and advancement. The wise question becomes "what is the best detour" for me to take at this moment with this setback or obstacle.

Desire Power—This is the power of our self-motivation. It is the fuel that propels and sustains our progress. It is an "I want to" versus the "I need to" state of mind.

Determined Decisions—Decisions that are proactive, as they are well-thought-out prior to doing something or saying something. They are the result of wise thinking before doing.

Dispassionate Clarity—An objective view of circumstances devoid of negative judgment. It is the seeing of "what is" in the context of empathy and boundaries without anger, jealousy, despair, or upset. This outlook sees an objective reality for what it is without bias, emotion, or judgement much like the Dr. Spock character in the Star Trek series would.

Dispassionate Consequences—These are introduced after we have achieved understanding and empathy for another. We next set boundaries with another's behavior which we find unacceptable, toxic, or harmful. We think out these consequences in advance. When our boundaries are encroached upon, we are resolute to implement them consistently without anger or upset. Following through with the consequence is essential, announcing why it is being implemented is of secondary value.

Durinfre—A measure of progress based on the *duration, intensity, and frequency* of things happening. The goal is to have greater degrees of it with good things and less of it with bad things. In some cases, it is objective and measurable, in other cases it may be subjective.

EBC Symbiotic 3—Three integral concepts that promote peace of mind, harmony, and progress with others; these three concepts are *empathy, boundaries, and consequences.* When facing an ongoing upset or conflict with another, it is important to approach this situation with empathy, boundaries, and consequences. All three must occur to be successful. It is critical with maintaining achieved progress and limiting, if not eliminating, regression.

Emotional Predispositions—These are inclinations we may have with becoming angry or feeling threatened, frustrated, wanting to be liked, or need for superiority. These can lead to right fights, blame games, or becoming defensive. They can limit our ability to learn or see things objectively and clearly.

Empathy—An objective understanding of why another became as they did. By taking into account their life experiences, environment, and their DNA, we conclude that it was inevitable that they became who they are. This is a consequence of seeing their behavior in the context of the *natural order of things* (NOOT).

Evolutionary Learning—Learning from our experiences after the fact, especially with mistakes and setbacks. It is experiential learning as opposed to learning through formal educational.

Fatal Mistake—By their very nature, fatal mistakes are those that lead to dire outcomes. They leave little room for learning, as these actions take us to a point of no return. Punching the boss in the nose would be a fatal mistake. Driving without a seatbelt then being seriously injured in an automobile accident would also quality as a fatal mistake.

Follow-Up Setback System (FUSS)—A system for recording upsets and setbacks shortly after they happen in a place called the FUSS log. This log is reviewed at a later time as during a *week in review* session to determine what, if anything, we will do to learn from this experience and handle it better in the future. By recording the upset, it gives us confidence the issue will be handled thoroughly at a later time, and as a result we can resume our activities by reducing anger and stop unproductive "could have" or "should have" thinking. We quickly pivot like a *school of fish* and continue to move forward *being the stream* with our progress.

Foundational Background—Preexisting knowledge and experience. It is the understanding needed to advance our ability to learn new information. Examples include:

- We need to understand algebra before we can comprehend trigonometry.
- Before we can improve our ability to convince others, we need to be effective relationship listeners and understand their point of view(s).

Golden Key Words—Wise empowering language, which uses the core foundational words and concepts that promote the philosophy of

Betterism with the achievement more good and less bad on our path of peace, progress, and healing.

Higher Truth—A wiser view of things than we previously had, especially with empowerment, harmony (with self and others), and achieving sustainable results.

Ice Cleats—Habits and routines you design, implement, and sustain to support you with your daily journeys to minimize backsliding. These are a proactive set of tools you hone and are mindful of each day. These ice cleats include a personal mantra plus three sacred habits:

(1) Have an empowering prayer/mantra/affirmation

(2) Sacred Habit: *Marvelous Start Morning Routine*

(3) Sacred Habit: *Week in Review session*

(4) Sacred Habit: *Follow-Up Setback System (FUSS)*

Intentional Simple Tiny Efforts for Progress (ISTEPs)—Incremental planned action(s) for making progress, often committed to as part of a daily practice as with the *Marvelous Start Morning Routine.*

Learning Distraction(s)—They limit our ability to learn, perceive, and think objectively. They fall into two subcategories:

- The first is with the *emotional predispositions*, where we have inclinations toward feeling threatened, wanting to be liked, or a need for superiority.

- The second has to do with being *preoccupied* with concerns or worries.

Learning Experiences for Growth (LEGS)—A view of experiences, especially undesired or unexpected ones, which sees them as learning opportunities we will leverage to become better in the future.

Legitimate Empowering Alternate Reality (LEAR)—An alternative empowering and very possible perspective that disentangles us from drama and negative emotion; this view promotes objectivity. It moves us away from seeing ourselves a victims and others as villains. It moves us toward being empowered and capable of achieving results important to us.

Listening From the Heart—Listening based on caring for another's fears, needs, desires, and dreams. It is based on having empathy for another. It leads to communications which convince another that we understand them and acknowledge their point of view.

Make it Streamlined and Simple (MISS)—Making the effort to simplify and distill a concept or focus into a limited scope. It minimizes tendencies toward perfection, which make achieving and sustaining results difficult. It allows us to determine and implement a few critical actions to make important progress without getting bogged down in excessive and unsustainable complexity.

Marvelous Start Morning Routine—This is a set of habits we follow each morning; the launch pad for getting ourselves off to a strong start each day with a mindset of optimism, confidence, and self-motivation.

Mutually Exclusive—The reality that one experience excludes another at a specific place and time, such as we cannot spend the same money on two different things at the same time, or we cannot be joyous when we are angry. We cannot be physically in two places at the same time.

Natural Order of Things (NOOT)—The inevitability that events and people's actions had to have become as they are.

Objective Empowering Acceptance—Acceptance based on objective understanding of NOOT; things and people were destined to be as they had become, and as a result of seeing this, we can best learn to interact and set boundaries with these situations. This view is in contrast to *resigned acceptance,* as it empowers us to focus and take action in areas where we ourselves can make things better and avoid wasting time, energy, or money on dealing with things we have little or no control over.

Opportunity Cost—The same money, time, and resource expended on one thing cannot be spent on another thing. Putting a resource in one area excludes our ability to put that same resource into another area.

Opportunity for Contribution—the view that someone else's interruption of our agenda may be an opportunity to serve them by providing acknowledgement, caring, guidance, or support for them. This may reduce their suffering and increace their peace, progress or healing.

Pareto Principle—A rule that says for many outcomes, 80 percent of consequences (or results) come from 20 percent of the causes (or actions).

Proactive Learning—Learning in anticipation of achieving something we desire; it is aspirational in nature. It is often limited by:

- *Foundational background*—preexisting knowledge and experience
- *Learning distraction(s)*—emotional predispositions and/or pre-occupation distraction

Relationship Listening—Here you realize that as your interest in another increases, your preoccupation with yourself decreases. As you focus more on concern for another, your anxieties and self-consuming thoughts diminish, and your listening becomes much more effective. Here you listen as the *student listener* with the intent to understand what and why something is being said. As a result, your ability to achieve and maintain a healthy relationship improves and you are better able to connect with, guide, and support others to help themselves.

Relationship Trinity—This states that there are three parts to a relationship between two people:

1. Our relationship with self, which we are 100 percent responsible for.
2. The other's relationship with themselves, which we are 0 percent responsible for.
3. Interactions between the two of us, which we are 50 percent responsible for.

Resigned Acceptance—Seeing that a reality is to be endured because it won't change; a defeatist perspective.

Right Fight—Interaction with another where each is determined to prove themselves right and the other wrong. It often neglects the value of a healthy relationship and can lead to long term damage in a relationship. Here you may win the battle (of the argument) but lose the war (with the relationship deteriorating).

Roads of Tyranny (ROT)—Language that divides, dehumanizes, distracts, and diminishes people.

Sacred Boundaries—Lines of demarcation that clearly identify unacceptable behavior. These boundaries go hand in hand with us having consequences we invoke each time these boundaries are encroached upon.

Sacred Habits—Essential habits needed to improve our peace, progress, and healing. They must rarely, if ever, be compromised except in the most extreme of emergencies. It is recommended that you have a *Marvelous Start Morning Routine, Week in Review Session,* and use the *FUSS* system. These three foundational sacred habits will promote your ongoing progress and ability to achieve successes for yourself.

Self-efficacy—A belief in one's own capacity and ability to follow through with actions in a manner that will achieve desired results.

Self-exorcism—A means of purging ourselves of animosity, hate, anger, and despair that resulted from a perceived past transgression. It recognizes that "forgiveness" is not a doable verb, but rather through understanding and empathy we can get past the hurt of a previous upset with another.

Self-motivation—Motivation that comes from within ourselves. It is our responsibility to keep this going. It can be nurtured and sustained through daily action and wise habits.

Silver Key Words—Wise empowering words which build on the concepts and definitions presented with the Golden Key words and terminology.

Simple Elegance—A condensed, concise, and streamlined perspective of processes and views for progress. Achieved by our focus on the "MISS" process.

State of Being—A way to see oneself with a visualization in a specific circumstance, such as "be the student listener," where we are mindful to listen to learn from another as opposed to trying to teach another.

Talking Stick—method used by Native American chiefs where the person holding the stick is the only one allowed to speak their own position. The speaker holds on to the stick until they are convinced that everyone present understands their point of view (not necessarily agreeing with them, though).

Ten Convictions—A set of values and personal principles that we develop and write out for ourselves; these are our core beliefs with what is right and wrong and important in our lives. This is our personal creed and a foundation for our conduct, decisions, and identity.

Trails of Progress—Strategies, trajectories, and directions for achieving progress.

Useless Words—Words that prevent progress with achieving desired outcomes and results; they are often based on good intentions but they are not doable verbs or achievable outcomes. They have us going round and round, as with the cycle of doing the same things over and over again hoping for different results and not making progress.

Velcro Learning—Learning that sticks and is easily retained by us, especially when we have the foundational knowledge that allows us to build upon it with new ideas and principles.

Week in Review Session—A scheduled weekly session we hold with ourselves to review the prior week and determine focus and actions for the upcoming week.

What is—A calm, objective, and unemotional view of things and occurrences, devoid of judgment or blame. It is seen with *dispassionate clarity,* and as such allows us to make the best decisions we can at that time. This view allows us to have *objective empowering acceptance* though our understanding of NOOT.

Win-Win—An outcome where both parties achieve a positive and desired result.

Wisely Empowering Words—Words that promote personal progress and harmony with achieving desired results and win-win outcomes.

STATES OF BEING

Be Like a School of Fish—Here we pivot quickly and move forward *Being the Stream*, as with a setback or mistake, we don't stall or derail emotionally. When an obstacle or setback is encountered, we record it in our FUSS log for later handling then move on knowing it will be properly addressed at a later time.

Be Like Betty—Acting in ways where we continually improve ourselves by taking action to make things better.

Be Like Moses—Contemplate and write out your top ten convictions. Review them frequently and be mindful to always act in alignment with them.

Be Michelangelo—To step back from a vague and drama-oriented current view of a circumstance and see the masterpiece within it, like seeing the magnificent statue within a raw block of marble. Work at removing the waste to reveal the goodness within. Make things simple and manageable by achieving empathy for others and finding a workable simple elegance with our strategies and plans.

Be on Autopilot—Having habits and routines that automatically promote and sustain healthy progress for ourselves.

Be Sacagawea—Act as a guide and beacon for others.

Be the Apprentice—See ourselves as a student who learns from life's experiences with its many twists and turns and the many detours and undesired outcomes that may be contrary to our initial expectations.

Be the Archaeologist—Working to discover and understand the reasons why people (as well as ourselves) are the way we are.

Be the Bloodhound—Ferret out tyrannical and dangerous language and notice it for what it is. Avoid falling prey to it or promoting it.

Be the Bookie—Work the odds in having probability work to your advantage with seeking wise outcomes.

Be the Brave Velcro Turtle—With proactive learning we build on our *foundational knowledge* and have the courage to face our inclinations for retreat or attack. We stick our necks out like a turtle coming out of his shell willing to be exposed and vulnerable. As a result, we are available to better learn and see what is actually going on around us.

Be the Diagnosing Doctor—Take the time and effort needed to achieve the right diagnosis of a problem before attempting to solve it.

Be the EBC Symbiotic 3—Boundaries, empathy, and consequences work together as one cohesive set of actions, like the three legs of a tripod that hold up one object. An effective way to deal with friction and contention in our interactions and relationships with others.

Be the Empowering Mirror—As we practice *relationship listening*, we listen to understand and reflect back to another what we hear them communicating. We do so in an empowering way that summarizes their point of view to their satisfaction. This helps them advance their clarity and expectations, as well as helping us best understand and acknowledge them.

Be the Exorcist—To conduct a *Self-Exorcism*, purging ourselves of views that cause us to harbor animosity or upset with another. This is done through a process of learning who they are and why they became as they did.

Be the Glass Half Full—Wherever you can, look for and seek out *Legitimate Empowering Alternate Realties* (LEAR).

Be the Good Poppy—Be resilient and blossom in the most arduous of circumstances, and as a result best promote healthy relationships with others.

Be the Scout . . . Be Prepared—Before making a decision or having an important conversation, prepare in advance and weigh out the best approach, then do it.

Be the Savoring Breath—A daily practice that can be done proactively, such as when we first awaken and at bedtime. It can also be done reactively, such as during the day when stress and upset are beginning. It couples a positive image with a breathing technique.

Be the Self-Motivation Maestro—Orchestrate your surroundings to keep yourself motivated by wisely selecting the people around you, your experiences, places you go, and the language you use. Surround yourself with things, people, and activities that excite and energize you. Here you focus on taking actions that build your *desire power*.

Be the Servant Leader—Serve and lead others with compassion, competency, and integrity.

Be the Stream—State of being where we are defined by our constant forward movement with our ongoing actions for improvement. We continually move forward and quickly adapt to obstacles and setbacks by going over, under, and around them.

Be the Student—We study and seek out new knowledge by building our understanding of a subject. We understand first then next challenge and test the concept to see if it rings true for us.

Be the Student Listener—We are mindful to listen to learn from another as opposed to trying to teach them. Here we seek to understand both the what and why of a communication with both the words spoken as well as the concerns that may behind those words.

Be the Umbrella Opener—Avoid anger or harshness when implementing consequences when a sacred boundary is being encroached or crossed. Just do it calmly, like opening an umbrella when it begins to rain outside.

Be the Waiter—Make your case wisely and succinctly, then move on. Avoid badgering or pursuing a dialog with repeated efforts to have another agree with us.

Be the Win-Win, Wisely Selfish Mediator— We seek and implement actions where you and another can both have a desirable outcome.

Be the Wise Frog—Be mindful to avoid letting the scorpion on your back so it can most likely sting you once again. Based on the story of the scorpion and the frog.

Notes

1. Ian Johnson, "Who Killed More; Hitler, Stalin or Mao?" *New York Review of Books* (February 5, 2018), https://www.nybooks.com/online/2018/02/05/who-killed-more-hitler-stalin-or-mao/.

2. Eisenhower Library, "World War II: D-Day, The Invasion of Normandy" https://www.eisenhowerlibrary.gov/research/online-documents/world-war-ii-d-day-invasion-normandy.

3. Elizabeth Wildsmith, Jennifer Manlove, and Elizabeth Cook, "Teenage Childbearing Among Youth Born to Teenage Mothers," Youth & Society (June 2012): 258–283.

4. Center for Disease Control, "Suicide Trends Among Youths and Young Adults Aged 10-24 Years" https://www.cdc.gov/media/pressrel/2007/a070905.htm.

5. Nora Voklow, "Drug overdose deaths in 2020 were horrifying. Radical change is needed to address the drug crisis (August 31, 2021), https://nida.nih.gov/about-nida/noras-blog/2021/08/drug-overdose-deaths-in-2020-were-horrifying-radical-change-needed-to-address-drug-crisis.

6. Our Father's House Soup Kitchen, "Six Cities with the Highest Homeless Populations" (February 24, 2022), https://ofhsoupkitchen.org/cities-with-highest-homeless-population.

7. Bill Hutchinson, "12 major cities hit all-time homicide records," ABC News (December 8, 2021) https://abcnews.go.com/US/12-major-us-cities-top-annual-homicide-records/story?id=81466453.

8. Susan Scutti, "21 Million Americans suffer from addiction," AAMC News (December 18, 2019), https://www.aamc.org/news/21-million-americans-suffer-addiction-just-3000-physicians-are-specially-trained-treat-them.

9. Sara G. Miller, "1 in 6 Americans Takes a Psychiatric Drug," Scientific American (December 13, 2016), https://www.scientificamerican.com/article/1-in-6-americans-takes-a-psychiatric-drug/.

10. Keith Chen, "The Language We Speak Predicts Saving and Health Behavior," Yale Insight (February 19, 2013), https://insights.som.yale.edu/insights/the-language-we-speak-predicts-saving-and-health-behavior.

11. Mayo Clinic Staff, "The South Beach Diet," Mayo Clinic website (June 9, 2023) https://www.mayoclinic.org/healthy-lifestyle/weight-loss/in-depth/south-beach-diet/art-20048491.

12. Samantha Scott, "6 Guides Who Changed History," *Travelstride* (June 19, 2016), https://www.travelstride.com/blog/6-famous-guides-throughout-history.

13. John C. Maxwell, *Winning with People: Discover the People Principles That Work for You Every Time* (New York: HarperCollins Leadership, 2007).

14. Plato, *Republic* (London: Methuen, 1965).

15. Executive Coaching Services, October 16, 2023, http://www.executivecoachingservices.net/.

16. G. A. Akerlof, J. L. Yellen, and M. L. Katz, "An Analysis of Out-of-Wedlock Childbearing in the United States," *Quarterly Journal of Economics*, 111, no. 2 (1996): 277–317, https://doi.org/10.2307/2946680.

17. Center for Equal Opportunity, "Percentage of Births to Unmarried Women," (February 26, 2020), https://www.ceousa.org/2020/02/26/percentage-of-births-to-unmarried-women/.

18. See, "Conducting a Week in Review Session" at www.executivecoachingservices.net.

19. See, "Using the Follow-Up Setback System" at www.executivecoachingservices.net.

20. Staff Report, "Chronic Stress Puts Your Health at Risk," Mayo Clinic, (August 1, 2023), https://www.mayoclinic.org/healthy-lifestyle/stress-management/in-depth/stress/ art-20046037.

21. GAO U.S. Government Accountability Office, section Behavioral Health: Available Workforce Information and Federal Actions to Help Recruit and Retain, Providers GAO-23-105250 Published Oct. 27, 2022, Under the subtitle "What GAO Found," https://www.gao.gov/products/gao-23-105250.

22. J. Daniel Couger, "Creative Problem Solving and Opportunity Finding," Journal of Creative Beahvior (September 1998), https://onlinelibrary.wiley.com/doi/10.1002/j.2162-6057.1998.tb00818.x.

23. "Andrew Weil, MD," WebMD, accessed August 25, 2023, https://www.webmd.com/ andrew-weil.

Acknowledgements

My wife Karen: Thank you for the hundreds of hours of reading, reviewing, and discussing the concepts and drafts of my book over the last several years. You have been my encourager and cheerleader over the ten-plus years this book took to complete. I thank you so much for believing in me and my message. Your selfless support has been critical with helping me make this mission to help others reduce suffering and increase their well being come true.

Teresa Velardi: Many thanks to Teresa Velardi, owner of Authentic Endeavors Publishing, for her many hours of coaching, editing, and feedback that kept me motivated to finish this book. She has been a genuine and skilled guide in the journey of getting my book up and running.

Vice Admiral Al Konetzni, Jr. USN (ret): Thank you for writing the forward to my book and the time spent reading the drafts of it along the way. You, perhaps more than anyone else, has been a beacon of kindness and empowerment for me over the last forty-plus years. My time spent serving under your leadership in the Navy was one of the most formative times of my life. Often, I would ask myself in the years and decades after I left the Navy submarine force, "What would Al do?"

Steve Harrison's Company, Bradley Communications: Many thanks to coaches Cristina Smith and Debra Englander with their help in refining and reducing my manuscript into a manageable book.

Chris Szaz: Thank you to my web page designer and maintainer who is owner of Charlemagne Web Designs. Chris worked closely with Teresa V. to integrate the Journey Into Peace worksheets into my Executive Coaching web page.

Gilbert Baker: Many thanks to my friend Gilbert for our breakfasts at Waffle House, where we discussed, and he critiqued, my drafts and challenged some of the concepts in my book.

Aljon Inertia: My patient and skillful illustrator who suffered through my many requests for revisions to the twenty-seven drawings used in my book.

Valerie Costa: thank you for the exceptional effort in editing my manuscript as well as your challenges of some of my conclusions.

Christy Day: Many thanks for the assitance with the multiple editing of the additions, corrections, cover design, and formatting of my manuscript.

Thank you to the following "First Readers" for your fresh perspectives and invaluable candid feedback:

Gilbert Baker
Jane Coyne
Donna Heindel
Rebecca Hart
Becky Hurt
Lindsey Kepka
Al Konetzni
Mary Ann Kempke Moloy
Karen Staroschak
Joan Ward

About the Author

MICHAEL STARR (a.k.a. Myron Staroschak) is an adventurer at heart. He loves exploring and "going where few have gone." While studying at Carnegie Mellon University, he and a friend canoed fifty-four days from Pittsburgh to New Orleans. The next year, he hitchhiked and bused for four months through the United States, Mexico, and Guatemala, living on $3 per day. He was interviewed by Admiral Hyman Rickover and later became a Navy Lieutenant on the nuclear submarine USS Kamehameha SSBN 642. After his military service, he became an improvement team expert and a productivity virtuoso in the manufacturing sector. He has coached hundreds through his business, Executive Coaching Services, and has published dozens of articles relating to personal improvement and relationships. His greatest challenge, however, was discovering how to have empathy for others and empower them to find a way to make things better. His progress occurred largely as a result of learning how to deal with addiction, mental health crises, interpersonal conflict, and his own character defects.

In 2018, he began preparations for summiting Mount Kilimanjaro in Tanzania. On July 19, 2019, at the age of sixty-nine years, he reached the summit of Mount Kilimanjaro at 19,341 feet. During his ten-day trek up and down that mountain, he had a spiritual awakening, documented with his poem: "On my way to Kilimanjaro, I found God was waiting for me there." He is an advocate of his philosophy of *Betterism,* which continually seeks more good and less bad with win-win outcomes.

You can learn more about Mike and his coaching business at www.executivecoachingservices.net.